"He is our cousin, Cousin"

To Ben
with many thanks for your help
and advice + for so kindly writing
a Preface.

Kind regards
Antony
June 2015.

Quacks Books
Q

"To my Friends pictured within"[1]

To my parents for their unfailing love and example
To my family for their support in this project
and
To the memory of my dear friend Ven Hart

Please note Footnotes pp i-xxvi are 1 to 10 and Footnotes pp 1-284 are 1 to 203

---

[1] With apologies to Sir Edward Elgar!

"He is our cousin, Cousin"

Antony Barlow

When Sir Laurence Olivier opened the memorial gardens round Sir Henry Irving's statue in London, July 1951, he said of Sir Henry:

"He died two years before I was born, and yet I am as conscious of him as if I had served as a member of his company." [2]

In writing this book, I too have been as conscious of my forebears as though I had lived, suffered and fought along with them.

Quacks Books
7 Grape Lane
Petergate
York
Yo1 7hu

Q

---

[2] Quoted in 'The Oliviers' by Felix Barker (Hamish Hamilton 1953). See disclaimer under acknowledgements p v

Published by Quacks Books, 7 Grape lane, Petergate, York yo1 7hu

British library cataloguing in Publication data
Antony Barlow
He is our cousin, Cousin
A Quaker family's history, from 1660
Great Britain

ISBN 978 1 904446 60 6

Obtainable direct from the publisher, bookshops or Amazon

Set in Times Roman and printed by offset lithography on a 100gsm book wove, section sewn
with drawn on cover at Jackson House by Quacks the Printer, 7 Grape Lane, Petergate, York
Yo1 7hu, t 0044 (0)1904 635967 info@quacks.info wwwradiusonline.info

Bibliography

Thanks to the following for kind permission to reproduce their pictures:

To The National Portrait Gallery for:

The Anti-Slavery Convention of 1840 (Inside Front cover), Richard II, Duke of Aumerle (p.xvi), George Fox (p.2), General Monck (p.24), The Passing of the 1832 Reform Act (p.35), Photograph of Sir Josiah Mason p.(127)

To the National Library of Congress for: The Funeral of the Duke of Wellington (p.35)

To the Royal Collection Trust / © Her Majesty Queen Elizabeth II 2015 for the picture of John Camden Neild (p.60)

All historic family photographs are from the Barlow family archive; all contemporary photographs of Antony Barlow's family are from his personal archive.

Thanks to the following for kind permission to quote from their publications:

Apologies to any parties not consulted in quoting the words of Sir Laurence Olivier cited in 'The Oliviers' by Felix Barker (Hamish Hamilton), but all attempts made to trace rights proved difficult, though Penguin, who took over the publishing rights, have stated that they 'have no objection' (p iii)

Carol Saker for permission to quote her sister Anna OHerlihy's poem *"On the death of a favourite Quaker Aunt"*(p.xx)

Oxford University Press to quote from The New Fowler's Modern English Usage First Edition by Fowler 1998, description of 'Yeoman'(p.xxii)

Britain Yearly Meeting to quote from the 2014 Swarthmore Lecture 'Open for Transformation' by Ben Pink Dandelion (p.xxiv)

The Quaker Tapestry at Kendal, to quote from 'Quaker Enterprise and the Railways' by Chris Bullard and Sheila Williams 2011(p.xxv) and also for allowing me to reproduce panel C4 of the Quaker Tapestry (p.xxvi) www.quaker-tapestry.co.uk

Random House Group Ltd to quote from 'Rich Desserts and Captains Thin' by Margaret Forster published by Chatto and Windus (p.20)

Sir Adrian Cadbury to quote from 'A Dear Memory' by Elizabeth M Cadbury (née Taylor) published by Cornish Brothers 1914 for private circulation.(p.34 et al)

The Institute of Historical Research, University of London, to quote from the Victoria County History, A History of Gloucester Vol 11, Editors, R B Pugh and NM Herbert (p.37)

The Gloucester Citizen and Gloucester Journal to quote from their archives on Samuel Bowly (p.41)

Leighton Park School to quote from 'Leighton Park' by S W Brown and 'Leighton Park, the first 100 years' (p.50)

HarperCollins Publishers to quote from 'Chocolate Wars' by Deborah Cadbury (p.78)

Rachel Malloch, daughter of Duncan Wood to quote from Duncan's book on 'Horace Alexander, Birds and Binoculars', published by Sessions 2003 (p.160)

Attempts have been made to trace rights to 'The Friends Ambulance Unit' by A Tegla Davies, published by George Allen and Unwin Ltd in 1947, now owned by HarperCollins Publishers Ltd, who have been unable to trace any contractual information but 'have no objection' to the use of quotes. Apologies to any next of kin of Tegla Davies (p.163 et al)

Geoffrey Carnell to quote from 'Gandhi's Interpreter, A Life of Horace Alexander' published by Edinburgh University Press 2010 (p.175)

Janet Pickard to quote from her Father's book, 'The First Five: The story of a school' 1987 by the late E J Brown, master at The Downs from 1932 and then Headmaster until 1974 (p.215)

Woodbrooke Study Centre, David Gray and Gillian Hopkins, to quote from 'Woodbrooke 1953-1978' by F Ralph Barlow (p.227)

Faber and Faber to quote from T S Eliot's 'The Journey of the Magi' (p.264)

My thanks for the use of photographs by - Michael Sessions and my sister, Rosemary Howells (p.xii); my brother, Stephen Barlow for the photograph of No 1 Willow Road in Bournville (p.139); Michael Darby for the photograph of his great Grandmother, Deborah Barlow's sampler (p.xxi); Carol Saker for the use of family photographs (p.102 & 120) & of John and Enid Barlow (p.118) Roger Barlow for the use of the photograph of our Grandmother in a Steam Car (p.107)

Apologies also to anyone else who I may have inadvertently omitted to mention.

Antony Barlow's direct family tree

JAMES LANCASTER (1618-1699) = MARGARET (1631-168?)
I
DINAH LANCASTER (1656-1718) = JOHN NICHOLSON (1656-1715)
I
JOHN NICHOLSON (1689-1737) = SARAH SARGENT (c.1690-1741)
I
JAMES NICHOLSON (1725-1806) = MARY HODGSEN (c.1723-1834)
I
THOMAS NICHOLSON (1764-1823) = BETTY SUTTON (1769-1834)
I
ELIZA NICHOLSON (1813-1894) = JOHN BARLOW (1815-1856)
I
JOHN HENRY BARLOW (1855-1924) = MABEL CASH (1868-1956)
I
F RALPH BARLOW (1910-1980) = JOAN M BARBER (1914-2007)
I
ANTONY BARLOW (b.1941)

See end of book for extended family trees

Contents

The publication of this book has been made possible with the generous financial support of:

The Sessions of York Trust for their very substantial grant

The CB & HH Taylor Charitable Trust]
The George Cadbury Trust]
The William A Cadbury Trust] for their very kind and considerable financial help
The Edward Cadbury Charitable Trust]
Sutton Quaker Meeting]
The Pollard & Dickson Trust]

The Quaker Family History Society, in the form of the Society's Small Research Award. For further information on this Society visit their website www.qfhs.co.uk or email info@qfhs.co.uk

Members of my immediate family and my cousins Roger Barlow, Carol Saker and Michael Darby for rallying round with additional finance to help to make this a reality.

The publication of this book would not have been possible without any of the above, for which I am most deeply grateful.

My parents

My parents, to whom I owe everything and who always encouraged me to do my best.

List of Illustrations

Blue plaque in memory of John Henry Barlow

Blue Plaque erected to the memory of our Grandfather, at their former home, 'Sunnybrae' on Bristol Road, Birmingham being unveiled by the author, Antony Barlow on June 17th 2014

Friends and relatives at the unveiling

Left:
Stephen Barlow with wife, Linda (in chair), their son, Christopher, Rosemary's daughter Jenny Howells, Sir John Barlow, Michael Darby (cousin), Rosemary, her husband, Richard Howells, their daughter, Lucy Claridge and grandchild, Summer, Carol Saker (cousin).

Right:
Antony Barlow, Mary Goodyear and Stuart Morton (Selly Oak Meeting), Duncan Cadbury (BVT), Rachel Malloch (Duncan Wood's daughter), Chris Rice (Civic Society), Sandra Berry (Woodbrooke), Anthony Wilson (Paul Cadbury Trust), Ruby Maw, Michael Sessions

Acknowledgements

This project began some ten years ago when my dear Mother was still alive and I was staying at home for a while. It was, of course, invaluable having her there as someone to consult on all matters family. I can't help, however, reprimanding myself for being so remiss as not to record her memories of her childhood and growing up with her brother and sisters and her Mother. How even more remiss of me not to have asked the same of my Father when he was still alive, though in 1980 this book was not yet on the horizon. So I have had to rely on what I remember of my parents' accounts of past events, the anecdotes they told us and my siblings similar powers of recall. My brothers and sister, have all been extremely helpful, offering suggestions, photographs, documents and stories and proffering encouragement and support when energy flagged. I would like to give special thanks to my elder brother David for his invaluable help as guardian of the family Bible and as the final proof reader; likewise my cousins, on both my Father's and my Mother's side. Of these, I must make especial mention of Sir Michael Rutter and his wife Marjorie, for their unquestioning support through difficult times, as well as their loan of interviews made with Michael's parents and loan of family photographs.

I am also greatly indebted to my late Cousin Anna OHerlihy, who offered moral support at all times, as well as many family documents and old photographs. Her sister Carol Saker has been equally generous in searching for historic family books, letters and other documents, plus invaluable photographs of our grandparents. Finally, my Cousin Roger Barlow, who has found other rare family photographs and accounts which have been of great assistance in filling in gaps and to my second cousins Sir John Barlow and Henry Barlow for their support and access to family archives.

Amongst others who have offered their unparalleled advice and historical expertise, I must single out Edward Milligan, former Chief Librarian at Friends House, to whom I am particularly indebted. He has given of his time and detailed knowledge of all things Quaker over the entire period of my research and writing, without stint and in addition provided a typically personal Introduction. My thanks to Ben P Dandelion of the Woodbrooke Study Centre, for correcting historical inaccuracies and for kindly writing a Preface. In addition, I am immensely grateful to my Publisher, Michael Sessions for his help and encouragement at all times, without whom this would not have seen the light of day.

I am particularly grateful for the advice of David Blake, the Head of the Library and Archives at Friends House, and his team of Josef Keith and Jennifer Mulligan for their research advice; to genealogist Anthony Adolph; to Doreen Hopwood, genealogist at the Leisure and Culture Department at Birmingham City Council, for her persistent research into the Barber and Eyre family history; to Pamela Clark, Registrar at Windsor Castle for allowing me access to the Royal Archives and the John Camden Neild papers; to M J Hinman at Coventry Heritage and Arts Trust, for supplying the Pedigree of the Cash family; to Cumbria Archive and Historical Research Service for access to their Quaker records relating to the Barlows and the Carr family; to Headmaster Michael Roden of King Edwards Camp Hill and Five Ways and Alison Wheatley, School archivist for information regarding my Mother's time at the schools; to Humphrey Dobinson for information regarding his Father's time as Head of KE Five Ways; to Rachel Malloch for very kindly supplying me with photographs of her Father Duncan Wood and Grandfather HG Wood; to Arthur Nicholls for his excellent pamphlet on Stramongate school; to Celia Wolfe at Ackworth School; to Alan Shrimpton, Archivist to the Bournville Village Trust; to Penny Wallington archivist of the Old Leightonians and to Chris and Janet Pickard of the Old Downians; and last but not least to Lucinda Gibson-House for encouragement at all times. If I have omitted anyone I implore their forgiveness.

Preface
Ben Pink Dandelion

This book is a treasure trove of carefully collected and selected family and wider Quaker social history. Whilst it is self-confessedly primarily a tribute to the service and ministry of Joan and Ralph Barlow, the earlier chapters tell us much about Victorian Quakerism and the nature of a dynastic Quakerism which is today less prevalent. Quakers married Quakers and their offspring were brought up as Friends. Quakers were indeed each other's cousins.

It may seem born of personal motives to write a family history but to do so, especially with such candour and assiduous detail, is of great service for those of us interested in the Quaker past. Tableux after tableaux provides new insights: the linear form of book seems almost constraining at times. In the later sections, we have the added bonus of being able to hear Antony's family speak for themselves, through extracts from letters and diaries. This is a rich resource and in the detailed chapters on Ralph Barlow's time in the FAU in World War Two and Joan and Ralph's connections with the Bournville Village Trust and Woodbrooke, we enter into a more recent past still largely untouched by academic study. We should be very grateful for Antony's work and for the affirmation it brings of a Quaker way of life and a Quaker set of values that continue to offer so many of us such strength and hope. Quakerism has changed and maybe it has needed to but we can still celebrate some of its essential insights and books like this are very much part of that process.

Woodbrooke Quaker Study Centre

1914   **Two generations**   **2014**

Millior, John and Ralph Barlow   Owen, Summer and Lucy Claridge

The author's Aunt, Uncle and Father   The author's niece and her husband and great niece

Foreword
Edward Milligan

The young eager, American postgraduate student was in the depths of despair. He had crossed the Atlantic to visit Britain, where he had never been before, because he wanted to write a thesis, maybe even a book, about a hitherto almost unknown nineteenth century reform movement. The century, was of course, full of them: the British and Foreign Bible society, the Society for the Promotion of Universal Peace, the ditto Anti-Slavery Society and so one could go on. They were all properly constituted bodies, with the committees reporting to the Annual Meeting, usually conducted with a member of the aristocracy in the chair. Quakers, he had been told, were involved in most of these bodies and he had been advised to visit Friends House Library in London as a first step.

He did as he was bid, only to receive a rebuff. The stern Librarian (me) told him bluntly that they did not have a minute book of the society, whose records he sought. And as if he had not had cold water enough thrown at his project, the librarian had the temerity to doubt if a minute book of the cherished society had ever existed. The dispirited American scholar sensed that the implacable librarian was thawing just a little and said, with a smile, that by good fortune the library did have the papers of two Quakers who, he knew, had been much interested in the work of this elusive committee. He assured the young American that the papers would of course be made available to him. He also suggested to the young scholar that he note every person mentioned in the respective paper and that he consult a typescript embryo dictionary of Quaker biography, noting that person's parents, and marriage and children (if any). The rich young ruler had (as we learn from the Bible) turned away sorrowful, for he had great possessions. The poor young would-be researcher, however, went away sorrowful too, for he saw no prospect of having any historical possessions at all.

But four or five days later, he erupted (there was no other verb good enough) into my room. "Ted", he cried (well he had heard my colleagues address me thus) "I see it all. I thought all that genealogical stuff was to keep me quiet. But I should have known you wouldn't do that and of course it's essential. Nobody interested in the reform movement, is further from anyone else than first cousin once removed. Of course there was no committee and no minute book. When one's family's cousins came to stay, they could deal with any outstanding matter over breakfast."

I had quite forgotten that episode of long ago until I read Antony Barlow's magnificent account of his family during four centuries. It is perhaps best summed up in the explanatory words which grace an illustration; "He is our cousin, cousin". And once we have been introduced to them, they move off stage with skill and grace, just before we need to be introduced to the next group. Antony Barlow's prose carries us at a steady and sedate pace, so that we are never breathless and never bored. It is a joy to welcome illustrations, selected with loving care, so that they are companions with the written word in this family journey. But the book is more than that. Throughout those centuries, there has been in each generation, one or other of the family deeply involved in some Quaker enterprise or other. The book is therefore, more than a family record, providing as it does some glimpses of national Quaker preoccupations during the last four centuries. The book deserves a wide readership.

Former Head Librarian, Friends House

Cousins

King Richard
Cousin Aumerle,
How far brought you high Hereford on his way?
Aumerle
I brought high Hereford, if you call him so, but to
the next highway, and there I left him.
King Richard
And say, what store of parting tears were shed?
Aumerle
Faith, none for me; except the north-east wind,
Which then blew bitterly against our face,
Awaked the sleeping rheum, and so by chance
Did grace our hollow parting with a tear.

King Richard
What said our cousin when you parted with him?
Aumerle
'Farewell:'
And, for my heart disdained that my tongue
Should so profane the word, that taught me craft
To counterfeit oppression of such grief
That words seem'd buried in my sorrow's grave.
Marry, would the word 'farewell' have lengthen'd
hours
And added years to his short banishment,
He should have had a volume of farewells;
But since it would not, he had none of me.
King Richard
He is our cousin, cousin; *but 'tis doubt,*
When time shall call him home from banishment,
Whether our kinsman come to see his friends.

Cousins – King Richard II and Duke of Aumerle, grandchildren of King Edward III
Scene as depicted by Shakespeare in *Richard II Act 1 scene iv* from where the title quote comes.

"He is our cousin, cousin!"

My mother, Joan Barlow died in 2007 at the age of 93, and so I became the custodian of most of the family archives. These had always intrigued me as a child; the old family Bible of 1616, family trees or old letters dating back some hundreds of years, plus first-hand accounts by, for instance, my Great Grandfather, Frederick Goodall Cash, of historical events such as Queen Victoria's coronation and Wellington's funeral or my Grandmother, Mabel Cash describing a visit to the House of Commons in 1889, but above all the striking painting of my great, great Grandmother, Elizabeth Petipher Lucas, which was hung prominently in our house and is now in mine and is the front cover of this book.

Our branch of the Barlow family comes from a long line of Quakers, dating from the very beginnings of the Society of Friends. Quakers it seems have been fairly assiduous in maintaining family records, making it somewhat easier for the present day genealogist to trace their families right back to that early time. Also, up until the late nineteenth century, Quakers only married within the faith[3], and hence any of our family trees will form an intricate network of interlocking families. So that, for instance, when I was at the Quaker school Leighton Park in the 1950's many of my peers were my close or distant cousins including such well known Quaker names as Cadburys, Darbys, Frys, Rowntrees, Braithwaites, Hoylands, Brockbanks, Taylors and Nicholsons[4]. Because of this interconnectedness of many Quaker families, it became customary for families to address each other by the title of 'Cousin', though they might only be second or even third cousins! Indeed when I was a child, I remember my Father's redoubtable mother, referring to members of her extended family, always by the prefix of Cousin. Not, as we might today talk of 'my cousin Michael' but almost as a title on its own, endowed with honour on its bearer.

This custom, so much an integral part of Quaker life of bygone days, gave me the idea of using a favourite quotation of my Father, Ralph Barlow, from Shakespeare's *Richard II,* as a title for this book[5]. The intricate relationships of the Houses of Lancaster and York, are so much a part of Shakespeare's history plays, that a full appreciation of the various dramas that make up the cycle are perhaps, only fully understood by some knowledge of who's related to whom. At the beginning of *Richard II*, after King Richard has banished his cousin Henry Bolingbroke following an argument, he questions another cousin, Aumerle, as to how Bolingbroke had seemed when he left him. Despite his description of Bolingbroke's friends' tearful farewell to their hero, Aumerle replies that he himself was unmoved and thought that his banishment should have been longer. The King, ironically reprimanding him, says but "He is our cousin, cousin"! So this book tells the story of many of my 'cousins' from the last 350 years!

This book, therefore, is not only a personal family history but also very much the history of the Society, since most of my ancestors have at one time or another been caught up in the great issues that have engaged the Society since its inception. From persecution and pacifism to temperance and anti-slavery one or other of my family have been leading champions. Along the way we also come across sailors and silk merchants, wool merchants and cheese merchants, pioneering businessmen and distinguished academicians, and all of them devout Quakers. It is a fascinating history and one of which I am very proud.

---

[3] See under Professor John Barlow and the Carrs for more on marrying outside the faith
[4] See photo of Dame Elizabeth Cadbury's 90th birthday in 1948 under chapter on George Cadbury with all these names
present as relatives
[5] Shakespeare's *Richard II* Act 1, scene iv, line 20

My late Cousin Anna OHerlihy née Braithwaite 1942-2011

Her lovely poem *On the Death of a Favourite Quaker Aunt,* seems to encapsulate so well the theme of the book and which I reprint here as a tribute to her memory.

On the death of a favourite Quaker Aunt
by
Cousin Anna OHerlihy[6]

Around the years of my life
They stood
Uncles, Aunts, parents
Respectable, respected, responsible
Substantial, not much troubled by time.

Now they have gone, all gone in the lapse of twenty years
In the end they all grew old and tired
They have gone into the deep mystery of death.

Once they were the grownups,
They were weighty and wise,
Solicitor, Photographer, Lecturer, Philosopher.

They sat on committees, were treasurers, chair persons, elders and overseers.
They wrote books and poems and gave lectures,
Painted, embroidered, potted, sewed, fabric printed
Fashioned and repaired,
Cultivated their gardens and reared their children.
They could initiate and keep to the long haul.
Their marriages endured
They ministered in meeting
Sang in choirs, played the violin and the trombone.

They were a religious generation,
Quaker, epiphany philosopher, or agnostic
They lived in the Quaker heritage
And walked in the paths of the individual conscience
Through the clouds of temperate protest.

Now they have all gone from us
And we have become the grown up generation
We stand between our children and the end
We try to smile in the face of their revolt.

And with sadness and with gratitude
I know my loss and I remember them all
My parents, aunts and Uncles
And I honour their long lives.

---

[6] Anna was Antony Barlow's first cousin, the eldest daughter of Alfred and Millior Braithwaite. She was married to Callaghan OHerlihy and died in 2011.

Deborah Barlow's sampler

The Sampler of my Great, Great Aunt, Deborah Barlow (1822 -1879)

Deborah Barlow married John Thistlethwaite and she is the great Grandmother of my cousin, Michael Darby, who took the photograph. The sampler belongs to Michael's sister Deborah Taylor, named after her forebear. Samplers were a common pastime, but here this one seems also to be an apt metaphor for my book, which illustrates ancestral samples.

Introduction
Antony Barlow

As I read back over this history, I am aware that all those described, appear to have led lives of unalloyed perfection and that I do not sufficiently discuss the exigencies of their daily existence. The truth is that I have no way of knowing precisely how these people lived from day to day, other than from the official minutes of the Society of Friends, which are often fulsomely praiseworthy, or from our family records and the occasional biography. Even the correspondence that I possess of my great grandparents or have had recourse to, such as the letters that Elizabeth Cadbury published of her Mother, Mary Taylor in the delightful book 'A Dear Memory'[7], are full of endearments praising their wonderful lives. Who am I to contradict?

Many of these minutes and records are simple encomiums such as that for William Cash's wife Mary in the year 1770: *"A very sweet old lady, given to much Bible study and beloved by her grandchildren."* And of Elizabeth Taylor's Grandmother, by her Monthly meeting in 1832: *"We do not write in the language of eulogy, but having known, so we speak, and it may be long ere the memory of one so loving and beloved should pass away from our lives."*

Just occasionally, however, one finds a slightly critical record of a life less holy, as in the testimony of John Cash in 1811, *"Our friend John Cash removed to Coventry in the 19th year of his age, where, residing in an exposed situation, the enemy of man's happiness was frequently permitted to lay temptations in his way which sometimes he fell in with, till it pleased the Lord, who is often unmeritedly kind to the rebellious and backslider, tenderly to visit him for the purpose of his redemption and salvation, which proved at last effectual."* That 'unmeritedly' carries a world of opprobrium one feels.

There is also a passage in the tribute to my great, Grandfather Professor John Barlow, expressing his parents' worries that he would get into wrongful ways during his studies in Edinburgh in the 1840's, especially when they learnt, that for a while he had not been *'regular in his attendance at meeting for worship'*, and trusted he would *"keep to the religious life and eschew mixing with wrong company."* John, aware of his *'seclusion from Friends'* replies that *"All things considered, I feel best satisfied to forego the associations you allude to and with right assistance to retrieve myself."* Yet the same minute concludes *"Modest, gentle and unassuming in his manners, he obtained the respect of all who came in contact with him."* So the return to religious ways are all the more virtuous for his having overcome temptation.

We do find occasional glimpses into their everyday lives, as when Elizabeth Taylor recalls an incident relating to our great, great Grandmother, Elizabeth Lucas: *"We liked to hear stories of their childhood; one I remember was of a visit of some young Friends one afternoon to the Lucas house. The daughters were demurely sitting by their mother with their sewing, when the visitors were shown in and wondered at the special object of their united call. Eventually they heard that there had been a debate amongst the Quakers of Westminster as to which was the prettiest girl in the Meeting and that all had voted in favour of Elizabeth Lucas."* A passage worthy of Jane Austen and proof that even Quakers were not immune from worldly thoughts!

There are other visits mentioned as well, such as to Elizabeth Lucas' sister, great Aunt Hannah, *"Our great pleasure when visiting her as children, was to hear her read aloud. Her voice was musical and the intonation and expression quite perfect"* which suddenly brings a

---

[7] 'A Dear Memory' is in the possession of my cousin Carol Saker. Elizabeth Taylor married George Cadbury.

world to life. And I have found several letters that describe the life at the family home in Peckham, which *"was a very hospitable home, and most Friends living in or visiting London found their way there."*

The comings and goings of the many cousins, relations and friends living at 'The Rye' was obviously a constant source of interest and pleasure. Elizabeth Taylor recalls an incident when she goes over to visit my great Grandfather's home on the Rye (see photo on page 29).

"I remember, for instance, one bright summer's day sitting in the schoolroom at home, struggling to study, and listening to the call of the birds, knowing that Mother had gone to 'The Rye' to greet a family passing through to the South. Suddenly a tap at the door, and in comes a bright boy cousin, saying 'Excuse me, but my Aunt says 'may Elsie come today to play with us?' Oh the joy to fling down books and slate and to go skipping down the hill to the beautiful gardens with the cedar trees and the winding walks and the summer houses and the swings. I feel again the spring of childhood, the abandon of irresponsible happiness."

In her introduction to her Mother's correspondence, Elizabeth Taylor alludes to the extensive cousinship in which she moved in the late 19th century, *"We were a clan of between seventy and eighty first cousins and the circle was enlarged by the inclusion of second and third cousins."* This interrelationship still very much obtained when I was a child and went, along with 150 other cousins, to Elizabeth's, by then Dame Elizabeth Cadbury's 90th birthday in 1948 (see photo on page 80) and examining my parents' lives I am very conscious of the considerable influence of the large Quaker diaspora, in the way they extended a hand to all its members.

In wondering about their everyday life, it is often easier to imagine the day to day existence of the men than the women, as their professions will usually give some immediate insight, though sometimes an unexpected name is referenced or an incident told that to our ears now sheds an amusing light on contemporary customs. Here again is Elizabeth Taylor for instance, talking about her family, describing her Grandfather, Henry Taylor of Whitby, born in 1737:

"As a boy, he was the playmate and friend of Captain Cook and many another worthy navigator. On one occasion, he and his wife were visiting Friends in Ireland, when his ship was in port, adding, 'We were often burdened with the luxury of their tables, especially their immoderate use of wine, and the matter lay so weightily on our minds that we resolved ever after, to drink only water'."

Like the Taylor forebears, the Nicholsons too were mariners and led an often precarious and dangerous life, with the wives sometimes accompanying their husbands on voyages, *"encountering terrible gales, once with our cabin being flooded, though my wife never showed any signs of fear."* But other early ancestors were described on their birth certificates as Yeomen. Henry Barlow for instance (1664-1720) of Alderley Edge, Cheshire is so described, which according to Fowler's 'Modern English Usage' usually indicates "a small landowner, a farmer of the middle classes, qualified by the possession of land to serve on juries and vote for a Knight of the Shire, though it was often hard to distinguish minor landed gentry from the wealthier yeomen."

Owning land was the main form of wealth in the 18th century and political power and influence was in the hands of rich landowners. At the top were the nobility and below them were a class of nearly rich landowners, known as the gentry. But in the early 18th century there was another class of landowners called yeomen, somewhere between the rich and the poor, though throughout the century this class would become less numerous, as other middle class people such as merchants and professional men became richer and more numerous. Thus some families like my Barlow ancestors became gentleman farmers and indeed my cousin, Sir John Barlow lives and farms in Nantwich, Cheshire, but a stone's throw away from where our mutual ancestors have farmed for generations.

On the other hand, many Quakers became businessmen, because in the 18th and 19th Century their faith forbad joining either the military or the church, and they were excluded by law from politics and large areas of public life, so found themselves going into industry. The leading families, such as many of my relatives - the Cash family weavers of Coventry, the iron founder Darbys of Coalbrookdale, the Cadbury chocolatiers of Bournville - were a close-knit highly inter-related community, with strategic marriages to secure family businesses, who supported each other and maintained high standards in their work.

Reading the diaries and letters of these businessmen, it is amazing to learn of how much they travelled, not only in this country but abroad as well. Mary Taylor writing to her friend Mary Jenkin- Brown in 1868 says of her husband:

"John had to travel to Berlin on business and was away a week and enjoyed the change very much, only had not the leisure he had hoped for to inspect the foreign attractions. He had hoped to spend a day or two on the Rhine, but had to be content with a visit to Cologne."

Then again the following year:

"John had again to visit Germany and went first to Düsseldorf and from there visiting iron foundries on the Rhine. Then he went to the town of Rotterdam and Sunday he spent in Antwerp and is charmed with the place, intensely admiring the cathedral and the churches, whose chimes he thought the softest and most beautiful he had ever heard and he loved the carvings and the frescoes. He had wonderfully calm passages across the channel."

But despite many of the 19th century Quakers being successful businessmen and well off, there are also as many accounts of dealings that went wrong. My Great Grandmother, Eliza Barlow was one such, who suffered badly when the money left to her by her beloved husband Professor Barlow on his early death at 40 in 1856, all disappeared as a result of ill-advised investments encouraged by Jonathan Carr, leaving her destitute, with three children to look after. Elizabeth Taylor also describes the sad circumstances of her father John's bankruptcy, who had invested badly as well, where:

"his guilessness and trust in others had brought him to grief, believing everything he was told by those miserable American railway magnates. Worried by the failure of one concern in which he had invested his own and his clients' money, he endeavoured in various ways to put matters right, only succeeding in becoming more hopelessly involved."

In my childhood we learnt about the history of our family and the story of the bible, and the long list of notable forebears were set before us as exemplars. It was a similar story in those same people's own childhoods too, as we learn from Cousin Elizabeth's account in 'A Dear Memory' of how our mutual Uncle Fred (Frederick Goodall Cash) proceeds to:

"Trace the descent of our family via the Hayhursts to General Monck's sister Lady Eleanor and the Plantagenets and by consequence from William the Conqueror. These histories were told us as children, with the idea that if we could really claim lineage with past 'makers of history', we too must do something for our country in our own day and generation."

Today the membership is no longer brought up in big Quaker dynasties and more people now join the Society in adulthood. There are no famous Quaker names running big companies any more, as the major family firms have been taken over and perhaps a more significant change runs parallel to this. Many Quaker businessmen concluded that maybe their very difference from others, was holding them back and so gradually began to convert to Anglicanism, the better to fit in with the business elite of the day.

Nonetheless, Quakers can still be found running small firms along Quaker lines and there are of course, many successful Quakers in business. But by and large, Quakers are now active in other ways, working for social change, often through the old Trusts such as those of the Rowntree family, and have become very involved in the setting up of the many non-governmental organisations such as Greenpeace, Amnesty International or Oxfam.

But today, Ben Dandelion, who has generously provided a Preface to this history, expresses some misgivings, in his introduction to the 2014 Swarthmore Lecture[8]:

"Now that we no longer begin our spiritual journey in the tailor's shop, being a Quaker is far easier than it used to be. We have a private life and personal beliefs; we pick and choose our understanding of testimony and our opportunities for service and how often we come to meeting."

We welcome all comers into membership including many who have only a tangential belief in God or even Christianity. So in looking at the history of this family of mine and our many 'Cousins' down the centuries, I hope I provide not only a glimpse into the lives of early Quakers but perhaps also find a way of returning to the certainties of their lives. For in writing this book, I have come more and more to believe, as Ben Dandelion so eloquently puts it in Chapter 2 of his lecture: *"that we have in places lost the heart of our faith and have diluted basic and central Quaker understandings within a desire to appease all of the varieties of doctrinal slants we now encompass."* Maybe the lives of these Quaker men and women of earlier generations, can encourage us to recover something, not only of their innate spirituality, but also the way they expressed that spirituality so positively in their everyday lives.

A memorial to the Quakers' wartime service was inaugurated at the National Memorial Arboretum in Staffordshire in April 2013. The Memorial, designed by Staffordshire sculptor and Quaker, Rosemary Barnett, serves as a focal point for commemoration of the humanitarian work conducted by Friends in times of conflict.

[8] 'Open for Transformation', the 2014 Swarthmore Lecture published by Quaker books, Friends House.

Quakers and Quakerism

The Religious Society of Friends was founded by George Fox (1624 -1691) in the middle of the 17th century in Northern England. He was an English dissenter, living at a time of great social upheaval and unrest, who rebelled against what he saw as the corruption of the religious establishment and the political authorities of the time. The name 'Quaker', originally a term of ridicule, derived from a statement of Fox's, when he told his followers "to tremble at the Word of the Lord", but before long became accepted as the name of the movement. He preached throughout Britain, North America and the Low countries and was persecuted and imprisoned by the authorities for his beliefs.

He believed that the light of God was in every person and that everyone could have a direct relationship with God without involving a priest or minister, with Quaker worship consisting of silent waiting and participants contributing as the spirit moves them. The passing of the Toleration Act in 1689, eventually allowed for freedom of conscience and so gradually Quakers became more tolerated, if not still totally accepted. Indeed some Quakers, such as William Penn, had already left for America to escape persecution, establishing their own state of Pennsylvania, with a legal framework, where power was derived from the people, much like a Quaker Meeting.

While comparatively small in its membership, the Society has nonetheless been hugely influential in the history of reform, and Quakers have played a significant role in such movements as the abolition of slavery, promoting education and equal rights for women, campaigning on behalf of gay rights, and working for the humane treatment of prisoners, famously through the work of the 19th century philanthropist Elizabeth Fry. Above all they have campaigned tirelessly for peace between nations, and in 1947, the Quaker movement worldwide was awarded the Nobel Peace prize on account of the relief work they did in both World Wars, particularly through the work of The Friends Ambulance Unit.

From the earliest days of the Quaker movement, constraints were placed upon them by varying acts of parliament, some of which were still in force in the early 19th century. The Test and Corporation Acts, for instance, restricted entry to the world of universities and public service, to members of the Church of England, which affected not only Quakers but other non-conformists and Catholics as well. In addition, Quaker principles of peace, truth and simplicity, often created their own difficulties regarding a career, closing options such as the military or arms manufacture. Of necessity, therefore, Quakers took up manufacturing and trade where their very honesty and straightforwardness brought them success. As Chris Bullard and Sheila Williams say in their booklet 'Quaker Enterprise and the Railways'[9] :

'In proportion to their small number, it is amazing that so many well-known companies and Banks were founded by Quakers....(but) Quakers had their own networks that could be used to enable, encourage and help sustain their businesses.'

Many of these, such as George Cadbury, Joseph Fry and Joseph Rowntree were successful, not only because they were trusted but also because they used their money philanthropically, caring for their work force, providing good conditions in which to work and in many cases pleasant places to live such as Bournville in Birmingham. Today Quakers work just as actively as ever to try and improve the human condition. Their particular concerns continue to be with human rights, with social justice and environmental issues, peace and freedom of conscience, being paramount. Though no longer dressed in the Quaker attire of the early years, they still seek to live simply, so as make this a better world.

---

[9] Published by Quaker Tapestry of Kendal 2011

The following words from The Quaker Tapestry illustrate the themes that run through my book and members of my family appear under most of the headings listed below.

This remarkable tapestry tells of Quaker events and insights and is a celebration of the significant contribution these quiet, non-conformists have made to the modern world. Telling stories from the forefront of the industrial revolution, developments in science and medicine, the abolition of slavery, social reform, all are revealed from within the stunning needlework.

The idea of a Quaker Tapestry came into being as a result of a chance question about the history of the Society, made by an eleven-year-old boy attending the children's class of a small Quaker Meeting in the South West of England in 1981. His teacher, to whom the remark was made, was Anne Wynn-Wilson, an accomplished embroiderer. She had the vision of a number of large tapestry panels telling something of the Quaker story and beliefs. In 1982 she mounted an exhibition of work in progress and her ideas and determination aroused an enthusiastic response from many Friends. Designers came forward, embroidery groups were formed, and training workshops were arranged. Enthusiasm for the project spread and more than 4,000 men, women and children in 15 countries 'had a hand' in the creation of the Quaker Tapestry. Completed in 1996, the result is 77 panels of narrative 'crewel' type embroidery on specially woven wool cloth. With each panel measuring 25" (635mm) by 21" (533mm) it is testament to the passion and shared sense of community of an amazing group of Friends.[10]

The above is quoted from the Tapestry's publicity.

---

[10] Quaker Tapestry © This image is one of the 77 illustrations known as the Quaker Tapestry which is a community textile of embroidered panels made by 4,000 people from 15 countries. The exhibition of life, revolutions and remarkable people can be seen at the Quaker Tapestry Museum in the Quaker Meeting House in Kendal, Cumbria UK.
Further information: http://www.quaker-tapestry.co.uk

Chapter 1
"To begin at the beginning"

'To begin at the beginning', to quote Dylan Thomas' famous opening of *Under Milk Wood,* seems as fair a place to start as any. For the Quaker family of Barlow, that beginning goes right back to the very birth of Quakerism, sometime around the 1660's, when its founder, George Fox was gathering his first followers about him and much of our earliest Quaker ancestry is gleaned from the family Bible, known as the Lancaster Bible, dating from 1616, after its first owner, James Lancaster. Lancaster, our earliest recorded Quaker ancestor (1610-1679), was amongst the first to join up with Fox, and this Bible, still stained by the salt water from when he dropped it as he was fleeing persecution across Morecambe sands, has been handed down through his daughter's family ever since and now belongs to my elder brother David. This book will tell the story of the nearly 400 years of our family history, since James Lancaster first acquired that Bible.

My Grandfather, John Henry Barlow (1855-1924), was the first to write a history of this Bible, in the Quaker publication, *The Quarterly Examiner,* in 1898 and I can't do better than repeat his scene-setting introduction:

"In the year 1616 the printing house of Robert Barker, 'Printer to the King's most excellent Maisetie', (sic) was busy with an edition of the Bible. It was only five years before this that the Authorised Version had been published and we may therefore suppose that when the sheets were finally bound into volumes, they found a pretty ready sale. One of these lies before me on the table as I write....."

James Lancaster was born in 1610, just six years before the printing of this Bible, on the island of Walney in what is now Cumbria. The island lies in the Irish Sea to the west of the Furness peninsula in north-west England and up until as late as 1974, both the island and the peninsula were a detached part of the county of Lancashire, but today the island is part of the borough of Barrow-in-Furness, having been connected by a bridge since 1908. Young James was a yeoman who lived in North Scale on the northern edge of Walney Island, a former royalist stronghold during the English Civil War. In fact Quakerism in the 17th century, was the natural refuge of those who disagreed with the Presbyterian organisation of the Commonwealth under Oliver Cromwell, though ironically, as it turned out, it was actually Cromwell who would become the most sympathetic to Fox's beliefs and who eventually gave the Quakers their religious freedom.

So in many ways, Cumbria could be said to be the birthplace of Quakerism; George Fox preached on Pardshaw Crag in 1653, drawing huge crowds and Pardshaw and Pardshaw Hall, near Cockermouth, became strongholds of Quakerism from its earliest days. Other preachers of the period, did not find Cumbria particularly conducive to their missions, but for Fox, it was exactly the reverse. When he allied himself with the 'Westmoreland Seekers', a group of spiritual dissenters, who met in private homes and public buildings to discuss scriptures and religious issues of the day, he found a ready audience. As Fox continued to travel throughout the region, these groups naturally coalesced and on Sunday, June 13th, 1652 on Firbank Fell, over a thousand people gathered in the open air, to hear him preach. This now famous gathering has often been recorded as the first ever Quaker Meeting.

After James Lancaster was 'convinced', as Quakers describe joining the Society, he went on to become one of the most prominent of the first Quaker missionaries and a member of that

Quaker associations

GEORGE FOX,
Founder of the Society of Friends.

George Fox, 1624 – 1691
Possibly by R. Sawyer
etching, late 18th to early 19th
century

The Author writes:
"Fox was an English Dissenter and
a founder of the Religious Society
of Friends, commonly known as the
Quakers or Friends."

©Reproduced by kind permission of the
National Portrait Gallery, London

Swarthmoor Hall
built c.1568.

The Author writes:
"This was the home of the Assize
Judge, Thomas Fell, and his wife
Margaret and family. Today it is a
Quaker retreat."

elite group known as the 'Valiant Sixty', the earliest leaders and activists in the Society. They were itinerant preachers, mostly from northern England, who spread the ideas of Quakerism throughout Britain, Europe and America during the second half of the Seventeenth Century. The first religious meetings of Friends, as we would recognise them, began in a private house in Cumberland in 1653. As the numbers grew, the meetings could not be contained indoors and for many years they met in the open air on Pardshaw Crag. But eventually, in 1672, a purpose built Meeting House was built at Pardshaw, which within a few years was already too small and by 1705 had to be further enlarged. Soon other Meeting Houses sprang up all over the county, such as those at Swarthmoor[1] near Ulverston, Brigflatts near Sedbergh and Kendal, which seemed to fit perfectly into the Cumbrian landscape. Today, meeting for worship still takes place in Kendal, in a building which stands on the land originally purchased for the first meeting house there in 1687, though the current building only dates from 1816 and now houses the renowned Quaker Tapestry.

Any student of the early history of the Society of Friends will soon come across the name of James Lancaster, for he became a frequent and trusted companion of George Fox, travelling with him throughout the country on his ministry. At what period of his life the old family Bible came into his possession it is difficult to say, but on one of the leaves at the front of the Bible is the following note written in 1780 by Mary Nicholson of Whitehaven, who inherited it from her great grandfather, John Nicholson who married Lancaster's daughter Dinah:

"James Lancaster was 'convinced' by George Fox in 1652 and in 1654 went on a gospel mission to Scotland and again in 1657; in 1665 he visited many of the Midland counties and in 1669 he went to Ireland. There was not perhaps anyone who was so much associated with George Fox as James Lancaster, often acting as his amanuensis."

James Lancaster was married to Margaret (b 1631) in 1652, and they had at least eight children, including Ishmael (1653), Dinah (1656), Deborah (1660) and Elisha (1664), the latter three of which are confirmed in the Quaker records at Friends House. Deborah married John Marshall, son of Nicholas Marshall of Biggar, Walney Island, at Swarthmoor in 1689, and Dinah married John Nicholson in 1678 at Pardshaw, Cumberland, both Quakers, and according to the Quaker archives[2], *"established generations of Quakers"*, amongst which, number of course, our many forebears, not to mention the current members of our family.

It is necessary, for a moment, however, to return to George Fox. He was born in 1624 in Leicestershire, and from an early age, mingled with many of the Dissenters who had broken away from the established church. But Fox was an individualist, who soon found himself in disagreement with the others and began to formulate his own beliefs, which would become the very heart of future Quaker thought. He believed that ritual was not important in worship, and neither were church buildings, for it was his strong conviction that 'God could be found everywhere'. Most importantly, he said that church ministry should not be confined to a professional priesthood, as anyone who was guided by the Holy Spirit, had a right to minister and to seek God's inner light in the individual.

By 1647 the Religious Society of Friends was taking shape and Fox was travelling around the country, preaching publicly in market-places, fields or anywhere he could find an audience, nearly always with James Lancaster at his side. He was a powerful and charismatic preacher

---

[1] Swarthmoor - it's original spelling was 'Swarthmore' but later changed to Swarthmoor, though the two often seem interchangeable. When the Bournville Village Trust was deciding on names for new Roads, one was called Swarthmore Road (sic) which was where the Barlow family lived for many years.

[2] Friends House Library

and he soon began to attract a substantial following. It is not entirely clear at what precise point the Society of Friends was formed, but certainly by 1650 there was already a group of people who regularly travelled together, calling themselves 'Friends of the Truth' and later simply 'Friends'. Also by this time, their style of worship had been firmly established, much in the form we are familiar with today, of a silent gathering 'waiting on the Lord'. Needless to say they attracted a great deal of attention, partly because of their distinctive, simple attire and partly because they refused to swear oaths or pay tithes to the established church. Fox campaigned against the paying of tithes, because, he said, these usually went into the pockets of absentee landlords or religious organisations, far away from the paying parishioners. This inevitably brought Fox and his followers into conflict with officials and the general public, who would whip and beat them to drive them away.Oppression by the powerful, was a very real concern for the English people in the turmoil of the English Civil War between the execution of Charles I in 1649, and the beginnings of the Commonwealth in 1653. And certainly Fox's beliefs, such as for instance, that you didn't need to have a university qualification in order to be a preacher, or in addition, his total disregard for the established church, were bound, sooner or later to bring him up against the civil authorities and before long he and many others were frequently being imprisoned.

In fact, Cromwell himself was quite tolerant towards those with different beliefs. This was apparent both by his decision to re-admit Jews into England and in his relaxation of the harsh persecution of Catholics. But though, in reality, he was sympathetic to Fox's views, meeting with him on several occasions, this did not guarantee Fox's or his followers' safety. Indeed, the authorities continued to ill-treat Fox and those around him and the many widespread inequities that they witnessed during their years of persecution, led to the establishment within the Society, of 'Meeting for Sufferings'. Such gatherings, would closely monitor the treatment of fellow Quakers, but at a deeper level, they also inspired within his growing movement an interest in social justice which would become a hallmark of so many Quakers, from prison reformers such as Elizabeth Fry and the campaigners against slavery such as our great, great Grandfather, Samuel Bowly[3] to the caring industrialists such as Cadbury and Carr, and 'Meeting for Sufferings' remains to this day, a vital part of Quaker practice.

During his many travels around the country, George Fox became a friend of the distinguished Assize Judge, Thomas Fell, and his wife Margaret and family, who lived at Swarthmoor Hall in the Furness area of Cumbria. Swarthmoor Hall had been built in about 1568 by Thomas' father, and was inherited by his son, so that when he married Margaret Askew in 1634, they were able to move into the family home. Fell was a travelling judge, later becoming Vice Chancellor of the Duchy of Lancaster and was an influential supporter of parliament. From Margaret Fell's first meeting with George Fox, she showed a great interest in his new teachings and arranged for him to come and preach in the nearby church in Ulverston. Before long, Margaret became 'convinced'[4] of his teachings and joined the new Society, and although her husband Thomas never did, he was always sympathetic and allowed Swarthmoor Hall to be used as an early meeting place, until eventually a new meeting house was built nearby. In 1658 Thomas Fell died and Margaret and George Fox continued working together, eventually marrying some eleven years later in 1669.

It was in 1651, when James Lancaster was 41, that he first met up with George Fox, just after Fox had been released from Derby gaol, where he had been imprisoned for twelve months and had endured a great deal of particularly harsh treatment. George Fox's *Journal* gives a good

---

[3] See Chapter 8
[4] A Quaker term for joining the Society

idea of the atmosphere of persecution of the time, as well as describing an incident relating to our own Bible, when Fox was badly attacked while crossing to Walney, not least by Lancaster's own wife, who mistakenly thought George had bewitched her husband:

"I went over in a boat to James Lancaster's. As soon as I came to land, there rushed out about forty men with staves, clubs and fishing poles who fell on me, beating and punching me and endeavoured to push me backwards into the sea. James Lancaster was lying over me trying to keep the blows and stones off me."

James managed to reassure his wife that no 'bewitching' had taken place, but felt that he should really stay behind with George Fox after this frightening event. However, he felt even more uneasy at the prospect of leaving his wife and baby on Walney Island and so decided to return to Cartgate, leaving home by night for fear of being set upon again. They travelled in a farm cart, carrying only their daughter Dinah, and their Bible, from Walney to Cartgate across Morecambe sands and James Lancaster records for us what happened:

"We were fleeing as fast we could, when the horse sunk in the sands as the tide rose and the sand grew softer and softer and ever more treacherous. The more the horse struggled the deeper it sank. Only by the grace of God did we narrowly manage to escape with our child and the Bible, showing clearly the marks where the salt water had stained its leaves."

One has only to recall the recent tragedy of the Chinese cockle pickers drowning in Morecambe Bay[5] to realise how treacherous the area can be, and John Henry Barlow in his account, explains why:

"Walney is only an island at high water; at low tide the sands are sufficiently dry for foot passengers. The island lies very low and in the old days the abbots of Furness charged themselves with the support of a dyke for its defence. But since the suppression of the abbey this has been neglected and the sea has made considerable inroads. We may therefore suppose that James and his wife and daughter unduly delayed their departure and that the tide advanced more rapidly than they expected."

So fortuitously, our distant ancestor James, survived to tell the tale, his daughter Dinah, to marry the seafarer, John Nicholson, and this old Bible subsequently to be handed down through the Nicholson branch of the family. As a final point on this incident, it is interesting to note that on one of the water-stained leaves of the Bible, their marriage is actually recorded and witnessed by Fox's wife, Margaret Fell, whose name is listed along with others members of the family. It may not I suspect, be Margaret's own handwriting, more likely that of James Lancaster himself, but nonetheless is an historical witness to the beginnings of our Quaker story.

Walney Island, is an island off the west coast of England, at the western end of Morecambe Bay. It forms part of the town of Barrow-in-Furness, and it is separated from mainland Barrow by Walney Channel, a narrow channel which is spanned by the Jubilee Bridge.

---

[5]February 2004 21 cockle pickers were drowned on the incoming tide.

From the front pages of the family bible.

The Nicholson family and their descendants.

See family tree at the end of the book, pp 265/6

The marriage of Dinah Lancaster to John Nicholson in 1678

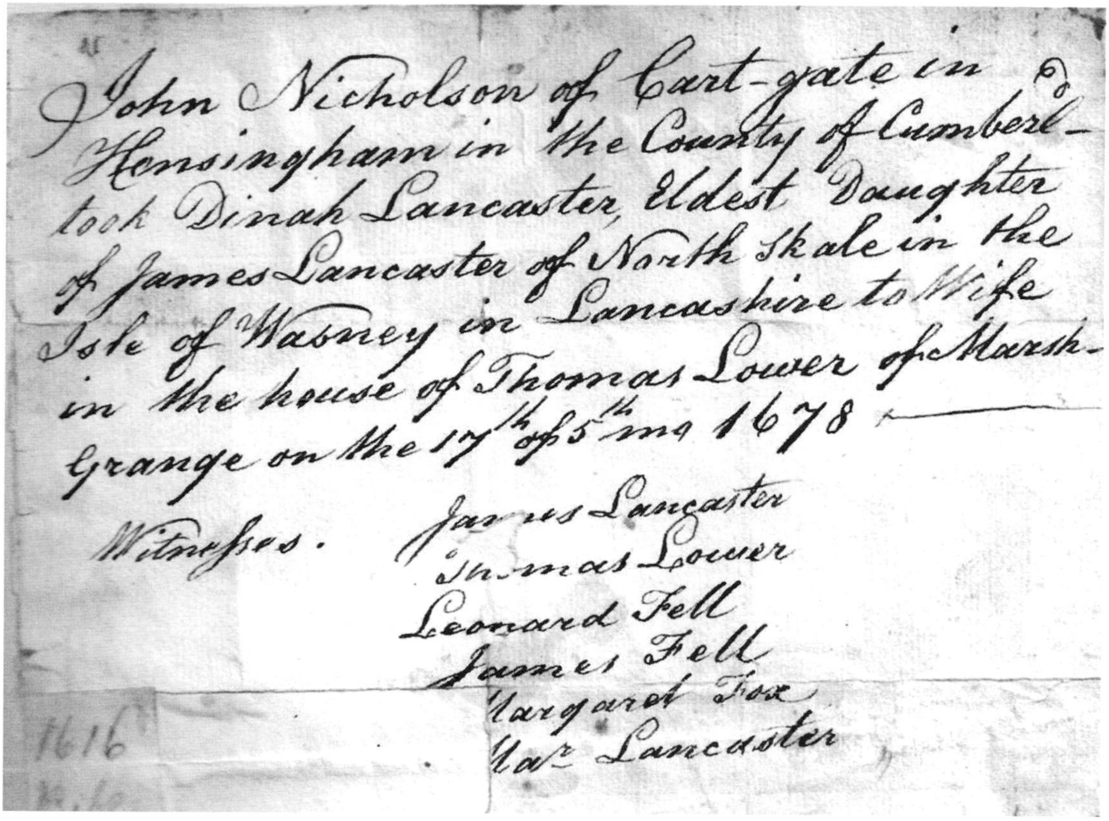

John Nicholson of Cartgate in
Hensingham in the County of Cumberland
took Dinah Lancaster, Eldest Daughter
of James Lancaster of North Skale in the
Isle of Walney in Lancashire to Wife
in the house of Thomas Lower of Marsh
Grange on the 17th of 5th month 1678.

Witnesses:
James Lancaster,
Thomas Lower,
Leonard Fell,
James Fell,
Margaret Fox (née Fell),
Margaret Lancaster.

The Nicholson's house in Cartgate, Whitehaven

Chapter 2
The Nicholsons

From the marriage of John Nicholson and his wife Dinah Lancaster, we can trace our descendants till we come to the next significant person, our great, Grandmother, Eliza Nicholson and eventually to the Barlow family from the Oak Farm Estate, from Chorley in Cheshire, the home of her husband, our great, Grandfather, Professor John Barlow.

The Nicholsons were a very old seafaring family, who for many generations had lived in or around Whitehaven and where many of the present family still live.[6] Whitehaven is a small Cumbrian coastal town, lying equidistant between Carlisle and Barrow-in-Furness and in the 18th and 19th centuries was a major coal mining town and a substantial commercial port on the back of this trade. Eliza Nicholson's father, Thomas Nicholson (1764-1823) was a mariner as was his father James Nicholson (1724–1784) before him, who had married Mary Nicholson, the lady whose comments on the Bible's history, appear in its early pages. In 1800 Thomas Nicholson decided to give up his sea-going life and went instead into business as a flour merchant in Whitehaven. He became a much respected member of the community, valued both as a businessman and as a good Friend and his obituary in the Quaker Monitor of 1823 records a devout life:

"In his outward concerns he was a man of strict uprightness and integrity, punctual and honourable in all his dealings, with compassion towards those in distress. These qualifications, combined with his humility and unaffected simplicity, gained him the love and respect of all with whom he was acquainted."

In 1793 he had met Elizabeth Sutton, known as Betty to her friends, who came from another old Quaker family from Scotby, then a village within the City of Carlisle. She was born in 1769, the fourth of seven children of William Sutton (1731-1815) and his wife Betty Robinson (1732-1813). I have managed to trace her lineage as far back as the 17th century, to Betty's great Grandfather, David Sutton (1670-1740), who married one Esther Bond, who all came from Scotby and all married local Quakers. Betty Sutton was a very devout and rather tiny, lady, much loved by all who knew her and she, and Thomas Nicholson had eight children including our great Grandmother Eliza, Jane who married Jonathan Dodgson Carr, the founder of the biscuit firm, Mary who married George Peile, and Sarah, who married John Wigham.[7] They were a close-knit Quaker family and as will become apparent, looked after each other in adversity.

Eliza, the youngest of Thomas and Elizabeth's children was born in Whitehaven in 1813, but when she was only two her parents moved to Springfield, Carnforth near Lancaster, where according to local records, they made a very happy home *'loved by all who lived there'*. Thomas sadly died in 1823 and Betty Sutton moved back to Whitehaven where she remained until her death in 1834. Eliza, however, now aged 21 but still single, was looked after by her married sisters, dividing her time between the Wighams in Edinburgh and the Peiles in Whitehaven. Her brother-in-law John Wigham[8], was a public-spirited man and a leader of reform in Edinburgh, where she was able to mix with all the leading thinkers of the time including John Bright, Sir William Trevelyan, Lord Macauley and John Cobden. Eliza herself shared actively in all such gatherings and was much respected for her own thinking and in 1849 she attended

---

[6] James Graham, a friend of my brother David comes from Whitehaven and has looked up several descendants.
[7] See further on for the Wigham family
[8] See Chapter 3 for Wighams

The Nicholsons

Eliza Nicholson 1813-1894 m. John Barlow 1851

Betty Sutton 1769-1834 m. Thomas Nicholson 1793

Jane Nicholson 1796 -1856
m. J D Carr 1833

Mary Nicholson 1798-1855
m. George Peile 1832

Sarah Nicholson (1803 - c. 1860)
m. John Wigham c.1830

the Peace conference in Paris, along with a large Quaker delegation. The International Peace Congress, was the popular name of a series of international meetings, held in various places in Europe from 1848 to 1853. Following a preparatory congress at London in 1843, a series of such gatherings were organised, called 'The International Congress of the Friends of Peace', or more informally "International Peace Congress", the first being in Brussels in 1848 and the second in Paris in 1849.

The Brussels Congress had been a great success and received a considerable share of public attention, along with the good wishes of peace lovers, especially Quakers. The Peace Congress of 1848, though it encountered opposition, was nonetheless historic, as it was the first of its kind, sowing the seeds of international co-operation and from which future peace conferences grew, another of which my Grandfather, John Henry Barlow was to attend in Holland some 60 years later during the First World War.

The 1849 Paris Congress, with Victor Hugo as chairman, was also noteworthy and Eliza was considerably prominent among the Quaker delegation at this conference, both as a speaker as well as being much admired as a lady of great beauty, with her blue eyes and dark hair. She was at the forefront in meeting the great hero of the hour and liberal thinker, Alphonse Lamartine. This French writer, poet and politician had virtually retired from politics by 1848, but was still the champion of liberal thinkers across Europe. This was because he espoused such Quaker causes as the abolition of slavery, the death penalty and pacifism, as well as the the principal of the right to work, and so he was the one person they all wanted to meet. He was a political idealist who supported democracy and pacifism and it was perhaps this stance which eventually caused some of his less radical followers to desert him, but Eliza met him and was much taken with his sincerity.

By the next year 1850, while staying in Edinburgh with the Wighams she had met John Barlow, then Assistant Professor at the Royal Dick Veterinary College, the son of another old Quaker family from Cheshire. In 1851 they were married in Whitehaven and settled in Edinburgh at No1 Pilrig Street, a house which is still there. It was an ideal love match and they were wonderfully suited to each other. They had three children, Alfred born in 1851, Mary in 1853 and John Henry, my Grandfather in 1855. John's career continued to advance and he was made a full Professor in 1855. During his time at the University, he completely revolutionised veterinary studies, first by introducing the microscope[9] and later in the study of pathology and systematic clinical teaching. He was widely recognised as one of the leaders of his profession and he was admitted as a Fellow of the Royal Scottish Society of Arts in 1852 as well as of the Physiological Society the following year. He wrote many treatises for leading journals that were ground breaking in their time and his standing among the scientific men with whom he mingled and worked and the appreciation of his talents and acquirements, won in the Edinburgh Schools of Medicine, was second to none. Indeed, talking to two present members of the University Veterinary School, Colin Warwick and Alistair Macdonald, they cited John Barlow's influence as one of their inspirations. Tragically, all this came to a sudden end in 1855, when Professor Barlow became seriously ill with a spinal infection, most likely an acute form of meningitis, and after a long and painful struggle he died on the 29th January 1856, leaving a grieving widow and three children and was mourned throughout the scientific world.

---

[9] When John Henry died my Uncle John and my Grandmother offered his microscope to the Royal Dick in Edinburgh in 1929. The Principal O Charnock Bradley wrote thanking her: *"The name of the late Professor Barlow is reverently remembered in this college as one who did inestimable service during the early years of our history and added lustre to the name of the college. Professor Barlow was the first to use a microscope in Edinburgh and this college has long taken pride in the fact that it was the first Veterinary College in which the use of the microscope was taught. So you will understand how happy we are to possess the original microscope. (Letter dated February 8th 1929).* I understand that this has recently been lost.

Eliza Nicholson

She married Professor Barlow in 1851

Eliza Barlow née Nicholson 1813-1894 in later life c 1870

Soon after his early death at the age of just 40, further catastrophe followed, as the substantial finances John Barlow had left his widow and children in investments, collapsed, due to the sudden insolvency not only of the Glasgow Bank but also the Cornish tin mines[10]. In those days of unlimited liability, she was forced to make continual payments, leaving her with very little to survive. But once again her sisters and their families, the Peiles and Wighams, helped her out and to begin with she divided her time between the two of them. But her other sister, Jane Nicholson had married Jonathan Carr in 1833 and with the success of the Biscuit business, they were in a position to offer Eliza and the children a decent home, with rooms of their own and eventually she decided to move the family to Carlisle. This generosity was partly tempered by a certain sense of guilt as we shall see, as it was Carr who had encouraged Professor Barlow to invest in the two companies in the first place.

One further disaster was also to befall the family, as their eldest child, Alfred died when he was only 6 in 1857, and suddenly Eliza's once idyllic home and great prospects had fallen apart, so that when their second son, John Henry, now head of the family, grew up, he had to leave Stramongate[11], his Quaker school at the age of 16, because of shortage of funds and to start earning a living. To begin with he went to work for the Clydesdale Bank, but after a while, his Uncle, Jonathan Carr, offered him a job in his now thriving biscuit company, and John Henry soon rose to become Secretary of the Company in 1889.

Eliza Nicholson was obviously a remarkable lady, not only bringing up the two children, but also devoting herself to the poor and to the Temperance movement and in 1870 to the war victims. This was the year that the British Red Cross was founded and many Quakers became involved in working with them including Eliza. It was a Swiss businessman, Henry Dunant who had first proposed that countries should create organisations to provide neutral, impartial help for the sick and wounded soldiers in wartime. This ground-breaking idea had come to him when he was travelling through Italy and had seen the carnage following the Battle of Solferino in 1859, between the Franco-Sardinian alliance and the imperial Austrian army. Some 40,000 wounded men lay abandoned on the battlefield until Dunant started organising local villagers to help them. His idea led to the creation of the International Committee of the Red Cross in 1863 and the first Geneva Convention in 1864.[12]

Soon countries across Europe began forming their own Red Cross National Societies, and in 1870, when war broke out between France and Prussia, the British Red Cross was founded. Colonel Robert Lloyd-Lindsay, who had served in the Crimean War, was very concerned about the suffering the war would cause, especially since the British government had ties with both sides and he wrote a memorable letter to The Times[13] on 22 July 1870 to propose that the country should create a neutral British aid organisation to help the wounded soldiers on both sides of the frontlines. As a result of his letter and the backing of people such as the Foreign Secretary, the 2nd Earl Granville, Florence Nightingale and a who's-who of prominent British people including a group of leading Quakers of whom Eliza Barlow was one, a meeting was held in London in August 1870 to discuss ways of helping survivors. At this meeting, the group passed several resolutions, which enabled the establishment of an organisation called the 'National Society for Aid to the Sick and Wounded in War', which later shortened its name to the 'British Red Cross' and from 1870, as John Henry was working and Mary was then over 20, Eliza had more time and was able to devote her energies to working on behalf of the new organisation.

---

[10] Jonathan Carr encouraged this speculation and felt great guilt when the mines collapsed. For more see under J Carr.
[11] See Chapter 10
[12] History of the Red Cross
[13] Times archives

When they first moved to Carlisle, although Jonathan Carr had generously given over a good portion of his large house to Eliza and the children, it was not their own. But not long after John Henry had started work at the Clydesdale Bank, he was bringing in a fair wage and the family were at last able to move to a lovely home of their own. This was Murrell Hill Cottage[14], on Murrell Hill in Carlisle, where she continued to live for the rest of her life, and where, according to a friend *'her sweet and loving presence made the house to be pervaded in sunshine.'*

Eliza obviously had a great sweetness of nature and a wealth of love, but she was full of playfulness too and her children adored her. Because Mary and John Henry had no father she lived for them and was their inspiration as much as she was to all those who came into contact with her. That John Henry went on to become himself such an eminent and leading Quaker in his own right, is in no small measure due to his mother's influence. Her life influenced people from many different backgrounds, for on her death in 1894 at the age of 81, it was remarked by a friend to her two children, John Henry and Mary *'Even bad people, I firmly believe, were influenced by just a glimpse of such a life as your Mother's. There was more in such a life than in a hundred eloquent sermons.'*

It might be appropriate to mention at this point a true story that links the generations and which has come down through the family, as related by my Father's Mother, in an essay she wrote for the Birmingham Essay Society. Many Quakers had similar groups, especially as other forms of entertainment were frowned on and many references exist among family letters to such occasions. In later years my parents also belonged to the Birmingham Essay Society, along with such other Quakers as Michael and Heather Cadbury, David and Marion Cadbury, the Southalls, Jeff and Margaret Gillett and Michael Darby and his mother. They were very formal gatherings for which evening dress was obligatory even in my parents' time and all the best silver and china came out, often indeed the china service mentioned below in the story. My Father, a very un-formal person, always hated the 'dressing up', though undoubtedly to us children as we watched our parents get ready, he always looked most handsome, even if latterly the evening suit was a little too tight for him!

Our Grandmother retells the following story as it had been told to her, a tale of an old romance concerning a great, great, Aunt Deborah Nicholson 1753-1847 as related by Mary Nicholson to her cousin Eliza. In this romantic story, mention is made of items including a seal, old family china and a Grandfather clock, all of which are still in the family's possession[15]. Mary lived with her two Aunts, Sarah and Deborah in Whitehaven and was herself suffering agonies of love over a young man, but to comfort her, her Aunt Deborah, told this story of her own sufferings of long ago and when she had finished the tale she said *'I wish thee to have this my dear, as I know thou wilt understand'* and gave her the Seal.

When Eliza announced her own engagement, Mary Nicholson was insistent that her cousin should have the seal on her marriage to John Barlow in 1851, and she wrote to Eliza as follows: *"To my beloved Cousin Eliza Nicholson, as a relique of my Aunt Deborah who died in 1847. She wore (the seal) from the age of 25 till her death in her 95th year, and in giving this seal (to you) it is my dearest wish that you (and John Barlow) may unite in full submission to the government of Him who through infinite mercy will present them faultless before the throne of His Father's glory with exceeding joy."*

---

[14] Murrell Hill Cottage – see under John Henry Chapter 13
[15] My brother Stephen has the Grandfather clock, now over 250 years old. I have the china service and my late Cousin Anna's family had the seal.

The story concerns the engagement of Deborah Nicholson to a young man she had met at Yearly Meeting in London, which was, as she describes: *"A union of hearts in the deepest sense. Vows were exchanged and we were to be married. Wedding gifts began to arrive including the pretty grey/blue china service that I always like to use still."* But unexpectedly, her fiancé had to postpone the wedding because of family business, though promising to come to Whitehaven before his departure for the Continent. He duly arrived and a few days later when he departed, he gave Deborah the seal:

"A white stone in a plain silver setting and deeply cut into it were two hearts each with a flame springing upwards from it, while above the flames was the word 'unite'. He asked me to wear it always for his sake...which I did faithfully for the next sixty years.... No more was ever heard of the young man despite endless searches and for long hours of the night I was unable to sleep and night after night I listened to the old clock as it sounded its clear bell. But one night I was aware of a presence and I heard with the utmost clearness the words 'Unite, unite'. 'Yes' I replied 'we are united no matter what has happened' and at that moment two strokes rang out from the old clock. From that moment I felt I could face life once more."

Eliza too wore this seal all her life and through our grandmother it came down to her daughter Millior and so to my cousin Anna Braithwaite. It seems perhaps overly sentimental to our present day sensibilities, but the fact the items mentioned in the 'Quaker Romance' as my Grandmother calls it, still survive and are very much treasured by the present generation of the family makes it a less sentimental and more moving story.

Whitehaven harbour with fishing boats

John Wigham

John Wigham, 1781-1862 in old age

The Author writes:

"John married Sarah Nicholson, our great, great Aunt and looked after Eliza and the two children in their Edinburgh home, after Professor Barlow died young."

Chapter 3
Family friends and relations - The Wigham family

I have already made several mentions of family relations, especially the Wighams and the Carrs, so for a moment let us just pause to look at these two families that proved of such importance to Eliza and the children after John Barlow died. In many respects, both families were paradigms of many Quaker families of the period; the Cadburys, Cashs and Bowlys being very similar. They were hard working, established good businesses through honest dealings, looked after their workforce, espoused good causes and cared for each other in times of trouble. Quakers, as has been stated, believed very strongly in looking after those in distress, whether they be immediate family or strangers. So it is typical that John and Sarah Wigham were particularly solicitous towards Sarah's sister Eliza when John Barlow died, as indeed were the Peile cousins and later the Carrs.

John Wigham was born in 1781, growing up in Scotland, and becoming a successful cotton manufacturer in Edinburgh, so that by 1811 'J & J Wigham, Manufacturers and Silkmen', had large premises at 6 Lothian Street, Edinburgh and by 1813 John had built a substantial home for himself at 10 Salisbury Road, Edinburgh where he continued to live all his life.

The Edinburgh shawl trade was almost entirely in the hands of Quakers, among whom the Wigham cousins certainly stood out. After his first wife died, John married our great, great Aunt, Sarah Nicholson, in 1830, at Whitehaven, in Cumberland. The Nicholsons had already made good money at sea and later when Thomas ceased being a mariner, he continued to prosper as a flour merchant and so when Sarah married, she was able to bring a sum of £2000 to the marriage, probably in the region of some £50,000 in today's currency. They had four children, John (1832), Sarah (1834), Anna (1836), and James (1838) all born at 10 Salisbury Road, Edinburgh.

Like all Quakers of the period, as we shall see with the renowned Samuel Bowly later, John Wigham was a staunch fighter against the Slave Trade and became Chairman of the Anti-Corn Law Association. He was a much respected businessman, and was appointed President of the Edinburgh Chamber of Commerce and along with other Quakers, took a leading role in prison reform, believing that rehabilitating prisoners, especially young offenders, was a better preparation for release than simply leaving them in prison unaided.

When he died in 1862 he was described by the Edinburgh Quaker Journal[16] as *"possessed of a superior understanding and good judgement, deeply founded on his religious beliefs, and was well qualified to be a guide to others. He was always ready to listen and tried to help others with his advice and counsel not only the poor, but anyone who applied to him, and he treated them all with goodness of heart. In spite of his many qualities he was a truly humble man."*

The obituary in the Daily Review[17] concluded: *"In the death of Mr Wigham, the Society of Friends has lost one of its brightest ornaments, and this city, one of its greatest and most enlightened benefactors."* He was buried at the Quaker burial ground in the Pleasance in Edinburgh where our great Grandfather, Professor Barlow was also buried.

---

[16] Friends House Library
[17] Edinburgh City archives

The Carrs

Jonathan Dodgson Carr, the founder of Carr's biscuits, and his wife Jane née Nicholson

Theodore Carr 1866-1931, (Right) family friends Theo with JHB, Mary and Lillie Monkhouse

The Author writes:
"J D Carr, married Jane Nicholson and looked after her sister, Eliza in Carlisle, after John Barlow died in 1856. JD's grandson, Theo took over the company on JD's death."

Chapter 4
More family friends and relations - The Carr family

The other significant relative for our ancestor Eliza, was Jonathan Dodgson Carr who married another Nicholson sister, Jane. JD as he was known, was extremely benevolent to Eliza after John Barlow died, offering not only a home but also later, employment for our young Grandfather, John Henry, when he left the Bank. Such a pattern of care, will be familiar to anyone studying Quaker families of this period.

JD Carr was born in Kendal, in 1806, the second in a family of four sons and five daughters of Jonathan Carr and his wife Jane Dodgson. His Father was a wholesale grocer and tea dealer, descended from an old Quaker family from Yorkshire of weaving stock, and his wife Jane Dodgson, was the daughter of another grocer from Kendal. Like our Grandfather, John Barlow, JD also went to Stramongate School, though his younger brothers were sent to Ackworth. Initially, he was apprenticed to a baker in Stockton, but soon found the commercial opportunities in his home town, to be distinctly limited and so in 1831, as legend has it, he walked the 50 miles to the city of Carlisle and then, perhaps with a little financial help from another Quaker tea merchant, Thomas Brockbank[18], he opened a bakery near the Cathedral. He did very well there and only two years later, felt he was well enough established to set up home, having met and fallen in love with our great, great Aunt, Jane, the eldest of Thomas and Mary Nicholson's daughters. Jonathan and Jane went on to have six children, two daughters and four sons, three of whom later became partners in the family business.

As with John Wigham, George Cadbury and other similar entrepreneurial Quakers, Carr energetically built up the business. He took advantage of the various forms of transport, initially constructing a factory near the canal basin in Caldewgate, but before long, he added a fleet of ships and as technology developed, when the new railway came, a line was built to the factory to transport his requirements of wheat, as by 1841 biscuits had become the leading product group and he was granted the royal warrant for them. Soon the factory was employing over 90 staff and as well as manufacturing biscuits, the business ranged from corn merchanting and flour milling to baking and retailing. Although some Quakers, as we shall see with Elizabeth Taylor before she married George Cadbury, lamented the arrival of the railways 'spoiling the quiet of the country' as she put it, and changing life for ever, most of the Quaker businessmen such as Carr and Cadbury in Birmingham realised the enormous benefits they would bring to their industries and many, including our Grandparents John and Mabel Barlow, invested heavily in the new companies.[19]

By1860 Carr was offering seventy-two varieties of fancy biscuit. The steady expansion of the business led to three of his brothers joining the firm of 'Carr & Co.', though in 1860, the youngest, John, departed to join rivals Peek Frean & Co., the London biscuit firm, to be succeeded at Carr's, by another son Arthur. Eventually, JD's Grandson, Theodore took over the family business when his Grandfather died in 1884. Theodore was the son of JD's son Thomas and grew up to be a great friend of my Grandparents when they were living in Carlisle. After going to a local school, Theodore went on to Owens College at Manchester University, where some 80 years later, I also went in the 1960's. In 1893, he married Edith Hobbs and became a highly successful leader of the firm, ending up as Chairman of the Company.

In 1918 he moved into politics, being elected MP for Carlisle and in 1920 was made a CBE. With the fall of the coalition in 1922, however, he lost his seat to Labour. According to my

---

[18] A descendant of Thomas Brockbank was at The Downs with me
[19] Granny Barlow lost considerably when, much later, the Railways were nationalised.

Grandmother, Theo Carr was quite a character, for as well as his other pursuits, he was something of an engineer and built a prototype steam car, in which, as a keen motorist, he took my Grandmother, all dressed in her best, on a rather precarious drive in 1895.[20]

Later in the new century another family member, Ernest Hutchinson, who had married my Grandmother, Mabel Cash's sister, Louisa, became works manager of Carr's and as Theo's other interests diversified, he virtually ran the biscuit company. Like other family firms, however, the Carr family members gradually dropped out and by 1972 the Company had been bought by McVities, part of the United Biscuits empire, much as Cadburys was taken over by the American giant Kraft in 2010.

Jonathan Dodgson Carr, JD to all, was a giant of a man, with a benevolent expression and full white beard in his riper years. To demonstrate his strength, it is told, he once carried three sacks of flour, the length of the mill and back. Like other Quakers, his treatment of the workforce was humane, the factory being clean and airy and he ensured personal cleanliness by providing a swimming-bath with hot water from the steam engine. He had a schoolroom, library, and reading room close by, and he gave religious instruction in his house on Sunday afternoons.

Annual outings to the Lake District, took place and once there was an excursion to Edinburgh. There were weekly employees' meeting, attended by one of the Carr family, at which matters to do with conditions in the firm could be raised. Although Carr never became a local councillor, he took a lively part in public affairs and as Secretary of the Carlisle Anti-Corn Law Association, he placed in his shop window both a taxed and a much larger, untaxed loaf. When the Corn Laws were finally repealed in 1846, he presented every inmate in Carlisle gaol with a fruit loaf, and had a silk waistcoat made, decorated with ears of corn marked 'FREE'.

He helped to promote gas and water undertakings in the city; as a founder of the Cumberland Co-operative Benefit Building Society, he spoke on housing conditions at its meetings, and he actively supported the Cumberland Infirmary. He took the initiative in developing the docks and railway in Silloth, to where the firm later transferred its flour milling operations. But closest to his heart as with other Quakers, was the fight against slavery, a cause in which his wife Jane joined fervently as well. As a businessman, Carr showed abundant energy and vision, and a rigid adherence to the Quaker principles of offering good-quality products at fair and fixed prices.

However, his strong-minded individualism did cause some friction in the Quaker community, as having become used to taking his Bible into meeting, he was censured on the grounds that reading any book during meeting, weakened worshippers' dependence on the promptings of the Holy Spirit. Then, although marrying outside the faith had been relaxed in 1859, customs linger long and his two eldest sons were disowned by the Society in 1880, for not marrying Quakers, and JD and his wife reluctantly resigned from Quakers and instead joined the Plymouth Brethren Assembly in Carlisle, soon becoming prominent members of the group. As Margaret Forster writes in her book on the Carr's[21] :

"This was a time of agonising significance in J D's life. His entire career, which had been so enormously successful and had made him, in Carlisle, an important and wealthy man, had been founded on and guided by Quaker principles. His religion and his worship within it, was the cornerstone of all his work."

---

[20] See Chapter 16
[21] 'Rich Desserts and Captains Thin' (Chatto and Windus).

The Carr family

JD Carr and family c. 1850 l.to r.: George, James, Eliza, JD, Lizzie, Jane, Thomas

The biscuit factory in 1860

Girls and young women working in the packing room of Carr's, all neatly dressed in regulation white aprons and with hair tied back.

Their decision to leave, was only taken after much prayer and deliberation, writing a typically simple but kind letter:

"While remaining individually attached to you with whom we trust to be ever united in the bond of Christian love, we realise sadly, that we do not see alike with you on some points of doctrine and practice and therefore, believe that it is not well to remain nominally, what we are not in reality, but we would wish ever to remain, with love, your friends."

My Grandmother records this event in her memoirs and how:

"Great pressure was put upon Mrs Barlow and John to leave also. But John possessed a strain of obstinacy. The more the relatives urged their tenets, the more he stood upon the defensive and it strengthened his adherence to Friends. His mother never faltered and rejoiced that her son stood firm."

Only a few years later Carr's health was failing and on April 6 1884 he died at his home, Coledale Hall in Carlisle. Jonathan Dodgson Carr, along with George Cadbury and Joseph Rowntree was one of a number of remarkable Quakers from the nineteenth century, who made a difference, both industrially and socially, leaving the world a better place for their having lived.

A popular old advertisement

Chapter 5
Royal connections

The recent discovery of the bones of King Richard III[22], the last of the Plantagenet Kings in a Leicester car park and the subsequent search for Plantagenet descendants to supply DNA, reminded me of our own links to the Plantagenets. During the turbulent times of the 17th century, when George Fox was establishing Quakerism and Cromwell headed The Protectorate (1654-1659), we encounter another branch of the family that derives from one of the crucial figures of the seventeenth century, namely General Monck (1608 – 1670).

General Monck was the man who was famous for restoring Charles II to the throne in 1660 and according to my Great Grandfather, genealogist Frederick Goodall Cash, ' *General Monck's sister Eleanor, married a German gentleman, William Hayhurst'* in 1680, and this lady, Eleanor Monck, was our great, great, great, Grandmother. It is a Quaker habit to keep the parent's surname as a forename in subsequent generations and our great Uncle, who was to emigrate to America in the 1880's, was called Oliver *Hayhurst* Cash. William Hayhurst and Eleanor had two sons, the latter named after Oliver Cromwell, presumably before General Monck joined the Royalists!

Their son, also William Hayhurst (1713-1793) had a large family and developed a business selling Artist's colours in Leicester Square, which did so well that he was later able to retire to Danvers House in Chelsea, which became the family home and left each of his three daughters, Elizabeth, Ann and Eleanor, a considerable fortune! Danvers House was in what is now Danvers Street near the Physic garden, though sadly the original house was demolished. It was their second daughter, Ann Hayhurst (1753-1829) who married Samuel Lucas and their daughter Elizabeth Petipher Lucas[23] (1796 -1894) who was our great, great Grandmother.

During the lead up to the restoration of King Charles II, debate raged over the succession and at one point, such was Monck's standing, that it was even contemplated offering the crown to him. Prior to the likelihood of such an event, however, much effort went into establishing his royal ancestry and a pamphlet was even circulated entitled 'The Pedigree and Descent of his Excellency General George Monck, showing how he is descended from Edward the 3rd by a branch of the White Rose of York and likewise his extraction from Richard Plantagenet' (now in the Guildhall Library). Sadly for our family, Monck refused the crown, probably for fear of the consequences!

King Charles II suitably rewarded Monck for his services in restoring him to his throne. He was made Gentleman of the Bedchamber, Knight of the Garter, and Master of the Horse in the King's household. He was also raised to the peerage in 1660 as Baron Monck of Potheridge in the County of Devon, Baron Beauchamp of Beauchamp in the County of Devon, Baron of Teyes in the County of Devon, Earl of Torrington in the County of Devon and Duke of Albemarle. His titles were inherited by his only son, Christopher Monck, 2nd Duke of Albemarle (1653–1688), on whose death they became extinct. As far as can be discovered, neither his sister Eleanor, nor indeed any of his family, appeared to benefit from George's ennoblement or closeness to the King! But this is not the only brush with the Royal family as we shall see nearly two hundred years later, when another ancestor and Chelsea inhabitant left a fortune to Queen Victoria![24]

---

[22] The bones were discovered in a Leicester car park in September 2012 and through matrilineal descendants of Richard's sister, Anne of York the DNA was found to match and the bones were reinterred in Leicester Cathedral in 2014
[23] See next chapter
[24] See under John Camden Neild

General George Monck

ILLVSTRISSIMO AC GENEROSISSIMO DN° DN° GEORGIO DUCI
ALBEMARLIÆ, COMITI de Torrington BARONI MONCK de Potheridge,
Beauchamp et Teyes, AUGUSTISSIMO CAROLO IIdo MAGNÆ
BRITANNIÆ FRANCIÆ et HIBERNIÆ REGI etc ab Intimis CVBICVLIS,
et Sanctioribus CONSILIIS, CAPITANEO GENERALI, Omniumqʒ Sacræ Regiæ
MAJESTATIS in Regnis Angliæ, Scotiæ et Hiberniæ, Exercituum SUMMO DVCI,
Magno Stabuli Magistro, et Inclyti Ordinis Aureæ PERICELIDIS EQVITI etc:
Hanc ipsius Effigiem manu sua ad vivam delineatam et cælatum submisso cultu D.D.D. D. Loggan. A° 1661.
Sold by Matthew Collings, at the 3 Black-Birds in Cannon Street.

The Author writes:
"General Monck restored Charles II to the throne in 1660. His sister Eleanor married
William Hayhurst in 1680. She was our three times great Grandmother."

Chapter 6
The Cash family

Elizabeth Petipher Cash (née Lucas), the lady who graces the cover of this book, was by all accounts a saintly woman. She was born in 1796 at the end of the 18th century when the Napoleonic wars were at their height and she died at the great age of 98 in 1894 just when the Lumière brothers were experimenting with film and Keir Hardie was founding the Independent Labour Party to become the first Labour MP. When she died, many tributes were written about this quiet, special lady including the following by her son, Frederick Goodall Cash:

"My mother, was one of the loveliest of women, of a sweet countenance, in later years of an imposing presence, a mind that thinketh no evil, a disposition of loveliness, gentleness, sympathy and unselfishness, to whom those in perplexity or trouble would instinctively go, sure of help, consideration and sympathy."

She was the youngest of ten children of Samuel Lucas (1748-1808) and Ann Hayhurst (1753-1829), the descendant of the William Hayhurst mentioned in the previous chapter. They lived in Warwick Street, just off Golden Square, in a house that is still there behind Liberty's, where their father, Samuel Lucas carried on the family business as a Corn merchant. It has been well said that corn was the equivalent of oil in today's world, the basis of the staple diet and hence when the protectionist Corn Laws came in, in 1804 many Quakers led the way in fighting for their repeal and Samuel Lucas and John Wigham were particularly prominent in the struggle. The Corn Laws were eventually repealed in 1846 in the Peel government, though it split the new Conservative party and forced Peel's resignation.

Samuel died when Elizabeth was only 12 in 1808 and not long after in 1809, their eldest child Samuel Hayhurst Lucas (1786-1873) got married to Hannah Smith and took over the Warwick Street home and their mother Ann Hayhurst Lucas moved with the other children to 'Highbury Barn' at the top of Highbury Fields, then situated in Tottenham, North London. Their home there, had literally been an old barn, dating from the previous century, and was a place where Londoners used to go on a summer's evening to take the waters or eat syllabubs[25]. Elizabeth Lucas was sent to a Quaker school in Croydon, where she did well. By all accounts she was fast growing into an attractive young lady, and in 1818, aged 22 she met William Cash (1792-1849) of Coventry, who soon proposed to her and they got married down at Westminster Meeting in St Martin's Lane; but for the marriage breakfast, it was back to Tottenham!

The Meeting is one of the oldest Friends' Meetings in London, though it has occupied several different buildings since Quaker gatherings started in the area in 1655. One of the earliest was in New Palace Yard, near the Palace of Westminster, and in a reference relating back to General Monck, Samuel Pepys notes in his dairy for the 7th of February 1660 *"In the Palace Yard, I saw Monck's soldiers abuse all the Quakers that were at a meeting place there; indeed, the soldiers did use them very roughly and were to blame."* Westminster Meeting is of course, still today, a very active one, though the old Meeting House, dating from 1779, which was on the opposite side of St Martin's Lane,[26] roughly where the present Duke of York's Theatre now is, was eventually pulled down when the lease expired. The present Meeting House, built at 52 St Martin's Lane opened in 1883.

---

[25] A dessert made of milk or cream, flavoured and sweetened and then whipped.
[26] Westminster Meeting has met on this same freehold site in St Martin's Lane since the late 19th century (previously it held a lease on the other side of the road, on the site of the Duke of York's Theatre).

Elizabeth Petipher Lucas

Elizabeth Petipher Cash (née Lucas) 1796-1894

The Author writes:

"Elizabeth, was the daughter of Ann Hayhurst and Samuel Lucas and our great, great Grandmother."

William Cash, had already set up in business acquiring a house in King Street, Cheapside and it was to this, at that time, slightly run down area of London, near the Monument, that William took his bride to live above the premises. But she never complained, as this was - as described by Frederick Goodall - *'a love match which grew in intensity with the years'*. William Cash came from the well-known Coventry-based silk-weaving family. His father was also William Cash (1749-1795) and he had married Mary Goodall in 1781 near Warwick and they had seven children of whom William junior was the fifth. Two of his sisters died in infancy and another sister and a brother died in their twenties. Their father was a wealthy stuff-merchant, a dealer in flax, and a prominent member of this Coventry family later to become famous for their nametapes, with which any boarding school pupil was familiar, as they were sewn into all clothes as ready identification. Sadly, along with many another old Quaker family firm, in January 2014, they went into administration after 140 years.

William Cash senior's pioneering Quaker cousins, John and Joseph Cash, began production of silk ribbons in Coventry in the early part of the 19th century. Coventry by then was already famous for its silk-weaving, brought over by the Huguenots fleeing persecution in Europe and bringing their jacquard[27] weaving process with them. The Cash's distributed the silk for them to weave, initially in their own homes but later in the famous 'Topshops', weaving factories in the Coventry district of Kingfield and like other Quaker Businessmen such as George Cadbury with his chocolate factory-in-a-garden in Bournville and Jonathan Dodgson Carr and his biscuit-making in Carlisle, the Cash brothers were pioneers of a more enlightened approach to employment, caring for the workforce and their well-being and for the social environment in which they lived.

William junior was only four when his father died and he didn't join the family silk business in Coventry, opting rather to go into the woollen business, serving his apprenticeship at Baldock in Hertfordshire. In 1818 he came up to London, the year he got married to Elizabeth and was soon engaged in the business of wholesale stuff, setting himself up as a woollen merchant. He remained in the wool trade in London all his life, first in King Street, Cheapside near the Guildhall and later at 39 Wood Street, further along Cheapside. William and Elizabeth had ten children of which our Great Grandfather, Frederick Goodall Cash, born in 1829, was the sixth. William built up a very successful business, which entailed a great amount of travelling, and usually he was accompanied by his wife which, as the Quaker Monitor recorded on her death in 1894:

"was doubtless a picture that we shall never see again in these days of rapid locomotion; the steady steed, the happy young husband and wife in Quaker dress; he full of spirits, sometimes leaving the chase to test his athletic powers, jumping over brooks or rivers; she repeating poetry to him as they rode through quiet lanes in the beautiful country which they so both so dearly loved."

The business prospered and after about four years they moved in 1825 to Peckham, South East London with one little daughter, the eldest son, a very bright clever child having died in 1823. Rye Lane, Peckham, in the early nineteenth century was a pleasant rural retreat and according to Elizabeth Cash in her journal: *'Nightingales sang among its trees on summer evenings.'* And Frederick Goodall writes:

"*My parents moved to 42 Rye Lane, Peckham and later, a few hundred yards further into the country to a large house where I was born in 1829. It stands in an old fashioned garden at the north east corner of Peckham Rye. The house* (now no longer there) *was known as Effingham House and had belonged to Howard Earl of Effingham in Stuart times.*

---

[27] Jacquard was a manufacturing process that used perforated cards to produce a pattern that could be replicated

Elizabeth Cadbury

Dame Elizabeth Cadbury's 90th birthday in 1948 with the present writer, Antony Barlow, aged 7 on the right of the photo, watching as Laurence Cadbury helps her cut the cake and his wife Joyce and their daughter and Virginia Cadbury looking on.

'Sunbury,' Peckham Rye 1871. Elizabeth Taylor is the girl under the window.

The Author writes:
"Elizabeth Cadbury was born Elizabeth Taylor and as a young girl she lived opposite her cousin, my Grandmother Mabel Barlow (née Cash) on Peckham Rye."

The Cash family's home in Peckham Rye

William and Elizabeth Cash's (née Lucas) garden in Peckham, South London 1850

The Author writes:
The family moved there in 1824 and engraved on the back of the photo, it says:
"A pleasant country place where there are farm fields and a few houses with lovely gardens and nightingales sing."

Left to right, some of their ten children and our great, great uncle and aunts:
Centre: Caroline Cash (1838-1924), Annie Cash (1835-1895), Thomas Cash (1827-1901),

Far left and right: The Parlourmaid and the Gardener.

The Author writes:
"The photograph clearly shows what a rural area Peckham was in the nineteenth century and the size of the garden would have reflected the size of the house, which must have been considerable for their large family. It was situated just on the corner of the Rye, directly opposite the Taylor's house, 'Sunbury' on the other corner."

Peckham was indeed a pretty country village and several Quaker families moved there, including the Cash's cousins, the Taylors. Frederick Goodall's sister, Mary Jane Cash had married John Taylor in 1855 and their daughter Elizabeth was later to marry George Cadbury in 1888 and was ultimately to become Dame Elizabeth Cadbury. As a young boy of seven, I remember going to Dame Elizabeth's 90th birthday party at her home at The David's, Birmingham in 1948, (see photo p 80). By pure coincidence and at the time totally ignorant of the family connections, I also moved to live in Peckham in 1982 where I stayed for nearly twenty years only a few streets away from where the homes of the Cash's and the Taylor's had once been!

A few years after their first move to Peckham in 1825 the family, as Fred says, moved *'a little further into the country'* with three children, to a house close by the Taylor cousins' house which was called 'Sunbury', opposite the pond on the corner of Peckham Rye. They were all regular attenders at the Quaker Meeting house which was in Highshore Road, just off Rye Lane, Peckham; a beautiful Georgian building, sadly now the Postal sorting Office. But this is where Elizabeth Cash was appointed a Minister and also became for several years, the Clerk of London and Middlesex Quarterly meeting. She supported her husband in all his good works especially on behalf of Total Abstinence, a cause common to most Quakers of the period, but also in relief work for the Irish famine as well as for the Anti-Slavery campaign. All her life she looked after the poor and the sick and anyone in distress; she was much loved as a kind and good woman.

Fred Cash recalls in his memoirs, the early travel of his childhood when *"Joseph Gurney came to call in a fine carriage drawn by two if not four horses."* (see picture on p.31) Of course, London businessmen of this period, including Fred's Father, William and Elizabeth Taylor's Father, John would drive daily into the city by a coach-and-four. But with the building of Peckham station in 1865 they were soon able to make the journey much more quickly, though Peckham would soon become a very different place, with more and more buildings going up and once the railway was completed, it ceased to be the quiet village it had been in the early part of the century. Indeed the arrival of the railway did not please everybody, witness Elizabeth Taylor's remarks in her journal in 1864: *'Our beautiful country view is quite spoilt by the railway embankment which is already, I'm sorry to say, fast coming on'*!

In 1849 Elizabeth's husband William, died of cholera, at the relatively young age of 57, still a common disease in London with its poor sanitation and Joseph Bazalgette's great sewerage system, yet to be built. His son, Frederick recalls him *"As my dear and honoured Father, one of the best of men and wherever known, widely esteemed and revered."* It was after his death that Elizabeth's character as a Mother became of special significance. She held strong views on the early upbringing of children and all hers could read well by the age of five. As she grew older and the children moved away and married, the big house in Peckham, became too large for her and she moved with her two unmarried daughters Mary and Ann, to Rose Hill Cottage in Dorking, a peaceful retreat for her old age. At 75 she remained an energetic lady, still adoring walking in the countryside and she was beloved in the area. After a time, one daughter got married and the other, due to ill health, moved to France, so for her last years she moved to Croydon, with her second son William and his wife Rachel. She died in 1894 aged 98 and is buried at Forest Hill cemetery, as the Peckham graveyard, where her husband was buried, had been closed. Elizabeth Petipher Cash was a remarkable lady, of considerable beauty, even in old age, who was revered by all who knew her, especially her children, as Frederick wrote:

"She was a true gentlewoman, friend, sympathiser and consoler; always unselfish, sweet in temper, a lovely Christian, a devoted Wife, Mother, Grandmother, daughter, sister, Aunt, going back, one, two, three generations!"

Horse drawn travel in late 18th and early 19th century

A painting by Samuel Lucas of Kershaw's renowned Hitchin Coach, which drove between London and Hitchin from 1741 to 1850 and on which young Fred Cash went to school in Hitchin and typical of the transport pre Railway.

Frederick Goodall Cash

Frederick Goodall Cash 1829-1909

The Author writes:

"Our maternal great Grandfather, married Martha in 1858, the daughter of Samuel Bowly."

Chapter 7
Frederick Goodall Cash – the early years

William and Elizabeth's sixth child was Frederick Goodall Cash, who was born at the Peckham Rye house in 1829, which he tells us used to belong to the Quaker John Fell. One can only surmise that he might have been a descendant of Judge Thomas Fell, the friend of George Fox, alluded to earlier. We must be grateful to FGC that he records his life in some considerable detail for the benefit of his children. In fact his account, written towards the end of his life in 1908, tells not only of his family life, but of events that he had witnessed or was part of, which now read like a history of the nineteenth century, from Queen Victoria's coronation to Wellington's funeral, and from the Great Exhibition of 1851 to Queen Victoria's death in 1901.

Fred was educated first at Isaac Brown's school in Hitchin (see Samuel Lucas' painting of Hitchin p.282) and he draws a fine picture of his time there.

"The year 1838 saw my Father driving me and my brothers down to Isaac Brown's school in Hitchin. We were three brothers together initially prior to William and Thomas leaving to go to Thomas Binn's school at Tottenham, but I stayed for nearly 4½ years and laid the groundwork of whatever was good in correct English and grammar that I may have been justified in priding myself in all my life. I also learned some Latin and Greek, which has very often been of service to me since. I was still so small in my first year there, that our favourite teacher, William Dawson of Hitchin, would toss me up on the top of the playground wall and catch me again."

In 1843 his parents determined that he should go onto Benjamin Abbott's school in Lewes:

"On my arrival, I was truly disappointed to discover a very small playground shut in by other small gardens and houses. But there was a splendid piece of sunken and level turf known as the 'frying pan' and inspired by my love of cricket, of which I had been such a devotee at Hitchin, I introduced the game at Lewes and many a time led it and won against all elevens that we could muster. One of my scores 'Cash's 120' was long remembered to my credit, if I mistake not, for a considerable time, after quitting the school."

Recalling the two schools after he had left Lewes at the end of 1844, he writes with an almost Dickensian relish of his time there:

"My recollections of Benjamin Abbott, after leaving his school were always pleasant. He differed widely from Isaac Brown, was more approachable, less unbending and would often stop the lesson, tap and open his snuff box, and taking a pinch, would with a twinkle in his eye and an amusing expression, relate some story, or incident which would be sure to amuse or interest his young hearers. One narration was the escape of his Father by 'cutting and running' from the mob of rioters in the Lord George Gordon[28] riots of 1780, when they burned down Newgate and committed other excesses.

He left Lewes at the end of 1844 following which he served for some time as an apprentice with J T Shewell, a linen draper and Silk Mercer. But in 1852 at the age of 23, he decided he would go into partnership with his brother, William as a Publisher in Bishopsgate, where he

---

[28] The 'Gordon Riots' were anti-Catholic protests in London against the Papists Act of 1778, intended to reduce official discrimination against British Catholics. The protest evolved into riots and looting including freeing prisoners from Newgate

33

stayed for five years and at the age of 28 was to meet the young Martha Bowly, then only 21. She was third daughter of the renowned Samuel Bowly[29] of Gloucester and Jane Bowly (née Dearman) and Fred writes:

"How well I remember in 1857, Samuel Bowly coming to Yearly Meeting with his daughter Martha. Little did I think of the close connection I was soon to have with that family."

Further meetings soon followed, both at the Cash's home in Peckham as well as on visits to the Bowly's famous house 'Horsepools', described by Mary Taylor in *A Dear Memory*[30] as *"being on a high hill, the valleys on either side and the hills beyond, all beautiful,"* situated between Gloucester and Stroud, with splendid views out over the Vale of Gloucester, across the estuary of the Severn and the outskirts of the Forest of Dean and on each side the range of the Cotswolds:

"One evening while walking together with Martha in the Spa grounds in Gloucester, I made known my wish to make her my wife.....to my great delight, she consented to my proposal."

In January 1858, Frederick and Martha were married in the little Painswick Meeting House and with an offer from his Father-in-Law to start work in the family Cheese business, they both moved to live in Gloucester, as Mary Taylor recalls:

"Fred is soon to move to Gloucester, as Samuel Bowly feels the need of him to become his business partner, which is a nice arrangement in many ways. Fred does, and will appreciate Samuel Bowly and such a man as friend or father would be a blessing to anyone. Jane Bowly will rejoice to have a daughter to settle near her. Dear Fred! We shall miss him intensely from our circle with all his liveliness and affection and kind and constant consideration for others."

They remained living there until Samuel died in 1884. To begin with they had a small home in Brunswick Street in Gloucester, but later, as the family grew, they moved to a larger house nearer to his office, which they called Radford House after his father's old house in Coventry, where Fred had lived as a boy and where they remained for the next eleven years. It was a happy marriage and they had seven children, though two of them sadly died in childhood but the youngest, Mabel was to become our grandmother. Poor Martha suffered badly from 'headaches', probably migraines, which was an inherited affliction and troubled her acutely over many years and Fred often mentions her 'acute sickness'.

One of the first of the many historical events that our great Grandfather recalls, is the passing of the Great Reform Bill of 1832:

"It is curious to reflect the unrest and excitement of those stormy times....the prolonged political strife, the near revolution that arose in the country stirred the pulse and caused many apprehensions as to what lengths the people would be carried if Parliament much longer pursued their foolish policy of 'no surrender'. At last the House of Lords gave way and the Reform Bill became law and the rejoicings were great."

And the destruction of the Houses of Parliament in 1834 :

"On the 16th October 1834 the old Houses of Parliament were burnt to the ground and great were the flames which we could see from the top of our house. At first it was thought to be the result of an incendiary, a second Guy Fawkes, but it was soon ascertained to have been an

---

[29] See Chapter 8
[30] 'A Dear Memory' by Mary Jane Taylor, limited edition 1914

Events and places described by Frederick Cash in his memoirs

Painting by Sir George Hayter in the NPG commemorating the passing of the Great Reform Bill in 1832
©Reproduced by kind permission of the National Portrait Gallery, London

Right:

"Wellington's funeral procession round Trafalgar Square to St Paul's"

Engraved by Emily S Drummond

© By kind permission of The Metropolitan Museum, of Art. New York

Left:

"The Great Crystal Palace in 1851, where I saw the Duke of Wellington," described by FGC

Unknown engraver

accident. While a careless worker was burning up some old disused wooden tallies[31] and a spark set fire to some furniture and soon the whole building was in conflagration. It broke out so suddenly and spread so fast that people only escaped with difficulty. Both Houses of Parliament, the offices, residences and other buildings attached, were alike reduced to hopeless ruin."

Or the day Queen Victoria came to the throne:

"I remember clearly the day in June when the young Queen came to the throne. As we were returning home over Peckham Rye, we heard the bells for the accession. Then later, on the 9th November, a large party of us, Father, Mother and several of us children went up to Cheapside to my Father's warehouse to see the young Queen pass in stately procession to the Guildhall for the Lord Mayor's Banquet with the Corporation and Ministers. So great were the crowds that we were unable to leave the building till after midnight and in those days there was still a great double turnpike gate stretching across the wide road at the Elephant and Castle at Newington and as we were so late we had to pay a second toll as it was already another day."

To the Great Exhibition which opened in 1851:

"This was the wonder of the world. Opened by the Queen and Prince Albert, the scenes and the excitement exceeded anything I had previously experienced. I had never seen the road at Hyde Park so crowded, crammed and impassable with carriages and people. The exhibition was a sight never to be forgotten. I visited it several times, including the last week when in one day there were 100,000 visitors and I saw the Duke of Wellington in the great Crystal Palace."

And the very next year, the death of Wellington:

"In 1852 the great Duke died and I remember on a very wet day in that October, going to Chelsea Hospital to see the lying in state and then later watching the imposing funeral procession on its way to St Paul's."

In 1869 he paid his first visit to the United States as a Quaker Minister and emissary on behalf of the Anti-Slavery Society to see the President of the United States:

"I was granted a special private interview with the President, Ulysses Grant at the White House, who showed me much kindness. This veteran soldier of the Civil War was most generous in listening to our beliefs on slavery and promised to consider our views most earnestly."

Ulysses S Grant was the 18th President of the United States (1869–1877) as well as having been military commander during the Civil War and post-war reconstruction periods. His presidency was somewhat marred by corruption but his reputation has since improved among scholars, impressed by the Administration's support for civil rights for freed slaves, encouraged by such missions as the Quaker one led by Fred Cash.

I have included these little glimpses of the great events of the century, as described by my great Grandfather, as they not only give a wonderful picture of the period he lived through, but help I think, to build up a portrait of the man as well. A kindly and caring husband, but also one who sees the world with an observant yet wry eye.

---

[31] Tallies were used in the old court of Exchequer....a piece of wood marked with notches for each item and then split in two with each person keeping a half.

Chapter 8
Samuel Bowly

My great, great Grandfather Samuel Bowly was born in 1802 and became one of the most influential Quakers of his generation. Frederick Cash, confesses to being in great awe of his Father-in-law and writes always with due deference! Certainly, from a very young age, amongst the many stories we were told of our forebears, the legendary funeral of Samuel Bowly in 1884, when his home town of Gloucester came to a standstill as thousands turned out to pay their respects, remains with me as one of the most memorable.

He was not only a much revered businessman in the town and a leader of the temperance movement, but more importantly for our history, was one of the prime movers, along with Wilberforce, in the abolition of slavery in the early years of the nineteenth century, and I discovered a painting of him, along with other campaigners, including many leading Quakers, in the National Portrait Gallery. (see picture inside Front cover)

In 1787 a small, mainly Quaker group led by Thomas Clarkson (1760-1846) formed *The Society for the Abolition of the Slave Trade.* At the time their cause seemed hopeless, as slavery was a such a crucial part of Britain's economy, but popular feeling was on their side. The French Revolution and the backlash against British Radicalism, had temporarily stalled the campaign for the anti-slavery campaign, but the Society's Parliamentary spokesman, William Wilberforce, finally oversaw the triumphant passing of the Abolition of the Slave Trade Act in 1807.

The Great Reform Act of 1832 had swept away many of the old pro-slavery MPs and the final emancipation of slaves in British colonies was effected in 1833. The huge painting in the National Portrait Gallery of the 'British and Foreign Anti-Slavery Society', already referred to, records the 1840 convention which was established to promote worldwide abolition. A frail and elderly Clarkson addresses a meeting of over 500 delegates, who include, as well as Bowly, many such leading Quaker names as Tapper Cadbury, the banker Samuel Gurney and his famous sister Elizabeth Fry, the prison reformer, Joseph Sturge and the Irish Radical, Daniel O'Connell.

Samuel Bowly's family like our own, also had a distinguished heritage and is not alone in claiming royal ancestry, as he could trace his family back to Henry the Seventh! Samuel himself came from Cirencester and was the son of another Samuel Bowly, a miller from Bibury in Gloucestershire, and his wife Sarah Bowly (née Crotch). Samuel Jr married Jane Shipley in 1827, the daughter of John Shipley of Shaftesbury and they had nine children including the third daughter, Martha, who was to marry our great Grandfather Frederick Cash in 1858.

Jane sadly died in 1868, after a lingering illness and considerable suffering, as Fred Cash records in his memoirs. Writing fondly of his mother-in-law, he describes *"a sweet lady, of a shy and retiring character, who was beloved by all who knew her and whose memory was cherished by all."* Sam Bowly later remarried in 1873, in Devizes, a lady called Louisa Cotterell, the widow of another Quaker, Jacob Henry Cotterell of Bath.

The Bowly family had been distinguished and important Quakers in the Gloucestershire area since George Fox's time, and the Victoria County Histories of Gloucestershire recounts how:

"A group of Quakers was established at Tetbury from the mid 1650's.....who were visited several times by George Fox. Many of the Quakers were persecuted and imprisoned. But in the1690's a meeting house was built adjoining the Bristol Road south of the town and..........

Samuel Bowly

Samuel Bowly 1802-1884

The Author writes:

"Our maternal great, great Grandfather, the Anti-Slavery campaigner with Wilberforce."

....the meeting flourished and by the early 18th century there were many leading members, most of whom were tradesmen including a cheese factor Jacob Wilkins."[32]

Jacob Wilkins' daughter Sarah, married Samuel Bowly's grandfather, and by the early eighteen hundreds the family were living in Gloucester. In 1829 young Sam had set up business as a cheese factor himself and the influential position which he acquired both by his business tact and Christian character, procured him the Chairmanship of many local companies including banking, gas, and railway and he was soon looked upon as one of the most important leaders in the town's commercial circles. However, commercial success was never his ultimate aim, as like many Quaker businessmen, Bowly was also a very caring individual and believed in helping his fellow men, which in his case meant providing cheap and universal education. Putting his money where he thought it could help most, he became one of the founders of the ragged schools, not just in Gloucester but throughout the country.

Perhaps, however, he will be principally remembered for his indomitable campaigning for the Anti-slavery campaign. As Frederick Sessions, another native of Gloucester, and the brother of my publisher, Michael Session's great Grandfather, remarks in his 'Life of Samuel Bowly':
"His love of freedom would have made him a nonconformist, even if he had not been born a Friend. It was this inborn love of freedom that brought him to the front during the later phase of the Anti-Slavery agitation."

It is perhaps sometimes forgotten how much the abolition of slavery owes to the Quakers and people like Samuel Bowly led the field in campaigning and supporting Wilberforce. It was in 1837 that he led a deputation to Downing Street, where they discussed with the Prime Minister, Lord Melbourne, the cruelties exercised towards the slaves under the apprenticeship system introduced in 1834. In 1838 he started a Society called the Central Negro Emancipation Committee and they made yet another deputation to Downing Street and this time managed to get a bill for the abolishment of slavery introduced into the House of Commons. The first was defeated but undaunted, they pushed another forward which was eventually carried by three votes against strong opposition.

Lord John Russell, for the government, still refused to accede to the national wish, but with incessant agitation from Bowly and others, they faced down the government and forced them to think again and so to sweep away for ever, the whole 'objectionable system'. But Bowly was not satisfied and proceeded to form 'The British and Anti-Slavery Society', to effect the emancipation of slavery throughout the world. Even in old age he was still fighting this cause, as The Gloucester Journal observed:

"It was not because these slaves were merely British subjects that we fought against slavery; it was because the weak and oppressed had nobody to take up their Cause. I am glad to say the English sentiment ever has been and I believe ever will be, in favour of protecting the weak against the strong. I have no faith in the regulation of the sale of strong drink. I think we want to get rid of it, and so I think with regard to slavery; that instead of regulating this Slave labour – a sort of forced labour – the best way and the only safe way, is to get rid of it altogether.....So, may we go on, taking courage that the God of all mercy will bless our labours ultimately to the freeing of all the world from this gross iniquity."

Like his father, Samuel became a leading member of the Society of Friends and throughout the 1850s spoke regularly at Yearly Meeting and in 1863 he was made a minister. In common with all Quakers, he was a staunch pacifist and during the early stages of the Crimean War, he

---

[32] Victoria County History, A History of the County of Gloucester Vol 11, Editors Ralph B Pugh and N M Herbert 1970

became heavily involved in the peace movement, braving much unpopularity, alongside such other luminaries as John Bright and Richard Cobden.

"During the Crimean war, Mr Bowly, retaining all his old courage, braved extreme unpopularity, with John Bright and others in protesting this iniquity. Never as long as memory lasts, shall I forget a scene when Mr Bowly stood upon the platform to plead for righteousness and peace, confronted by a wild and howling mob of men, headed by some leading citizens. Ever and anon the poor fellow would pause for breath and Mr Bowly would say, in his stentorian voice, a few more words, only to be hooted at more vigorously than before.

Calm and stately he stood there for an hour or more and never once was he goaded, other than a shout and a wave of his right arm – "This is English liberty!" But very many of those who thus stifled free speech, lived to rue the day that ever the war broke out. Gloucester as a port, was largely dependent upon Russian imports from the Baltic and corn from the Black sea, which all ceased and starvation came into many a workman's home.

This episode in his life is one of the most honourable to him and stands in contrast to the ovation he received on his 80th birthday, some thirty years later, from those same working men as well as from the Mayor, the Bishop and other civil and social leaders. But Samuel Bowly took honours with the same calmness that he took persecution and affronts. Glory or shame were nothing to him, if only the cause he chiefly loved, could be thereby promoted."

To have some idea of his presence one need only read another passage from Sessions' 'Life of Samuel Bowly':

"Many will remember his tall, spare figure and his venerable features crowned with the glory of his snow-white hair, as he rose to address some enormous teetotal gathering. Nor will they soon forget the grand, strong tones that literally rolled over the room and carried to the farthest and deafest listener, the loving and persuasive words of that practical common sense which was the special characteristic of his oratory. People seemed to love him at first sight and to realise by instinct, even before they had heard him speak, that what he said would be right, wise and convincing. To his commanding presence and unusual voice, he undoubtedly owed much of his success as an advocate of temperance."

His love of human freedom was his ruling passion and he was often comparing human slavery of the body to the slavery to strong drink and the above reference to temperance is important, as he will be also be remembered as a strong fighter for that cause. Mary Taylor's letters in *'A Dear Memory'* makes many a mention of Samuel Bowly visiting the family in Peckham:

"As Samuel Bowly has made no engagements at Peckham, we are hoping to have the pleasure of his company as long as possible and I hope he will interest himself in our Temperance cause here in Peckham as we have had poor attendance of late."

Taking the pledge of course survived long into the next generation, indeed Sam Bowly's granddaughter, our Grandmother Mabel Cash, like most Quakers of the period, signed the pledge as did my Father, he told me, though this was not a pledge he was to keep all his life as I can often recall him enjoying a pint of beer or a good glass of wine in later life!

As a sign of just how Bowly was revered at home as well, there is an account by one of his servants, who had lived with him for many years:

"Mr Bowly shone more brightly as a Christian in the family circle, than anywhere. He never had an unkind word for anyone and when he was obliged to reprove, it was an evident pain to

him. One could sometimes see he had been deeply wounded by unkind words or the thoughtless conduct of others, but never did you hear an angry word in return or any bitter retort."

All those who worked for him were deeply attached and remained with him all his life and he regarded them as part of his family. So throughout out a long life of service not only to business but to the whole community, he had become possibly the most revered of all his fellow citizens, no matter what their creed. And naturally the family archives contain many an account of his famous funeral in 1884, preserved along with several copies of the national press as well as the local papers, Quaker and temperance journals. The Gloucester Citizen, for instance, recorded:

"On the 27th March 1884, the ancient city of Gloucester was stirred to its depths by the public funeral of one of its most illustrious sons. On this memorable day the Cathedral bell was tolling. All the office, shops and factories were closed and thousands of mournful spectators lined the streets as a long cortege of carriages and deputations followed the hearse, the Mayor and Corporation preceding it. In this procession were men and women of all classes and creeds. The Bishop's carriage was there and great numbers of clergymen of all denomination with leading members of the Society of Friends. Naval and military officers, Members of Parliament, the rich and socially influential and the poorest of the poor. All were represented to mourn a friend and neighbour, highly honoured and much beloved especially by the humble and lowly as they had lost one, who to many of them was more than a father."

In his memoirs, Frederick Cash really manages to capture the scene and to encapsulate what his Father-in-law had meant to everyone:

"My dear father-in-law's funeral was a remarkable demonstration of the love and esteem of his fellow citizens witnessed by thousands and taken part in by all classes from the highest to the poorest. A great congregation in the Shire Hall, Gloucester and then the multitudes in the cemetery at the rest of the solemn ceremony, the clothes shops and even the public house along the route closed or blinds drawn, altogether a striking evidence of the respect and love felt for the family figure so long in their midst."

The Old Shire Hall, Gloucester
The scene of Samuel Bowly's memorial service in 1884

Frederick Goodall Cash and his wife Martha Bowly

Fred and Martha c. 1859

Chapter 9
Frederick Goodall Cash – the later years

To return now to the later years of my great Grandfather, Frederick Goodall Cash. When Samuel Bowly died in 1884, Fred and his wife moved back to Highgate, north London, where they stayed for nearly another six years before moving to Highbury, until Martha, died in 1901, when he finally gave up his London home, to live with his various children and relatives and their families. Perhaps a few other incidents from FGC's fascinating memoirs, are worthy of note for present day historians. Having written of watching the young Queen going to the Guildhall, he later records the Diamond Jubilee:

"In 1897 the Queen's Diamond Jubilee was celebrated with great and imposing ceremonies including a thanksgiving service in the Abbey. A great many foreign, royal and noble visitors took part beside a vast number of the sovereign's own loyal subjects. It was a striking time in an illustrious reign, a reign in marked contrast to the House of Hanover that preceded it. The Queen had had many sorrows, notably the deaths of her husband, Prince Albert in 1861 and of her much loved daughter, Princess Alice of Hesse."

And then the following year, the death of Mr Gladstone:

"In 1898 died, in May, one of the most illustrious statesmen of those who governed our country. At the lying in state in Westminster Hall, thousands of people passed before the closed coffin; an impressive sight which I witnessed more than once. Later a vast public funeral took place in Westminster Abbey at which I was a privileged member of the congregation. By the death of William Ewart Gladstone who had spent 65 years in the service of his sovereign and fellow countrymen, the greatest man of the age disappeared. A great Christian, an eminent theologian, an almost unrivalled orator and Parliamentary debater, it is little likely such another will arise in the present or another generation soon."

Later he expresses solid Quaker anti-war sentiments on the Boer War, with much indignation:

"In 1899 the South African war broke out, in my opinion one of the wickedest and most wanton wars in which our country has been engaged. The mine owners and the millionaires fanned the flames in their own interests. The two men who must bear the chief blame and who were determined on bringing on the conflict were Joseph Chamberlain and Sir Alfred Milner. Let their names go down to posterity with the infamy attaching to them. All the efforts that Friends and other peace lovers could use were powerless to avert the struggle in the mad frenzy that overtook the country. The disasters that attended our armies during the first twelve months were serious enough and might well have been fatal. In the result, the loss of thousands of lives, untold suffering to tens of thousands, the expenditure of two or three hundred millions of pounds coupled with incredible cruelty to brave foes by burning their homesteads and destroying their property, brought victory such as it was, but no credit to our armed forces. To the conquered Boers, honour and pity may well be extended. Let no one before whose eyes these my poor recollections may come, refuse credence to the testimony of many Friends who have nothing to gain by misrepresentation or distortion of facts, nor let such place credence in the stories of others who tell a different tale. It is with a lasting sense of shame that this ever took place with the sacrifice of health, limb and life on both sides as to baffle calculation and all this to gratify personal greed, ambition and revenge. A large portion of the best and most enlightened opinion in the country, as well as most European countries condemned it as indefensible."

For most of 1903/4 he went on a long trip to America to visit his two sons Oliver and Herbert, sailing to New York from Southampton on the St Paul and then on to Los Angeles, where he

Martha Cash and her son Herbert

Martha Cash and her son Herbert Cash

The Author writes:
"Herbert Cash and his brother Oliver, who both emigrated to America in the 1880's. Herbert died in 1920 aged 49 and Oliver died in 1931 aged 56. Oliver and Eva had 3 children, now deceased. There are two grandchildren, Janet and Robert Cash who live in California."

greeted by his much loved youngest son, Hayhurst and his young wife Eva:

"I had not seen him for nine years. I stayed for nearly eight months having a most wonderful welcome with everything that could be done for my comfort and happiness. I later met my elder son Herbert who came to see us in LA. We then went on a long trip to Yosemite....a most beautiful and interesting trip. They later settled in their new home on Chelham Mountain about 5 miles from Newberg, Oregon. I can never forget the love of my two dear children. I eventually took a fond farewell of Herbert, realising that this may be for the last time in this life and then of Hayhurst and Eva as they accompanied me to Buffalo. I went on to New York and in May of 1904 I again boarded the St Paul exactly a year after I had left England. "

His last entry records:

"I recall a striking celebration on November 9th 1907 at the Guildhall. Seventy years before in 1837 as a little boy of eight, I was taken to my father's warehouse in Cheapside to see the show and especially to see the young Queen Victoria, go in state to the Guildhall to the Lord Mayor's banquet. In those days it was thought not safe to leave, so great were the crowds. At last guarded by the new Police we were able to get to Queen Street, Southwark Bridge where my Father's chaise awaited to convey us home to Peckham. The streets, the houses and the costumes, the uniforms of the soldiers and the police, the oil illuminations were all totally different from those of the present day, but that distant memory will never be effaced from my mind's eye. And so to November 9th 1907 which saw me gazing once more on this pageant but this time joining the throng in the Guildhall as an honoured guest, where Sir Henry Campbell Bannerman, the Prime Minister made his last public speech before his lamented death in 1908....."

When in 1901 his beloved wife Martha died at their home in Highbury Park,[33] aged 65:

"It was a terrible shock for us all and I doubt I could have managed but for the help of Lou and Gertie. Though her health had been frail for some time, nonetheless when the end came it was terrible for all of us, especially the two boys in America. Missed by us all, she was much mourned by the many friends who knew and loved her for her quiet loving and gentle spirit, her Christian life, her artistic gifts, especially her beautiful and exquisite paintings which were admired and praised by all who saw them."

Following her death it was agreed by his children that they would all have him to stay in turn and his daughter Mabel, our Grandmother, records in her memoirs:

"My mother died very suddenly in March 1901, so when we were building our new house 'Sunnybrae' in Selly Oak, Birmingham, we set aside one room for my father, which we furnished with his own furniture. A similar arrangement being made with Aunt Caroline Barrow at their home Rokesley, so that he could come and go with us, as well as to Gertie and Lou in Carlisle as he wished, and he gave up the London home."

Frederick Goodall Cash died in 1909 aged 80. For much of his life he had worked in Gloucester for his Father-in-law's cheese business but also pursued interests of his own such as his fascination with genealogy. He was a devoted Father and through his descriptions of visiting his sons in the States, obviously missed them both greatly. He was on the Board of Sidcot School and his visits there were much appreciated and like his father-in-law, he worked assiduously for the Anti-Slavery Society. He was widely respected and his obituary recorded a *'pre-eminently broad-minded man, always ready to see and acknowledge the good in others'*

---

[33] 9 Northolme Road, Highbury Park, where they had moved to from hilly Highgate, a more level area for his wife's health.

Quaker schools

Sidcot School in the 1850's

Sidcot as it is today

Ackworth School then and today

The site of Stramongate School which occupied premises beyond this passageway.

STRAMONGATE SCHOOL

This school, founded by the Society of Friends in 1698, occupied premises beyond this passageway from 1792 to 1932. It has connections with two famous scientists:

JOHN DALTON,
founder of the atomic theory and 'father of modern chemistry', who taught here from 1781 to 1793

and

SIR ARTHUR STANLEY EDDINGTON,
pioneer of stellar structure, author of "The Expanding Universe", former Chief Assistant at Greenwich Observatory, Professor of Astronomy at the University of Cambridge, who was born here in 1882, his father then being the Headmaster.

Sponsors: The Royal Astronomical Society.
The Institute of Physics.

KENDAL CIVIC SOCIETY

The commemorative plaque outside the site of the old school

'This school, founded by the Society of Friends in 1698 and occupied premises beyond this passageway from 1792 to 1932.'

'It has connections with two famous scientists: JOHN DALTON, founder of the atomic theory and 'father of modern chemistry', who taught here from 1781 to 1793 and SIR ARTHUR STANLEY EDDINGTON, pioneer of stellar structure, author of "The Expanding Universe", former Chief Assistant at Greenwich Observatory, Professor of Astronomy at the University of Cambridge, who was born here in 1882, his father then being the Headmaster.'

Chapter 10
Quaker schools

Inspired by Fox's teachings, Quakers set great store by education which was always for both boys and girls and Quaker schools feature largely in our story, so at this point, I think I should say a little about the history of these distinguished schools. Though some of course, have disappeared, there are seven which are still going strong. Our relatives have attended Quaker schools all over the country, including Elizabeth Petipher Cash who went to Croydon School about 1811 which had begun in Clerkenwell in 1702 and then moved to Islington in 1825 and finally from 1879 to Saffron Walden before closing in 1968. Great Grandfather Frederick Cash went to first to Lewes and then to The Woodlands at Hitchin in Hertfordshire in the 1840's, which closed in 1889. Our other great Grandfather, John Barlow went to Ackworth in Pontefract in West Yorkshire in 1825; his son John Henry Barlow went to Stramongate in Kendal in the 1870's; his wife Mabel Cash went to Sidcot and to Edgbaston High School; their sons, our Father Ralph and his elder brother John went first to the Downs School in Colwall near Malvern and then to Leighton Park in the 1920's (to both of which my brothers and I also went) as did another Uncle, Alfred Braithwaite who was there between 1915 and 1919; my Father's sister, Millior, who later married Alfred, went to Edgbaston High like her Mother. Our Mother, Joan Barlow (née Barber) and her sister Winifred and brother Reg all went to Sibford at Banbury in Oxfordshire; and our cousins Michael and Priscilla Rutter went to Bootham (opened in 1823) and to The Mount (1784) in York, respectively, as did our Braithwaite cousins, Anna and Carol and these schools are still going strong.

As we have seen, the Society was a non-conformist dissenting group, whose members turned away from Anglican Worship, many being arrested and imprisoned during the reign of Charles II. One consequence of this persecution was that Quakers realised that they would have to set up their own Schools for the education of the children of members of the Society. Indeed George Fox saw that education would be vital in supporting and advancing the cause of the Society of Friends.

He persuaded other Friends therefore, to help establish such schools around the country and Sidcot was amongst the oldest, founded by a group of local Quakers in 1699. The oldest of the present school buildings dates from 1838 and although the campus has been developed and modernised since then, the principal of the School remains the same; 'the provision of a boarding and day School in accordance with the principles of the Religious Society of Friends.'

Ackworth, where my great Grandfather John Barlow went in 1824 when he was 9 years old, is another very old Quaker school, being founded in 1779 by John Fothergill. As it was originally constituted, the Board of Governors, is still accountable to the Society of Friends to this day. Like other Friends' schools it was established for the children of their families and the Quaker Christian ethos, with its emphasis on quiet reflection and the search for God within oneself and within others, still lies at the heart of all Quaker Schools.

Stramongate School in Kendal, where John Henry Barlow went in the 1860's was another ancient Quaker school, opening in 1698 and continuing right up until 1932. Today, it is just commemorated by a plaque on the wall, near the passageway that led to the school. But the beginnings of the school are well recorded in the local archives.

A memo in the minutes of Kendal Quarterly meeting of 1695 states the aim of educating the children of the Society:

"This meeting having had under the care of consideration, the erecting of a school for the education of their children, and agrees that Kendal may be the place...."

A little later the principles by which the school were to be run are also clearly adumbrated:

- To train the mind and body as a means to the development of a strong Christian character
- To awaken the love of the open air and the natural beauty and simple pleasures of the exploration of the Lake District
- To develop an international outlook through a study of history, geography and current affairs
- To encourage hobbies for the leisure hours

To start with, a room was set aside in the old meeting house, which opened in 1698 and by 1728 it was already accepting boarders. But by 1772 it was already too small and a subscription was raised to pay for a new building. This was erected behind a row of small cottages and in 1785 Jonathan Dalton took over the school and his brother John Dalton later to become the famous scientist, was a teacher there. By the time John Henry was a pupil at the school one Henry Thompson was the Headmaster who was strict but much respected and loved by everybody.

Edgbaston High School, was not strictly a Quaker school but similar in its outlook and was founded much later in 1876 by George Dixon and many distinguished local families from the Quaker and Unitarian traditions including the Albrights, Chamberlains, Martineaus and Mathews went there. The founders were keen to make available a broad, liberal education, much like that already experienced by their sons and EHS has always been characterised by its non-denominational approach to teaching and learning. It was originally housed at the junction of Harborne Road and Hagley Road under the headship of Miss Alice Cooper but within two years had doubled in size and moved to the Laurels at 280 Hagley Road.

The School aimed always to be at the forefront of girls' education and this was reflected in the curriculum right from the start; a school inspector in 1878 was impressed by the girls standard "and their healthy freedom from silliness, tittering and affectation"!

After she left Sidcot, my Grandmother went on to Edgbaston High School in 1884, living with her Uncle and Aunt, Caroline and George Barrow in Edgbaston. Her Father FGC recorded:

'Edgbaston High she much appreciated and enjoyed and made a great many friends. She pursued her studies with industry and avidity and made excellent progress.'

Perhaps because I and many members of my family went to Leighton Park School it is of particular interest to me. But also, I believe, its history dating back to 1828 and the earlier school Grove House is in many ways illustrative of the changing mores of the Society. In 1828 a group of remarkable Quakers including William Allen, Samuel Gurney the Banker brother of Elizabeth Fry and John Hodgkin bought Grove House in the village of Tottenham. Tottenham was then a Quaker centre as Peckham in South London was to become later in the century. Tottenham was where, for instance my great, great Grandmother, Elizabeth Petipher Lucas moved when her brother married and took over the Golden Square house. Among those donating money to the new school were such worthy Quaker names as the Bankers Barclays and Lloyds and Richard Darby of Coalbrookdale. From the start the curriculum was all embracing including not only Latin and Greek but Mathematics and Science.

At the time this was considered extremely modern, combining a sound classical education with the new and unusual subject of science. These Quakers believed in finding out 'truth by experiment'.

More Quaker schools

Grove House School in the 1830's

Leighton Park School – as it is today.
This main building, then known as Central, included Peckover Hall, and classrooms.
It was opened in 1915 and just referred to simply as Peckover ever since.

It is interesting that one of the outstanding pupils of Grove House was Lord Lister, who was to become a close friend of my great Grandfather, John Barlow, himself Professor of Veterinary studies at Edinburgh University, evincing an early trend towards medicine that was to continue at Leighton Park. The school prospered for half a century, but gradually the founders died and the influence of new Board members became less until in 1877 the then Headmaster Arthur Abbott joined the Church of England and the school was sold to him and the sale helped to finance Leighton Park.

During the next twelve years Quakerism itself was undergoing a big change. Many of the young, university educated intellectuals of the Society were abandoning the distinctive sober dress and the old speech customs of 'thee' and 'thou'. Many were attending art galleries, going to concerts and the theatre and as a result many young Quakers were seeking a better education for their children. Oxford and Cambridge had removed the earlier religious tests and so were now open to Friends. Other customs were being abandoned too; whereas the Carrs had been pushed out of the Society for marrying outside the Society, this was now relaxed. One of the visionary Quakers of the period was John William Rowntree, himself educated at Bootham. He was one of those who challenged the Society to embrace the new scientific evidence and to use it to build a future "that would drive man forth with the apostolic fervour of the early church."

With the money from the sale of Grove House still in Trust, it was decided to use the money – some £7,000 along with donations from other wealthy Quakers such George and Elizabeth Cadbury – to purchase some land to build the new school, on an estate, White Knights Park, not far from the centre of Reading. Leighton Park, named after the area, opening its doors in 1890, belonged to this modern world, quite different from the old certainties that had inspired the opening of Grove House in 1828, although its links with the old school were perpetuated by naming one of the houses, Grove, but as S W Brown puts it in his *History of Leighton Park:*

"The new school represents a new beginning with much of the zeal, the purpose, the honesty and the vision of the Quaker revival so strongly influenced by John Rowntree."

As noted, the teaching of young people has always been a priority for Quakers and from the late seventeenth century onwards, many were involved in establishing schools for their own children and others in need. Leighton Park was opened as a public school for boys, and along with high academic aims it also set out to encourage them to think for themselves and to develop self-reliance. It was nicknamed 'the Quaker Eton' at the time and has always sent a high proportion of its pupils to university, especially Oxford and Cambridge.

With only four boys when it opened in 1890 it soon increased and by the 1920's there were well over a hundred and by 1970 there were 300 pupils. In 1975, along with many other schools, they decided to admit girls to the sixth form and today there are nearly 500 pupils from all over the world.

From the start the Quaker faith has been central to the school and today this is still true with its daily 'Collect', the morning meeting which is similar to that of 'assembly' in other schools, where the whole school gathers together and which finishes with a silence. Also once a week instead of 'Collect' there is a meeting held in silence as in all Quaker meetings.

So in many ways, from 1828 at Grove House in Tottenham, to today's Leighton Park in Reading, the school has continuously adapted itself to meet the mores of the time, yet maintaining its essential Quakerism that inspired its founding.

Old Downians at a School reunion

Mum with David, Stephen and Antony outside The Downs School 1999

The Downs school today

A school that always had particularly close links with LP is The Downs School which was founded only ten years later in 1900. Its strongest link was its founder, Herbert Jones and his wife Ethel who had previously been headmaster at Leighton Park. Like LP it opened with four pupils, and slowly expanded, with some 40 pupils by 1918. It soon established itself as a 'feeder' school for Leighton Park.

In 1920 Jones died and was succeeded by his second master, Geoffrey Hoyland, who had married Dorothea Cadbury and were thus able to use the Cadbury family's wealth to expand and improve the school during his tenure as headmaster. He built new buildings, introduced student self-government and an innovative curriculum with, as we saw at LP, an emphasis on science and the arts.

Also under his supervision, the pupils built and maintained a miniature railway, the only one in any English school at the time, which still survives to this day, long maintained by Mr Boyd who died in 2003. Among the notable masters he hired, were Maurice Field, known as Parsey a remarkable teacher and artist himself, who later went on to teach at the Slade. Among his pupils was the artist Lawrence Gowing.

My Uncle, John Barlow was at the school with Jones but my Father's time coincided with Geoffrey Hoyland, known to all as GH. Even in my own time at the school, as well as that of my brother David's period there, under GH's half-brother, Frazer Hoyland, it was always an occasion when GH was the speaker at Sunday Evening meeting. Frazer became headmaster in 1940 and placed a lot of emphasis on music and drama, which I greatly loved, learning the violin and taking part in many plays. Like LP and most other single sex schools, The Downs became co-educational in the 1990's and added a nursery, kindergarten, and pre-prep school to the original preparatory school and it has now merged with Malvern College.

Although some schools like Stramongate and Croydon have long ceased to exist, it is nonetheless, a tribute to the value Quakers have always put on education for both girls and boys, that there are still seven of these schools thriving today and which are still making a very vital contribution to the general educational mix; a mix that is still based on Quaker beliefs with a Morning Meeting very much at its heart.

Two remarkable head-masters and their wives. Left: Herbert and Ethel Jones. He went to Ackworth before going up to Cambridge; he was the 2nd head of Leighton Park, before having the vision to start The Downs school in the Malvern Hills. They were there from 1900 – 1920 and were succeeded by Geoffrey and Dorothea Hoyland (1920-1940) GH as he was known to all, was 'an educationist of genius, whose creativeness and imagination made The Downs a very special school.'

Frank Heyworth Talbot, Chairman of the Governors

Chapter 11
The Barlows

We can now turn to the family which gives me my surname, the Barlows! My paternal great Grandfather, John Barlow belonged to a Cheshire family and was born on the 20th September 1815 at Chorley near Alderley in the old gabled and picturesque house known as The Oaks, a rambling place with polished floors and diamond paned windows, standing on the estate which had been in the possession of the family for about 200 years.[34]

He was the eldest of seven – three sons and four daughters – children[35] to John Barlow (1789-1846) and Deborah Neild[36] (1790-1850). By all accounts he was a very affectionate brother. He went away at the age of nine to the Friend's school, Ackworth and was acknowledged to be "the cleverest boy in the class" as well as "the kindest and most amiable" according to a fellow pupil. John was from childhood of a rather sedate and grave demeanour and became interested in religious matters from an early age. His daughter, Mary writes in her diary:

"In 1824 at the age of nine, my Father went to Ackworth School in South Yorkshire, where he remained for four years. This was not the age of holidays in Friends' school and when he returned home, so altered was he that his mother, who had not seen him since he first set off for school, did not recognise him!"[37]

John's father was a Farmer and it was always assumed that when young John grew up, he too would remain at home and help his father in the running of the farm, which for some time he did. But he always had a strong love of animals, particularly of the farm cows and during the years on the farm he spent much time in the study of those diseases to which domestic animals are prone. And it was this which guided him into the choice of profession that later took him to Edinburgh. He also developed a fondness for poetry and was himself an original writer exhibiting a deep love of nature and of home and he was a much cherished eldest son in Chorley.

Eventually his own devotion to study was too strong and brought about a change in his life. By the time he was in his twenties, he decided to go to Edinburgh to study veterinary science and in 1842 he enrolled at William Dick's Veterinary College in Clyde Street, Edinburgh. He gained his diploma there in 1844 and was awarded a prize for the scientific paper he wrote 'On the Present Epidemic among Cattle' and a silver medal *"Awarded to Mr Barlow as the student most distinguished at the examination for diplomas."* That same year he was awarded another silver medal for his essay on 'Puerperal fever in the Cow'.

An article that appeared in the *North British Agriculturalist,* refers to the work of the next few years:

"After attending two sessions at the College he obtained his diploma, having been the most distinguished student of the course. The following session he acted as demonstrator and in

---

[34] In a note from a book on the Family Barlow privately published in 1911 it states: 'The Oaks is known to have come into the possession of the family when it was sold by the Hough family to a John Barlow, who died in 1658. The greater part of the property was sold after the death in 1846, of (the then) Sir John Emmott Barlow. A small portion still remains in the family.' It was pulled down in the 1875 to make way for the railway line.

[35] John's brother Thomas born in 1825 married Mary Ann Emmott and their son John Emmott Barlow married the Hon Anna Denman who I remember visiting in her London flat in Grosvenor House when I was about nine or ten. John Emmott was made a baronet in 1907 and became MP for Frome in Somerset. The present holder of the title is his grandson John Kemp Barlow of Bradwall Hall.

[36] Deborah Neild was a cousin of John Camden Neild, an eccentric, who left his fortune to Queen Victoria – see Chapter 12

[37] Carol Saker's archives

Professor John Barlow

Professor John Barlow 1815-1856

The Author writes:
"Our great grandfather, Professor at the Royal Dick School of Veterinary Studies, Edinburgh, with a slight air of Heathcliff about him!"

1845 was appointed Assistant Professor and lecturer on zootomy,[38] including the anatomy and physiology of domesticated animals."

He later moved full time to Edinburgh and it is obvious that he found a conflict in the Christian way of life in which he had been brought up and that his parents wished him to follow. This often led him to eschew the more convivial side of university life, and he wrote to a friend:

"I did not seek these (friendships) just for the sake of spending time with them and far less for the sake of simply forming connections; I sought (their company) for the quality of the people, intellectually estimated. Still all things considered, I feel best satisfied to forego the associations alluded to, for I was often compelled to countenance customs to which in reality I am averse."

One can only presume he might be alluding to women and drink! But William Dick immediately realised his academic potential and straight away employed him first as a demonstrator and later as Assistant Professor of Anatomy and Physiology. John became a notable figure in the intellectual and literary society of Edinburgh, a group who were all strong Liberals in politics. A particularly close friend of his was another Edinburgh Quaker, Joseph Lister, who later reformed surgery with the use of antiseptics. John was soon elevated to the title of Professor and his short successful career in Edinburgh was summed up by his illustrious peers. Professor William Gardner who became Glasgow's first Medical Officer of Health described John Barlow as a: *'great and original thinker, so truthful and unselfish'.*

Sir James Simpson the pioneer of chloroform wrote:

"He was a man destined to advance and elevate veterinary medicine'; while Professor Goodsir, wrote: *'John Barlow was a man of very remarkable ability who helped establish a course every bit as eminent as the School of medicine.'*

Mr Dun who taught Diatetics wrote:
"I never knew anyone whose influence on those with whom he came into contact was so wholly and powerfully good," adding that *"Professor Barlow's scientific investigations and writings were well to the front of his profession. He was in all a man greatly beloved, nay revered by his students."*

William Williams in a speech made at the opening of a new college, declared that: *'John Barlow was the pioneer of Veterinary science...a man living one hundred years before his time. Others were rule-of-thumb practitioners, while he brought the light of science to bear upon his profession."* Headley

He was highly regarded and his published papers in the Veterinarian and as veterinarian correspondent for The North British Agriculturist, were widely read and still form the basis of modern research. He sadly died before his time, probably from Meningitis which spread to his spine and his last weeks of illness were extremely painful. He first began to be seriously ill on New Year's Day 1856 when he was only 40, though initially it was thought that it was only rheumatic fever, and that he would recover. But it was in fact a very serious spinal infection and he soon became extremely sick and after a great deal of suffering, he died on January 29. But that is to pre-empt matters. John Barlow was an active member of the Edinburgh Meeting House in the Pleasance, where in 1851 he met Eliza Nicholson of Whitehaven whom he eventually married. Eliza it will be recalled, was the descendant of the family that possessed the Bible. It was a close knit circle as we have already seen, with Eliza's sister Sarah marrying another Friend, John Wigham of Edinburgh and her sister Jane, marrying Jonathan Carr.

---

[38] The anatomy, especially the comparative anatomy, of animals.

Professor Barlow's and Eliza's home in Edinburgh

The gracious front living room of No 1 Pilrig Street as restored by its present owner John Campbell.

On New Year's day, 1851 he and Eliza Nicholson were married and according to our Grandmother *'entered one of the most perfect unions that earth affords.'* They moved into No 1 Pilrig Street, where their three children were born. This was and still is a fine Georgian house, built in 1805, the first in the street and from the outside, has a rather stern and formal exterior, somewhat reflecting the demeanour of its one time occupant. But it in no way prepares one for what awaits inside the house, now lovingly restored by the present occupant, John Campbell. For, to echo Howard Carter's response to Lord Carnarvon's famous remark 'Can you see anything?' at the entrance to the tomb of Tutankhamun, one can only say, with him, 'Yes, wonderful things'. A hallway that opens on to the most splendid spiral staircase, which curves and winds its way up three floors to a fantastic oval cupola that lights up the whole central area of the house. From the spacious and elegant front dining room to the exquisite drawing room at the back, with its fine bronze fire place and tiled hearth, which still warms the room, itself given added grandeur by a dramatic curved end wall, with shuttered windows that overlook a beautiful long garden, is redolent of a more gracious age. Ascending the staircase one reaches a large master bedroom and several children's rooms and at the very top, still sizeable maid's quarters, while below the hallway is a huge basement where the old kitchen and storerooms would have been. There is still an air of tranquility about the house and sitting in the room where John Barlow died so painfully, I suddenly felt close to a person I had only previously read about.

Their three children were Alfred who died when he was only six (1851-7), Mary (1853-1899), and John Henry (1855– 1924). So Mary was only three and John Henry only four months when their father died and certainly JH would have had no memory of him. But according to both the pamphlet produced by Quakers when he died and by Granny Barlow's account *'he loved his dear children almost to idolatry'*. To all who knew them, it was a very happy marriage and John *'seemed the beau ideal of all that is noble and truly manly.'*

John and Eliza remained in Edinburgh and he continued his work at the College where he had studied and was appointed Professor in 1855 introducing microscopical[39] research and writing many treatises that were ground breaking in their time. He had been admitted as a Fellow of the Royal Scottish Society of Arts in 1852 and also as a member of the Physiological Society. The standing he had among the scientific men with whom he mingled and worked and the appreciation of his talents and acquirements won in the Edinburgh Schools of Medicine was second to none. In 1856 he was engaged in compiling the first ever text-book of veterinary science when his last illness began and he died that same year.

As The Scotsman later stated:

"Nothing was ever more wanted than a good anatomical text-book for the veterinary student. The late lamented Mr Barlow had begun one but sudden death took away one of the best of anatomists, of teachers and of men and for a time, our hope of a text-book."

His death was widely mourned both in Edinburgh and throughout the medical world. His achievements were perhaps best described by Professor Sir James Simpson, Professor of Anatomy in the University.

Writing in The North British Agriculturalist, he said:

"His character was indeed of a very high order both intellectually and morally. He was wonderfully informed on many of the most intricate modern questions in anatomical science. He was a man destined to advance and elevate veterinary medicine; and we all deplore his loss, the more so as he has been removed from among us while scarcely in his prime. ....People who knew him well respected him deeply, not less for his amiability and kindliness of heart, than for his great talents and high intellectual cast of mind."

And another colleague, Dr Fleming wrote to Professor Barlow's daughter Mary:

"I was a student under Professor Barlow from 1852 to 1855 and he had not long been married when I went to the college. My remembrances of him are particularly vivid; for his instruction, manner and almost paternal kindness and interest in the students, made him greatly beloved, nay revered by them. He stood in the forefront of scientific men of his generation. In the veterinary profession of those days or even since, there has not, in my opinion, been his equal; and his all too premature removal from our midst was one of the heaviest misfortunes that has befallen our branch of medicine.....He won the hearts of all the students, never begrudging time or trouble in helping or looking after them.....A testament to his outstanding ability from my own experience when I was with the Army during the Crimean war. The fact remains that there have only ever been six principle veterinary surgeons since it was taught in colleges in this country and of these, three studied under your father which must be gratifying to your mother. To me he has always been an ideal image of goodness and perfection and in my own professional career I have always had it before me."

When he died John left ample provision for his widow with shares in tin mines in Cornwall and the Glasgow Bank, but both of these were to crash.[40] These were the days of unlimited liability and Eliza Barlow had to pay out again and again to creditors until she was left with only £200 a year with which to bring up and educate the children. In addition, as if this were not enough, not long after, their eldest son Alfred died. As the wife of a Professor and with the Nicholson money she would have brought with her, she had been used to a relatively easy and

---

[39] When John Henry died my Uncle John and my Grandmother offered his microscope to the Royal Dick in Edinburgh in 1929. For more see page 9

[40] See under J D Carr p 42

comfortable life with maids to look after them, but this financial debacle meant that they had to move to a smaller house in the city nearer to their cousins the Wighams in Salisbury Road who were very kind, especially 'saintly Sarah Wigham', who taught the Barlow children for a while. As with many Quaker families, they tended to look after each other and in accounts of John Henry and Mary's childhood holidays, one often reads of them - Eliza's sister Sarah and her husband, John Wigham - all going away together, often on sailing trips to Scotland. Granny Barlow writes in her memoir:

"Sometimes big parties of cousins were arranged, Barlows, Carrs, Wighams, Ashbys, Peiles with JHB acting as courier and financier....Mary, full of fun and very racy....and John, quieter but apt and quick in repartee."

Eventually Eliza moved to Carlisle to be near her eldest sister Jane and her husband Jonathan Carr, where she and the two children lived in the upper part of a big old fashioned house above the baker's shop that Carr had first opened on his arrival in the city, just opposite Carlisle Cathedral. It maybe that there was a certain amount of guilt involved here, as JD Carr, against good Quaker principal had indulged in a speculation in 1850, investing in a Cornish tin mine, encouraging others, including John and Eliza Barlow to do likewise.

As already stated the tin mine crashed and all who had backed, it lost their money. JD always felt he was responsible and resolved to reimburse other investors, selling the family home and using the money to recompense the other investors. Housing Eliza and her children was his way of helping to make amends.

For the rest of his life Jonathan Carr rented a house, Coledale Hall in Newtown, as though *'doing penance for a piece of uncharacteristic vanity....protecting himself from delusions of grandeur'* as Margaret Forster puts it in her book on the Carr family.[41]

The author with the present owner of No 1 Pilrig Street, John Cambell 2014

---

[41] 'Rich Desserts and Captains Thin' (Chatto and Windus).

'Saintly Sarah' and John Barlow's microscope

'Saintly Sarah Wigham'

The Author writes:

"Sarah Wigham, (née Nicholson) the sister of Eliza, (who married Professor Barlow) and Jane (who married Jonathan Carr), described as 'saintly' by our Grandmother, for the way she cared for the children.

As with close Quaker families of the period, when troubles befell a relative, they all rallied round and when Professor John died at the age of only 40 and Eliza was left with the children and declining finances, she and the children initially stayed with the Wighams at their Salisbury Road house, before moving to Carlisle to live with her other sister Jane in part of the Carr house."

The Professor's microscope

The Author writes:

"Professor John Barlow, was appointed Professor of Veterinary studies at the Royal Dick University in Edinburgh in 1855 and introduced microspical research. On his death our Grandmother, Mabel Barlow donated his microscope to the college. Sadly, it appears to have been lost."

John Camden Neild

John Camden Neild, son of James Neild 1780 – 1852.
He donated all his money to Queen Victoria in 1852, the year she purchased Balmoral Castle.

The Author writes:

This unexpected windfall came as somewhat of a surprise to the young queen, especially since the Hanoverian Kings who preceded Victoria, had left the monarchy in considerable financial straits. In her diary, she makes only a brief reference to the inheritance, remarking that: *"A very handsome fortune had unexpectedly been bequeathed to me by a Mr John Camden Neild. He knew I would not squander it."* Considering the size of the fortune, it is a little surprising that this is her only comment, but I do like her certainty that he knew she 'would not squander it'!

Reproduced by kind permission of the Royal Collection Trust/© Her Majesty Queen Elizabeth II 2015

Chapter 12
John Camden Neild

Here might be the right point to mention the extraordinary story of the Neild family. Whilst researching the family archives, my elder brother David, happened to mention that one of our ancestors had given away a fortune to Queen Victoria. This all sounded an unlikely story and certainly one I had never heard before. But I decided to investigate some of the boxes that I had inherited from our Mother, that still remained unopened and there I chanced upon a document from the 1880's detailing the life of the eccentric John Camden Neild.

For this story I am indebted to an account that our great Grandmother, Eliza Nicholson had written for the family. Her father-in-law, our great, great Grandfather, John Barlow (born 1790) had married Deborah Neild in 1820, a first cousin of John Camden Neild. John Camden was the son of James Neild and Elizabeth Camden and was born in 1780. But the story really begins with his father James, who was born in 1744 and was famous as a penal reformer. His own father had died young and left James' mother to bring up the four children. As a consequence James had only a brief education and by 1760 managed to obtain a position with a London jeweller, where he learned to engrave and to draw as well as to fence. In 1770 an Uncle died and left him a large legacy which enabled him to set up as a jeweller in St James's Street in London. The venture proved very successful and in 1792 he retired with a fortune to 5 Cheyne Walk in Chelsea, a house built in 1792, that is now owned by the Cypriot High Commission. He had also invested his fortune in a great deal of other property outside London, which was estimated to be worth £250,000.

After his retirement he became actively involved in penal reform, visiting many prisons up and down the country as well on the continent and in 1773 he established the 'Society for the Relief and Discharge of Persons Imprisoned for Small Debts'. For the rest of his life he continued to visit prisons in and around London and to help release those imprisoned for petty offences. He also published many accounts of his visits and was granted the freedom of several cities for his good works, serving also as a JP for Westminster and being appointed High Sherriff of Buckinghamshire.

James had married Elizabeth in 1778, the daughter of John Camden of Battersea, then still in the County of Surrey and they had three children, a daughter Elizabeth, who died in childhood, William (1779-1810), and John Camden Neild (1780-1852). Following a family row, James had disinherited his eldest son William, who had moved abroad, and so when James Neild died at his Chelsea home in 1814, his younger son John Camden succeeded to the property and thereafter proceeded to live the life of a recluse, and when he died in 1852, was found to have left the whole of his great fortune to Queen Victoria.

Much unfriendly criticism has inevitably been directed against the younger Neild, not least from his relatives, but there are those who have maintained that his retirement from public life was quite possibly due to personal disappointments. It is said that he had a great veneration for the memory of his father and maybe felt that he was unable to measure up. It was also alleged that when he left his wealth to the Crown, he was genuinely unaware that he had any relatives, who might have had a possible claim upon his generosity. Whatever, the reason, there is no escaping the fact that this once knowledgeable man of letters, was undoubtedly eccentric and had become in later life, a confirmed miser. Inheriting a fortune of some £250,000 from his father, he left property worth at least double that amount to Queen Victoria, and here is what Eliza Nicholson says, corroborated by the Royal Archives at Windsor Castle:

"Cousin John Camden Neild was born in 1780 and educated at Eton (1793-1797) and Trinity College, Cambridge 1801, called to the Bar 1805. When his father died in 1814, he inherited the whole of his vast fortune, amounting to £250,000. But during the last 30 years of his life, he became a confirmed miser and spent his time accumulating wealth. His large house at No 5 Cheyne Walk, Chelsea[42] was meanly furnished with not even a bed to lie on. His dress consisted of a blue swallow tail coat with gilt buttons, brown trousers, short gaiters and shoes which were patched and generally down at heel. He never allowed his clothes to be brushed for fear of destroying the nap. He continually visited his numerous estates, always walking to avoid expense and insisted on sharing their food and lodging with them."

There follows a passage describing how he once tried to cut his throat and was only saved by the quick action of a tenant, Mrs Veale. It continues:

"He died at his residence in Cheyne Walk in 1852 and was buried in the chancel of North Marston church in Bucks. In his will he left the whole of his fortune, valued at half a million,[43] to the Queen, with the exception of a few trifling bequests. The Queen, provided for his servants, for whom he had made no provision and secured an annuity for Mrs Veale who had saved his life. In 1855 the Queen restored the chancel of Marston Church at a cost of £3000 and inserted a window in Neild's memory. As the Queen decided that there were no 'near relations' she accepted the fortune from this eccentric man, who during at least one period of his life was certainly insane."

To give his legacies some context, it is perhaps worth repeating, that when John Camden's cousin, Professor John Barlow, died tragically young aged only 40, his widow and children were forced to move to live with Eliza's sister Jane, as their entire fortune had disappeared, following the collapse of both the Glasgow Bank and the Cornish tin mines. I also discovered, on my inspection of the Royal Archives, that despite considerable representations made by various relatives, the Queen, after adjusting a few bequests, was quite dismissive of other relatives who had wanted to sue for some financial equity. As a final indignity, it was in 1852, the same year she had received this generous bequest, that Queen Victoria bought Balmoral, almost certainly with the proceeds of this legacy and it occurs to me, that at the very least, her descendant might allow the family the occasional stay at their Highland retreat!

**1900 print of Balmoral Castle, which was bought in 1852,
the year J C Neild left his money to Queen Victoria**

---

[42] Now the Cypriot High Commission
[43] Some £5 million in today's money

Chapter 13
John Henry Barlow – 1855-1900

John Henry was only a few months old when his Father died suddenly on January 29th 1856, having been born on October 3rd 1855, while his elder sister Mary (1853-1899) was just three. The eldest child, Alfred was born in 1851, but sadly died at the tender age of 6. Their Mother, Eliza found herself in a parlous situation, with no funds to support her two young children and forced to move out of Pilrig Street. Luckily they had caring Edinburgh cousins, the Wighams, who rallied round and for a while they stayed at their Edinburgh home at 10 Salisbury Road.

However, this would not be a satisfactory solution for long, and following an invitation from her other sister Jane, they moved back to Carlisle, where they could have their own separate corner of the Carr family's large house. Jane and Jonathan Carr had met at Quarterly meeting and married in 1833 in the rather grand premises of Whitehaven meeting house. She was three years younger than her husband and looked very small besides the towering six foot figure of the biscuit magnate! By this time Carr's biscuits had become hugely successful and as they prospered the family soon grew to six children, who grew up to be close companions of Eliza's two children.

Eliza and Mary and John Henry had the two upper stories of the house with their own private staircase opening onto Castle Street, which gave them much more privacy than they had been able to enjoy in Edinburgh. As their fortunes improved, Eliza and the children eventually moved to Burlington Place, where the children took great delight in building a boat in the outhouse which they launched on the Eden river. John Henry loved the river as well as swimming, fishing and skating, which became one of his favourite pastimes.

John Henry was sent to the old Quaker school, Stramongate in Kendal where the Carr boys went and he seems to have been very happy there, writing many affectionate and lively letters home to his Mother and beloved sister Mary (see p.68), as well as to their nurse Mag. These are full of typical schoolboy things such as cricket, pillow fights and exams, so I am inclined to think that his later very serious demeanour probably masked a jollier nature. In the photograph of him during his school days, he even seems to fancy himself as a bit of a dandy!

Sadly, because of the family finances, he had to leave school early, to become the family earner, which meant he was unable to pursue the medical career that he had hoped for, to follow in his father's footsteps. Instead he entered the Clydesdale Bank, where he did very well and the extra income soon enabled the family to prosper and in 1881 they moved to Murrell Hill Cottage in Carlisle, a lovely home where Eliza was to remain for the rest of her life. The front faced the street but at the back was a beautiful garden with a millstream at the bottom and the side windows looking out on to fields and beyond to Skiddaw.

My Cousin Carol Saker (née Braithwaite), has researched the life of our great Aunt Mary from papers in her possession and with her permission, I quote from some of her findings:

"I came upon some diaries and correspondence, written by great Aunt Mary, which have shed some light onto my maternal antecedents.....Mary Barlow lived from 1853 to1899 in Carlisle and in 1886 at the age of 33, started to write her own memoirs, which she called 'An Autobiography'. However, Mary's memoirs, rather disappointingly, are less about herself than about her parents and their heritage, the old 16th century farmhouse, The Oak in Chorley, where her father had been born in 1815. The Oak was near the railway station but sadly, was pulled down in 1875, but in its rafters was found hidden a crock of money from the time of Charles I, probably placed there during the Civil War.

John Henry aged 15 in 1871, looking a bit of a dandy!

One wonders what became of the 'crock of money'! As quoted in Chapter 11, Great Aunt Mary talks of her Father not having holidays from school and of his Mother hardly recognising the grown up boy. But as Carol goes on to observe:

"Her Father had not seemingly suffered from his long absence from home at such an early age and was always an affectionate son and brother and later after his marriage to Eliza Nicholson in 1851, became a Father too, whose daughter, although she was only 3 when her Father died, says she could just remember that 'he always had a keen appreciation for and enjoyment of fun and humour.'"

John Henry and his sister Mary stayed at Murrell Hill with their Mother for some years, a close knit family unit, with the two siblings enjoying many outdoor pursuits. In later years, when John was nearly 40 and had met his future wife, Mabel Cash, it was Mary who first encouraged her brother in his courtship after their Mother died in 1894. Being unmarried herself, she generously offered to move out, so that the newlyweds could live together in the house. Mary however, had always been of a delicate disposition, cared for throughout her short life by her Mother. Sadly, after Eliza died, Mary only lived another five years, dying in 1899 and so never living to see in the new century or knowing her nephews and niece.

As John Henry grew older he devoted more and more time to good causes, often talking to the Temperance League with his cousins Bertram and Theodore Carr, and quite soon becoming an extremely well-known figure for the great social work he did in the City among the poor communities, especially at Willow Holme, then a run-down area of Carlisle. In 1889 he left the Bank to become Secretary of Carr's Biscuits and his Bank colleagues presented him with a book-case on his leaving as a token of their esteem.

Another family friend from Gloucester, Ernest Hutchinson also moved to Carlisle in 1885 to join Carr and Co's business as the following year he was to marry Frederick Goodall's second daughter Louisa Cash – Lou for short – and she too left the Gloucester family home to join Ernest at his new home in Goshen Road, Carlisle. This road with its somewhat odd sounding name, for some reason became emblazoned on my mind, and I remember visiting there with Mum and Dad en route North on one of our many trips to Scotland.

John Henry and Ernest decided to revive the good work that J D Carr's eldest son, Henry had begun, but which had by then somewhat languished. It was a dark and dangerous neighbourhood, with '*drunken brawls and horrible fights between women as well as men; and terrified shrieks issued as wife or child was being ill-treated...*' writes Grandmother, but the love and energy of these two along with Lou produced great results. Others came and helped including Richard Cadbury and it was here that many young people received their first lessons in reading and writing; there was also a club room for the boys where John Henry used to go and read stories and organise games for them. Our Grandmother recalls in her book written for my Father, Aunt Millior and Uncle John:

"We turned the downstairs into a club for the boys who had nowhere to go and nothing to do and I remember once looking in and all was strangely quiet. Stumbling along the worn flagged entry and opening the door, I saw a picture which is vivid still. A low room lit by a swinging oil lamp, a stove, near to which sat John surrounded by boys, some lying along forms, some scrunched on the floor, others close beside him, all listening with breathless attention to a story he was telling."

After Lou and Ernest Hutchinson had married in 1883 and they were settled in Carlisle, Lou's sister Mabel, our Grandmother, began to visit her there and soon became involved with the work they undertook, and it wasn't long before she met John Henry... *'the Prophet'* as she called him'. Although, she describes herself as *'young and shy,'* their friendship soon developed and John Henry often used to go over to the Hutchinson's house 'Glevum' and join in the games and general liveliness there. Writing later, she recalls a man...*'who could act excellently and express so many emotions by changes of face and figure, which used to convulse us with laughter.'* And from a letter of January 22 1895 from John Henry to his future wife, he says: *"Monday night I spent with the boys again and told another story, as I had promised that I would tell them two this week."* Obviously, this 'serious minded' Quaker could also be great fun, and as if to reinforce the picture, Granny later describes evenings in Birmingham after their marriage, when they entertained friends, saying how...*'John used to act excellently in charades; making a capital actor.'*

From his childhood he had always loved bathing and sailing, which he continued to enjoy all his life, often diving off the boat deck into the sea and in later life his favourite hobbies were cycling and walking through the countryside, which he would often do with his sister Mary and later with his wife, *'to get right away among the mountains, amid the wild beauties of Cumberland.'* as he put it. These outdoor pursuits he handed on to his children, especially my father, who in turn passed them on to us his children.

It is coming across such little incidents in studying John Henry's life, that a completely different image emerges than the rather austere picture that looks out of the later photographs and it becomes increasingly clear that the often described 'solemn-faced' Quaker is not the whole picture. He could also be the naughty schoolboy having pillow fights, as well as the story-telling actor. Our father and Aunt Millior described a somewhat strict and evangelical household, but there was evidently much love and fun as well, and above all he patently took great joy in his children, as Granny describes a wonderful father:

"When the children heard his latch key in the door, there were shouts of 'There's Daddy' and a dash into the hall to greet him. He loved to read aloud to them as they got older, especially from Pilgrim's Progress, which Ralph appreciated so much he asked for it to be read again. And often when reading a Scottish story he would give it the correct lilt and accent."

Perhaps as I have suggested before, the serious face may have been to do with the long exposure time needed for photographs then, as inevitably it would have been easier to look serious for the necessary time, than to hold a smile for a long period, or maybe he just felt it suited his image as a senior Quaker!

In the Spring of 1894, John and Mary's mother, Eliza Barlow died at the age of 81. Coincidentally, it was almost exactly the same date as Elizabeth Petipher Cash, Mabel's grandmother, died aged 98, who would have been JHB's grandmother-in-law. Eliza had brought the two children up single-handedly and she and her two children had been a very close unit, especially since their father, John had died before the two children were old enough to have known him. John and Mary both felt the loss keenly, as their Mother had been a woman of remarkable strength of personality and yet a woman of *'quiet and beautiful character'*. After their Mother's death, brother and sister remained close and stayed on in Murrell Cottage together. Ever alert to John's thoughts, it was Mary who first realised her brother's growing feeling for Mabel, and encouraged the courtship of his future wife and it was she who suggested that Mabel should come and stay, following which it was not long before her father Fred Cash, went to visit his daughter Lou, and John went over to ask his permission to marry Mabel.

Mary and John Henry Barlow

Brother and sister, Mary and John Henry Barlow in 1860 aged 7 and 5

Letters by the young John Henry

The Author writes:
Letters written while at school in Stramongate, Kendal to his sister Mary in 1870

Left
"I am afraid you will think me very forgetful in neglecting to (write) at the proper time so often, but when I once get into a good game of cricket it is very hard to leave off....We have been having examinations in the last day or two but it is not yet finished so that I do not yet know my fate...we have just geography to go now and I hope it will soon be over."

Right
"I believe I did not tell in my last letter that a day or two ago after we had gone upstairs to bed, I with the other boys in the room had a bolster fight in which I had my thumb put out of joint, but they sent for the doctor and he soon pulled it in again and now it is much better….......I am top of the French class now, though I don't know how I did that....I will conclude now with dear love to Mamma and Meg."
(Meg was a favourite Nurse)

They were married on July 17 1895 at Holloway Meeting House...'*and a very nice and solemn occasion it proved*, writes FGC, *with valued ministers and many others present. Afterwards we had a large company at a midday meal at Northampton House in Highbury and later, afternoon tea at our own house. We eventually took leave of our dear child with sad hearts, especially on her beloved Mother's part who would acutely miss her cherished daughter from the family home...'*

A letter from Mabel's sister Lou, describes the occasion: *"I wish you could have seen May, she looked lovely, her dress was pure white silk and she wore a wreath of white stephanotis and maiden hair and had Aunt Carrie's veil on. She also wore a few flowers in her dress, but carried none......Bevan Braithwaite prayed very soon after they came in, so lengthily that poor May very nearly fainted, she told us after!"*

The guests included Thistelthwaite's, Cash's, Carr's, Ashby's, Elliot's, Taylor's, Barlow's and Cadbury's including George and his wife, Cousin Elizabeth. The reception at Northampton House *"looked beautiful, with white flowers everywhere and the table was most sumptuous, with salmon, chicken, pigeon pie, oyster patties, salads, jellies, cream, ices, and fruit..."*

They spent their honeymoon at Pension Kaufmann in Lucerne and there are a number of letters that they both wrote home during those weeks. One from John Henry to his Father-in-law is especially poignant, bearing in mind that he never knew his own Father and all that such a loss had meant to him:

Pension Kaufmann, 24 July 1895

Dear Father
For the first time in my life I begin a letter with those words, and I think you will understand something of the feelings, the mingled sadness and thankfulness, with which I use them. I am indeed thankful, not only to have Mabel as my wife, but to have entered into such close relationship with others whom I love and esteem so highly. Hitherto this close relationship so far as I have been concerned, was limited to Mother and sister, and for the last sixteen months just to my sister, but now at a step, I have gained a Father, Mother, sister and brothers. How greatly I value this is difficult to fully express, but I earnestly pray that I may in some measure show myself worthy of the great goodness of God.........with much love,
Your affectionate son, John

In such touching words, the stern Quaker minister comes immediately alive and present to us. Then there are letters from Mabel to her parents, again expressing the emotions of any young bride; this one written on the same day as the previous letter:

July 24, Lucerne
Dear Parents, you gave me a very happy wedding day and did everything you could to make it bright and enjoyable. Things all went well and without a hitch and I am so glad people enjoyed themselves.....Indeed I must thank you, dearest Mother and Father for all you have done for me all my life and for my happy home......

Then a little incident that must have happened to many a new bride, who finds herself with a new name!

"A letter to me was calmly appropriated by John this a.m. and opened. I did not say anything but just wondered if I might no longer call even my letters my own! (There's a meek and wifely spirit for one to possess). But when he found out his mistake, he apologised profusely, as he

had not recognised the name 'Mrs J H Barlow' as belonging to me. Nor I must say did I at first!!......My dearest love to you both my precious parents, ever your most truly loving daughter May"

As mentioned, Mary had sweetly decided to move out of the cottage and went to live for a while in a small house called The Nook near Cousin Lizzie Carr at Coldale Hall. So on returning to Carlisle, the newly married couple were able to move in to Murrell Hill Cottage, and Mabel writes of her welcome, though I am particularly intrigued by the last mentioned incident of her and the piano, as I cannot recall my Grandmother ever subsequently playing the piano!

"Does a bride ever forget her homecoming? I shall not as long as memory lasts........what a welcome as my husband brought me in and Aunt Mary and Uncle Ernest and Aunt Lou, Irene and Maurice all greeted me...when at last they had all gone, I opened the piano and played 'Home, sweet Home!'"

Among the many wedding presents received was a fine silver salver presented to them by a branch of the YMCA, The Pleasant Sunday Afternoon Association, which my parents passed on to me.[44] After her marriage to John Henry *'there followed six years of exceeding happiness.'* Grandfather was already an enthusiastic cyclist and soon after they were married Granny describes learning to ride and becoming one of the earliest woman cyclists:

"Aunt Lou and I purchased a bicycle between us and John taught me to ride. There were only about four other women in Carlisle with bicycles at the time....I had a costume made; a 'Norfolk coat' and a specially designed skirt, which stopped it from blowing upwards! John was an excellent teacher and we went glorious rides about that beautiful country, sometimes even going out after supper for a moonlight ride."

Not long after Mary's move away, her health sadly deteriorated and as she grew weaker she moved back to a house nearer to her brother, where she was soon confined to her bed and died in 1898 at the age of only 46. It was a great shock to John as they were so united and the two of them had had such a close bond with their mother, never having had a father to help in their upbringing. Perhaps, in order to erase the pain, John buried himself in his work. While continuing at Carrs, he was also involved with so much else, from Willow Holme to Bible classes to public speaking, and he soon realised that he would have to give up some of this if he was to have any home life. In 1898 Granny's parents FGC and Martha paid their first visit to stay at Murrell Cottage.

"Mother helped so much in making the house pretty by her beautiful needlework, embroidery and paintings. Also she was such a keen gardener that she gave me many hints about that too."

News of John's social work in Carlisle soon spread among the Quaker community and others such as Richard Cadbury came up from Birmingham to help, and see for themselves and then out of the blue, one day in October 1900, they received a letter from their cousin George Cadbury asking if John would be willing to undertake the position of Secretary and Manager of the Bournville Village Trust.

"One day in October 1900, John came home to dinner and found a letter awaiting him which amazed us both. It was from Cousin George Cadbury, asking if John would be willing to undertake the position of Secretary and Manager of the Bournville Village Trust in Birmingham."

---

[44] Sadly, on close inspection, though very fine, it turns out to be only EPNS!

Grandfather and Grandmother at Jordans

Grandfather and Granny Barlow at Jordans in 1923

The decision was not an easy one and *'involved much prayer for guidance'*. So much still depended on him in Carlisle and the scale of the task in Birmingham was great indeed. Eventually it was decided to make the move, much to the Cadbury's delight, as George's son Edward Cadbury writes in a letter in November 1900 to JHB:

"I am delighted that you have accepted the appointment of Secretary to the Estate Trust. I know we shall work together, as our objects are the same, to help to raise the poor. I also hope that you and your wife will join Dorothy and myself in the work at Selly Oak....it will be an immense help to have thy counsel and the guidance and Christian experience of one like yourself."

When the news became public that Mr Barlow was leaving Carlisle, Grandmother wrote, somewhat emotionally!

"There is mourning and lamentation...in many houses I visited, people were weeping. I was so proud to be his husband.....and many years later when I returned on a visit, people still told me how no one had replaced him."

John went to Birmingham ahead of Grandmother and initially stayed at the Manor House, the Cadbury's home, where we often went as children for parties. I remember particularly Christmas time, when the eldest member of the family used to dress up as Father Christmas and give out presents to us all. George Cadbury drove my Grandparents round parts of Bournville but they couldn't find a house exactly suitable, so George decided it best to build them a house on the Bristol Road, just above Woodbrooke College which had been the Cadbury's home and where they stayed while their house was being built. By the end of November 1901, 'Sunnybrae', as they named it, was ready and their eldest child, John Cash Barlow was born. After Grandfather died and Granny moved to 6 Swarthmore Road, the name went with them. This is the house on which Birmingham Civic Society erected a Blue Plaque in June 2014 in honour of my Grandfather. (see p. 88 for more and photo p. vi)

Pension Kaufmann, Lucerne, in 1895, where my Grandparents spent their honeymoon

Chapter 14
George Cadbury

Perhaps it is worth at this point to digress a little, and to say something of the life of George Cadbury and of Bournville, the village he created. George with his brother Richard, was the co-founder of Cadbury's chocolate company, but in my view, he was above all a social reformer and philanthropist, as well as a politician and an integral part of Birmingham society throughout his life. For although he was a successful businessman, he was as we saw with JD Carr and other Quaker entrepreneurs, a pioneer in building decent housing for his employees and for establishing, what has been described as a private social security program for their benefit; a welfare state before its time. He believed strongly that responsible leadership should be for the sake of others and he applied the principles of his Quaker faith in business, politics and his personal life. He and his second wife, Elizabeth Mary Taylor[45], were both leading philanthropists and their six children have done their best to follow in that tradition.

From an early age, George, who had been appalled at some of the housing conditions he found in Birmingham, decided that he wanted to place the welfare of his workers before anything else and invest in the community which was what enabled his company to succeed. He believed that if workers enjoyed a happy home life in attractive and sanitary surroundings, with a garden in which they could grow food, both they and the company would benefit from the esprit de corps that this would encourage.

In 1878 the brothers moved the struggling factory from the small premises in the centre of Birmingham, to some four miles south of Birmingham, where they had purchased fourteen acres of land in open country to start to build a new factory. By 1897 the Cadbury brothers began to produce a chocolate that became known as Cadbury's Dairy Milk, which was soon to become the most popular in Britain, taking on their Quaker friends and rivals Joseph Rowntree in York and Francis and Joseph Fry in Bristol.

Over the following years they acquired more land and began to develop their ideas for a model village, which became known as Bournville after the local river and the French word for town. By 1900 the management of the Bournville Estate was established under a separate Trust, becoming the Bournville Village Trust, of which my Grandfather, John Henry Barlow was the pioneer Manager and in 1940 my Father Ralph became the third[46]. It was designed primarily by a very notable, young architect, William Alexander Harvey, appointed by Cadbury in 1895 aged only 20, to provide low cost houses both for the factory workers and for the people of Birmingham.

In all, the brothers eventually purchased 120 acres next to the factory. Influenced by the Arts and Crafts Movement, many of Harvey's designs incorporated novel features such as stepped gables and small Venetian windows over slanted bays, with timber corner porches below dormer windows, with concave little leaded roofs. The village was all low rise development, providing both public and private open spaces, with each house having its own garden, pioneering the Garden City idea, that later developed in Welwyn and Hampstead, which aimed to introduce the benefits of a rural environment into the urban context. William Harvey, was the first and most influential of the architects of the Estate and undoubtedly set the style for future development.

---

[45] He had previously married Mary Tylor, daughter of Quaker author Charles Tylor. She was the mother of George junior, Mary Isabel and Edward. She died in 1887. In 1888 he married Elizabeth Mary Taylor, a 1st cousin of our Grandmother. They had six children together: Laurence John, George Norman, Elsie Dorothea, Egbert, Marion Janet and Ursula.
[46] When JHB retired in 1922, Leonard Appleton succeeded.

George Cadbury and Elizabeth Taylor

George Cadbury married twice. First in 1872 to Mary Tylor, who died in 1887 by whom he had 5 children; and secondly to Elizabeth Taylor in 1888 by whom he had six children.

First Marriage

George junior and Edward seen here standing at the back, Isobel and Eleanor sitting, and Henry sitting on the floor in front.

Second marriage

This photograph was taken shortly after the second marriage and the birth of Norman, who is seen on Elizabeth's lap, while George is holding Laurence, born the previous year, on his lap. Dorothea, Egbert and Marion were born after this photograph was taken in 1892, 1893 and 1894.

George (1839-1922) and Elizabeth (1858 – 1951) about 1888 the year they got married.

My Mother often said that when she married my Father, she hardly had to change her surname – just from Barber to Barlow. George Cadbury's first wife Mary Tylor and his second wife Elizabeth Taylor differed only in a syllable!

When George died in 1922, Dame Elizabeth, as she became, assumed many of her husband's duties, amongst which was Chairman of the Bournville Village Trust, a position she still held in the early part of my Father's tenure of the post of Manager of the Trust.

It is interesting, looking back at our family histories, to learn what large families they all had. George Cadbury was by no means alone in having 11 children; William and Elizabeth Cash had ten children and Fred and Martha had seven. Of course there was much infant mortality from cholera and the like, but I think many of the pioneering Quakers of the nineteenth century, where also in the business of building dynasties and making strategic alliances!

Bournville Rest House and the Infant's school

The Author writes:
Top:
"The Bournville Rest House, designed by William Harvey, was built to celebrate the Silver Wedding Anniversary of George and Elizabeth Cadbury in 1913 by donations from Cadbury employees and is based on the medieval Yarn market in Dunster.
Bottom|:
"The laying of the foundation stone of the Infant school by George and Elizabeth Cadbury with their youngest child Ursula in 1910. The main architect of Bournville, William A Harvey is on the right."

As already stated, Cadbury was a devout Quaker seeing a link between his faith and his civic responsibilities and in 1903, he donated the former Cadbury family home to the Society of Friends as Woodbrooke Quaker Study Center[47]. Woodbrooke was from the beginning open to people from any faith and focused on peace and reconciliation, spirituality and other areas of special interest to Quakers. Later, Woodbrooke would become a constituent college of the Selly Oak federation.

Woodbrooke has always been very much a part of my life. When my grandparents were invited by George Cadbury to run the BVT, they initially lived there, until 'Sunnybrae' was built for them just a little way up the hill on Bristol Road and JHB was a founding Trustee. So perhaps as children, we felt slightly proprietorial about it! Many of my parents' friends lived or worked there, so as children, we would nearly always walk through the grounds on our afternoon walks and loved to wander about in the woods, and later play hockey or tennis or simply walk round the adjacent Yachting Pool[48]. Many Quaker gatherings took place there, so we were constantly in and out, and in later life my parents studied there. In 1980 during an evening prayer meeting, my father died there aged 70 and later still my Mother became secretary to the Old Woodbrookers' Association. So since its inception, in one way or another and for over a hundred years, our family has had very close and fond associations with the College.

In 1890, George Cadbury purchased what was then known as New House on the Bristol Road near Northfield. He made extensive alterations, involving the rebuilding of the main house into a rambling Tudor mansion, renaming it the Manor House, where they would reside until the early 1950s when it was sold to the University of Birmingham[49]. As a child we would often frequent the house and grounds, skating on the pond in winter or for Christmas parties. Also as mentioned in an earlier chapter, I clearly remember going to another Cadbury House, 'The Davids', in 1948 when I was 7, for Dame Elizabeth Cadbury's 90th birthday, along with over 150 other relatives (see photo p.80). This was probably one of the last occasions on which such a large gathering of Friends, all of whom were related Cousins, was assembled.

George Cadbury died in 1922 at the age of 82, still very active, but in frail health. As a devout Quaker and a pacifist, he had been greatly depressed by the tragedy of the Great War and its thousands of dead, and later his wife, Elsie (Dame Elizabeth) became very interested and involved in establishing the new League of Nations and went to Paris for the Treaty of Versailles.

But for George, the twin undertakings of chocolate and social reform were strongly established. The firm was in the hands of the second generation, Laurence and Edward with new ideas and a fresh competitiveness; and Bournville itself was equally established and had influenced the beginning of the garden suburb movement with Port Sunlight in Liverpool, Ebenezer Howard's ideals at Letchworth and Henrietta Barnett creating Hampstead Garden suburb in north London.

He had successfully put into practice his beliefs, not only providing pleasant conditions for his work staff but also ensuring that the company was run on Quaker principals. Inevitably, as time went on, the company, like the other Quaker family firms such as Carrs, Rowntrees and Frys, fell victim to the pressure of the times. Family members gradually dropped away, the companies no longer remained completely in family hands as shares were issued to raise capital and the companies were subject to the demands of shareholders and hostile takeovers as Frys (which had merged with Cadburys), Terrys and Cadburys which were all taken over by Kraft.

---

[47] John Henry Barlow was one of George Cadbury's close circle, who were responsible for setting up Woodbrooke College
[48] In 1926 George Cadbury jnr had commissioned an area of marshland on the BVT Estate to be reclaimed and a concrete pool of even depth was constructed. It also gave work to some of the local unemployed.
[49] It was badly damaged by fire in July 2014

The Cadbury homes

Woodbrooke, former Cadbury home and now a Quaker Study Centre.

The Author writes:

"Our grandparents lived there when it was the Cadbury home, while 'Sunnybrae' was being built."

The Manor House, Birmingham, badly damaged in an arson attack 2014

The idealism of their founders, where business success went hand-in-hand with social responsibility had given way to short-termism and the making of quick profit where the hedgefund 'shareholders' knew nothing of the company and cared little for what it had stood for. An extraordinary period of Quaker entrepreneurship had come to an end.

But as Deborah Cadbury points out in her excellent book *Chocolate Wars*[50]:
"Whatever lies in store for Britain's chocolate industry, the trusts created by the pioneer chocolatiers still survive. George Cadbury's Bournville Village Trust has grown into a thriving enterprise that is still run principally by the direct descendants of George and his brother Richard.[51] The trust is responsible for more than 8,000 properties and 1,100 acres across the West Midlands and Shropshire as well as 2,500 acres of farmland to preserve the green belt around the south-west of Birmingham: a small piece of England that cannot be signed away......Apart from the BVT, the Barrow Cadbury Trust and other family trusts between them give over 250 grants a year.....A force for good, surely, a quiet, sane voice that is still there for those who want to hear it in this noisy century.....It is hard to imagine today's business leaders giving more than a passing thought to the claim of George Fox that the inner light is within us all. But those nineteenth-century entrepreneurs who made this their quest, did succeed for a brief period in putting the remarkable Quaker movement in the spotlight. In the process they illuminated a different work ethic, on a more human scale, between master and man."

That in itself is a great achievement and I am proud that both my Grandfather and Father were a part of that amazing creation.[52]

Before I end this chapter on George Cadbury and Bournville, I think I should explain how the Quaker spirit and the Bournville ethos affected one family – my mother's. I shall go into more detail about her and her side of the family later, but my Mother and her parents were very much children of the Bournville experience. Both my Mother's parents - her Mother's family the Eyres and her Father's family the Barber's - came from very humble backgrounds and grew up in the poorer suburbs of Birmingham. Ellen Eyre, my maternal grandmother, along with her sister Emily and brothers William and James had been orphaned at a very young age and I am quite sure that if it hadn't been for the Quakers, their future would have been entirely different.

Though I am sure they would not have thought so at the time, looked at from a later perspective, it was nonetheless, fortunate that Ellen and her sister found themselves in an orphanage which had Edward Cadbury on the board. This was Crowley's Orphanage, which was visited regularly by a Quaker lady by the name of Emmeline Wilson. She it was who took these two children under her wing and I am convinced that it was her benign influence that so helped my Grandmother. Emmeline organised trips to the country for the two girls; she found them work in a Quaker household in Birmingham; and later she facilitated my grandmother's meeting with my Grandfather out at Coleshill near Meriden. Finally, in 1900 she attended their wedding and later in their married life helped them to move to Bournville from Smethwick and Coleshill and when Grandfather died in 1922 she continued to help by finding my Grandmother a smaller house.

My Grandmother, known to us as Granny Barber, became a Quaker herself, partly out of gratitude, but also I am sure because she could see, that through the Society, she could find a lifeline out of her previous existence to a better life. My mother went to the Bournville village primary school built by George Cadbury, then, like her sister and brother had done, was enabled

---

[50] 'Chocolate Wars' by Deborah Cadbury, (daughter of Kenneth and niece of Michael) published by Harper Press 2010.
[51] Roger Cadbury, Christopher Cadbury's son who was at The Downs and at LP with my brother and I, was the last Chairman of the BVT. The present Chairman is Duncan Cadbury, Michael's son, also at school with my brothers and me.
[52] See next chapter

to go to the Quaker boarding school Sibford with financial help from Quaker bursaries and later met my Father through Quaker circles. I also learnt recently[53], that Cadbury's paid for my Uncle Reg to go to Manchester University where he studied Economics and where later I was to study too.

Obviously, Emmeline recognised something in my Grandmother, but she too, took full advantage of this help. In addition she was a very ambitious lady, determined that her children should better themselves and not remain in the same poverty that she had been born into. As a result of her ambitions and Quaker assistance, two of her children married men from well-known and successful Quaker families. My Mother married Ralph Barlow from a family linked, as we have seen to the very origins of the Society and a cousin of George Cadbury, while Winifred married Dr Llewellyn Rutter scion of another equally historic Quaker family.[54] The other two, Bobby and Reg married outside the Quaker circles, though Reg joined Cadburys as a young man and continued to work there all his life.

Perhaps one of the most fascinating aspects of my Grandmother's story is to realise that within a hundred years, all her hopes for her children had been amply fulfilled, as two of her Grandsons attained great professional success. My Cousin, Michael Rutter the son of my Mother's elder sister Winifred and Dr Llewellyn Rutter, was knighted in 1992 for services to psychiatry; whilst my brother, David Barlow rose to the top of the BBC after nearly 30 years with the Corporation, becoming Secretary of the BBC and Controller of Regional Broadcasting. These are extraordinary examples of social mobility and a tribute to the Quaker belief in helping those less well off, as well showing how Smilesian self-help enabled my Grandmother and her children and grandchildren, to take advantage of all that came their way.

Michael Rutter

David Barlow

---

[53] Letter from Reg's son Chris Barber
[54] The Rutters or Le Roter were Normans who came over with William 1 and Thomas Rutter, Llewellyn's ancestor of Kingsley Hall, Cheshire was disinherited when he joined Quakers in c.1665. (The Family of Le Roter or Rutter. Privately pub. 1966)

Dame Elizabeth Cadbury's 90th birthday 1948 at The David's

Dame Elizabeth's 90th birthday in 1948 – Dame Elizabeth seated centre. To her left are children Dorothy and Edward and to her right are George and Henry. Sitting 4th from the left in the front row is the writer Antony Barlow next to Virginia. Roger and Peter Cadbury. Behind Virginia is my Grandmother Mabel Barlow. Others featured are Hoylands, Crosfields, Gilletts, Gamans, Taylors, and Wilsons. Some 140 family – this is possibly one of the last occasions so many Quaker families were gathered together in one place

For complete identification of all present, see pp 275 and 276

Chapter 15
John Henry Barlow – 1900 -1924

In 1900 George Cadbury had fully established the Bournville Village Trust and my Grandfather had become its first Secretary and Manager, with the injunction to maintain and develop the village with the ownership invested in the Trustees. In his welcome George wrote:

Dear Cousin,
My sons and I will receive you like a brother and together we will face some of the great problems, on the right solution of which, the future of our country so largely depends. I know thee to be a man who grasps the underlying idea of our grand scheme, who is a man of sound judgment and of good experience. The experiment is being watched with increasing interest by other landowners and it will be a great relief to us to know that it is in the capable hands of one we trust and who shares our spirit. Your attached Cousin, George Cadbury[55]

At the beginning, John Henry had worried that his lack of specific knowledge in this field would be a handicap, but he set about his new role at Bournville with typical urgency and dedication. He was soon travelling all over Europe to housing conferences such as the deputation he led in 1902 to Germany where he headed up a Housing conference in Dusseldorf as well as visiting other developments in Holland. In fact before long he became a much respected authority on housing problems, often being asked by Lloyd George to advise the government. In 1916 for instance, he was requested by LG to help in deciding what should be a fair rent for the houses being built across the country for munition workers. John travelled all round England inspecting the houses and preparing a report for him and such was his success in this that they were soon adopted throughout the country.

Dear John
The report that you have drawn up after visits to Birtley and elsewhere, proves to be of the greatest possible service and we are most grateful.
David Lloyd George, Westminster

The work of the Village Trust made great strides and John Henry gave enormous help to the many people who came to live on the Estate. Very often it was remarked how he seemed to fill the role of Father to a large family. His office became a resort for those in trouble or perplexity and for those who sought guidance. Often he was called upon to settle disputes between neighbours, between parents and children, sometimes even between husband and wife! People came to him because they trusted his judgment. As usual, he had thrown himself into the new work with his customary intensity and made the Bournville Village Trust a practical working reality with a sound business footing. His immediate successor Leonard Appleton later remarked after JHB's retirement *"How much we miss him and how much we owe to his guidance. One thing is certain, the great tradition and pervading influence which he created, will never die."* Typical of the impact he had in Bournville was a letter he received on his retirement from a resident, Mr Harold Boughert:

Dear Mr Barlow,

We should like you to know something of the regret with which we view your departure. For the ten years we have resided on the Estate, you treated us with an unfailing and uniform kindness and consideration we should find it difficult to forget.

---

[55] Barlow family archives

John Henry Barlow

John Henry Barlow about 1900
"First Manager of the Bournville Village Trust and leading 'Quaker Statesman'."

Painting of John and Mabel Barlow's home, 'Sunnybrae'
Made for studio magazine 1901

'Sunnybrae' built by George Cadbury for John Henry Barlow and his wife Mabel, in 1901 on Griffins Hill, Selly Oak, just up from Woodbrooke Quaker College, where a Blue Plaque was erected for his services to peace and the FAU
(Reproduced by kind permission of Carol Saker)

They have been years of great importance to us and much of our own success has in a large measure been due to the firm knowledge that our minds could be free of anxiety, so far as our home was concerned, so long as the administration of the Trust remained within your responsibility.
Affectionately
Harold

Something of what John Henry achieved at Bournville can be gathered from the tribute paid to him by Dame Elizabeth Cadbury on my Grandfather's retirement in 1923.[56]

"The Trustees of the Bournville Village Trust, wish to record this expression of their high appreciation of his devoted service.....for over twenty years he has directed the administration of the Estate and fostered its expansion and development. His faithful performance of these duties and his public work in other spheres have won for him the honour and respect of all with whom he has come in contact. Above everything do the Trustees value the loyal fidelity with which he has interpreted and carried out the intentions of the Founder of Bournville and his ideals for the establishment of village life in an industrial area. They know that the work that John Henry Barlow has so lovingly performed has not only served the community which has immediately benefited by it, but will act as an example for all who follow this pioneer movement for housing reform."

Then there was also a fine tribute from Mr Henry R Aldridge, the then Director of National Housing and Town Planning:

Dear John,
I am quite certain that your work has been of vital importance to the whole housing movement. Indeed it is hard to imagine what the movement would have been without the example of your work at Bournville. Also in my preparation of the manual for those engaged in the essential task of town planning schemes, my thanks are especially due to you.

National Housing and Town Planning Council.
41, RUSSELL SQUARE, LONDON.

There were also appreciations from the building firms with whom he dealt, in particular from the Quaker firm, Tangye, Glaisyer and Atkinson:

"Your retirement severs a personal association of over twenty years…I would like to say how much we have deeply appreciated the invariably high standards you have maintained."

Many other letters paid tribute to his achievement at Bournville including one from Henry Cadbury which is both personal and apposite:

Dear cousin John,
I find it quite difficult to express my own thoughts to you on all the work you have done at Bournville, but the way you have helped Father to get the Village founded in its larger sphere of activity, is beyond praise.
Your affectionate cousin,
Henry

Perhaps one tribute above all, gives some indication of the wider importance of his work at Bournville. This was from Dame Henrietta Barnett, the great social reformer, educationist and

---

[56] BVT archives

"We record your devoted service"

Dame Elizabeth Cadbury

Lloyd George, President of the Board of Trade 1906

The Author writes:
"When John Henry retired from the Bournville Village Trust in 1923, he received tributes from everyone from President of the Board of Trade, Lloyd George to Social Reformer, Henrietta Barnet and from Dame Elizabeth Cadbury to the ordinary inhabitant of the Bournville Estate."

Lloyd George: *"Your work has been of the greatest possible service, for which we are most grateful."*

Dr Henrietta Barnett wrote:
"Thank God that I knew John Henry Barlow. His example has helped me to treat my enquirers with equal courtesy and patience as I received from him and so his great spirit goes marching on."

Dame Elizabeth summed it up in her tribute:
"Your work has not only served the community which has immediately benefited by it, but it will act as an example for all who follow this pioneer movement for housing reform."

Dr Henrietta Barnett, Social reformer and founder of Hampstead Garden suburb

founder, with her husband, Samuel Barnett, of Toynbee Hall, the first University settlement in the East end of London and the progenitor of Hampstead Garden Suburb:

"Thank God that I knew John Henry Barlow. In the early days when I was struggling with the difficulties of creating Hampstead Garden suburb, John Henry was extraordinarily kind to me. I had to ask such elementary questions which would naturally have tried an expert as he was, but he made me feel that he was always ready to help. His example has helped me to treat my enquirers with equal courtesy and patience as I received from him and so his great spirit goes marching on."

But as well as Bournville, George Cadbury was always insistent that Grandfather should, as he wrote in a letter to him in 1900 *"devote time to the philanthropic work for which we know you have a special gift"* and more and more he became deeply engaged with helping in issues that impinged on his Quaker beliefs. In 1914 for example, the question of the Women's movement came up at Meeting for Sufferings as Friends were thought to have the experience needed to help. In Quakerism from the very first, women were given an equality in the ministry and conduct of affairs which other churches had not afforded them. At the beginning of 1915 a meeting was arranged when John spoke, presenting the need of the Society to give help and support for the women in the present crisis.

From the very beginning, he was also intrinsically involved with the development of Woodbrooke as a Quaker college. When the family first moved to Birmingham, George Cadbury had made Woodbrooke, which was then their home, available for them to live in prior to a house being built for them. One Sunday, George called and told them how he was filled with the idea of starting a Quaker college. *"The Society of Friends needs more trained ministry if it is grow"* he said. As Thomas Kennedy recounts in his book 'British Quakerism 1860-1900'[57]

"What George Cadbury envisaged was an academy where dedicated individuals would engage in brief but intense study of scripture and the principles of Quakerism, to prepare for service in the Society of Friends."

John too, had long believed that ministry should, for some, be a 'first charge' on their lives, as he put it. Long recognised as 'the greatest minister in the Society' and known for the preparation he gave to his ministry through reading and study, John Henry also firmly believed that weekdays too should also be turned towards the coming Sunday.

From an address he gave to Yearly Meeting in 1909 he said:

"I am not pleading for a professional ministry. Far from it. But I am convinced that we need a fuller acknowledgement of the claims of the ministry....too often we come to our meetings having given little thought or prayer to them. Others give of their best to other forms of work; some should be prepared to be at their best in the meetings for worship."

So George was knocking at an open door and when John and his family had moved into 'Sunnybrae' and George and Elizabeth moved to the Manor House in Northfield, Woodbrooke and the grounds were given over into the hands of a Trust for the purpose of developing a Quaker college. John Henry was one of the first of the Trustees to be appointed and who, from the beginning, gave the experiment ungrudging help. From 1903 to 1915 he was Secretary of the Woodbrooke Committee and remained Secretary to the Trust and Chairman of the Settlement Committee until his death. The work of the College was very dear to him and he devoted an immense amount of time working on its behalf.

---

[57] Oxford University Press 2001

In 2014 the Birmingham Civic Society erected a blue plaque outside 'Sunnybrae' (see p xii) as a tribute to my Grandfather as part of the commemorations of 1914. John Henry Barlow was referred to in the Obituary in The Times in 1924 as 'The outstanding Quaker statesman of his generation' and to summarise his achievements in 2014, I wrote as follows for the occasion:

"He was Clerk of Yearly meeting for an unprecedented seven years from 1913 at a crucial time for the Society, especially throughout the war years, when much Quaker opinion was seriously divided on the correct response to the war; in 1915, he led a peace mission to Holland to try and find a basis for Peace negotiations; the same year he also led members of the 'No-Conscription Fellowship' to successfully secure 'the exemption clause' in the 1916 'Military Service Act', which enshrined the right to claim exemption from military service on grounds of conscience; in 1920 he was chosen to head up a Quaker delegation to Ireland to appraise the situation during the uprising of the Black and Tans and written up in The Times of October 5; and in 1922 he was the obvious choice to act as the British representative at the Five Year Quaker conference in Richmond, Indiana.

It is probably not an exaggeration to say that it was largely due to John Henry's breadth of outlook, wisdom, sympathy and patience, as well as in the words of The Times 'the power of decision and the judgment in presiding over deliberations of a large body of people of varying minds' that the Society of Friends was able to come through this taxing moment in its history."

It is instructive to look at each of these events individually. Perhaps one of the most crucial moments of this period, especially for Quakers, was the passing of The 'Defence of the Realm' Act in 1914, during the early weeks of World War I. This gave the government wide-ranging powers during the war period, such as the power to requisition buildings and land needed for the war effort, or to make regulations creating criminal offences. Of especial concern to Quakers was the fact that it ushered in a variety of authoritarian measures, such as censorship which would have curtailed the publication of the anti-war pamphlets issuing from Friends House. Regulation 27C, for instance, ordered that no pamphlet or similar publication dealing with the war or the making of peace should be issued without being first passed by the Censor. It was decided by Meeting for Sufferings that to submit to this would be to give up the whole case for liberty of speech. Following much heated discussion, John Henry carefully drafted a minute, which said[58]:

"The Executive body of the Society of Friends, after serious consideration, desires to place on record its conviction that the portion of the recent regulations requiring the submission to the Censor of all leaflets dealing with the present war and the making of peace is a grave danger to the national welfare. The duty of every good citizen to express his thoughts on the affairs of his country is hereby endangered, and further we believe that Christianity requires the toleration of opinions not our own. Beyond this there is a deeper issue involved. It is for Christians a paramount duty to be free to obey, and to act and speak in accord with the law of God, a law higher than that of any State and no government can release men from this duty. We realize the rarity of the occasions on which a body of citizens find their sense of duty to be in conflict with the law and it is with a sense of gravity of the decision that The Society of Friends must on this occasion act contrary to the regulation and continue to issue literature on war and peace without submitting it to the censor and is thus acting in the best interests of the nation"

---

[58] Friends House archives

So Friend's Committees continued to issue pamphlets on behalf of the Society such as 'A Challenge to Militarism', which contained information about people who had been imprisoned for their beliefs and general opposition to the war through such leafleting. As the war continued, the censorship became more and more strict and under The Defence of the Realm Acts, freedom of speech was almost non-existent. The outspoken document issued by the adjourned Yearly Meeting in 1916, dealing with the burning issue of Conscription, seemed likely to run the risk of infringing the law and with the state of public opinion at that time, such a statement might be considered dangerous. Friends were naturally concerned about this, questioning if it were fair to allow the Clerk alone to sign the document, in which case, prosecution with probable imprisonment would fall upon him.

This was discussed for some time and eventually John Henry rose and with his customary gesture of drawing himself up and throwing back his shoulders, his voice rang out across the crowded hall:

"Surely at such a time, no one is playing for safety; The Society is not and nor am I, concerned with what is safe, but what is true and right and I propose to sign the document."

Our Grandmother records:

"In absolute silence, a silence full of prayer and praise, he then read the whole document out aloud ending with the words, 'signed John Henry Barlow, Clerk' and in those minutes, I knew he faced anything that might be in store for him and I faced it with him – knowing so well that his thoughts were with me and that we were both willing to suffer if necessary."

In a letter my Grandmother wrote to her daughter Millior while she was at school, regarding the signing against The Defence of the Realm Act, saying:

"Father agreed to sign…an appeal to the government and the nation about the repeated imprisonment of Conscientious Objectors…if Quakers are challenged under The Defence of the Realm Act, Father may be summoned and may have to undergo imprisonment…but we may be proud and glad that he is willing to make such a stand for liberty of conscience. It will be very hard for us to let him go, but we shall be still more proud of him than we are now."

As a result of this John Henry and the others who had signed this anti-war leaflet, infringing the law, were brought to trial in 1918 at the Guildhall. John Henry headed a group of Quakers which included Barrow Cadbury, to make a stand for free speech against the Act and it was above all, John Barlow's voice that was the voice of conviction and courage.[59] The court was convened on May 24 1918, as yearly Meeting was in session, with John Henry Barlow as presiding Clerk and read the minute as quoted above. When the Aldermen retired to consider the verdict, John Henry's clear and commanding voice was heard asking for Friends in court 'to devote themselves to silent prayer.'

The memorable occasion was written up in the New York Evening Post[60]:

"At the Guildhall Court, one of two Police courts of the City of London, at which the presiding judge is always one of the city aldermen, there occurred a few days ago an unprecedented scene. The defendants in the case were prominent Quakers, and the body of the court contained a large number of Quakers. Then the magistrate retired to consider his decision and the Clerk, of the Yearly Meeting, John Henry Barlow, rose and invited Friends who were present to engage in silent prayer. For a time, the court then became a Quaker meeting, during which the silence was occasionally broken by a few words of vocal prayer. As one of the reporters present remarked: 'It was like a throwback to the 17th century.' The incident was not only curious in itself, but is likely to be historic.

---

[59] 'Conscription and Conscience' by John W Graham, George Allen and Unwin 1922
[60] Barlow family archives

Future historians may record it as a landmark in the relation of the British churches to the State. It is probably the first occasion since the Stuart period on which an organized religious body has deliberately challenged the State's authority."

A member of the Cabinet, the Rt Hon Augustine Birrell remarked of the case:
'The first thing that attracted me to Friends was that they had never succumbed to the most pestilent and dangerous heresy of our age – that the State occupies the supreme throne over the consciences of men. And further they believe that you can never save civilization by the sacrifice of liberty....for when the war is over, it may be very difficult to reconstruct that liberty."

John Henry did not eventually have to go to prison, as on November 11th 1918, peace was at last declared to everyone's rejoicing, and in another letter written whilst Millior was away at school, though this time from her Father, he talks emotionally of the declaration of Peace on November 11th:
"I was sitting quietly on Monday when suddenly came the boom of a gun and then a hooter sounded and sirens joined in and more guns. I leapt to my feet and threw open the window to listen...and called out 'the guns, peace has come!' I stayed alone and wept and prayed. There came such waves of sadness, remembering all the loss and sorrow, and it tempered the gladness."

To return to those early years of the war, there had been little to warn the ordinary people of Britain in 1914 that war was about to break out. Quakers, outside their local meetings, were very involved in domestic matters – for example with the Adult School movement in the UK. As there had been no European war for some time, it was, according to Wilfrid Littleboy, "a shock to everybody, Friends included" when war broke out. Littleboy was a Quaker who was imprisoned in Wormwood Scrubs and later in Dorchester Prison for the duration of the war. He was a member of Selly Oak Meeting which was John Henry's and our family's Meeting and I well remember as a child, the imposing presence of Wilfred and his wife Winifred. When the prospect of Conscription loomed, Wilfrid records that he remembers saying "Oh well, I shall be going to prison"- taking that as a matter of course.

It was to prove a very difficult time for Quakers and with the question of finding a peaceful outcome to the conflict very much on everyone's mind, John Henry was asked in 1915 if he would go on a secret mission to Holland to urge those in authority to join with other neutrals to find a basis for peace through negotiation. He was accompanied by Sir John Fry, an American Friend, well known to President Wilson. It was an anxious time for everybody, especially for his family, as he crossed the North Sea with all its dangers, recalled here in the record of another Quaker, Isaac Sharp prior to their sailing:

"My thoughts turn to the responsible nature of the undertaking immediately before you. I trust you may all be supported with a sense of the Divine presence in whatever is before you and that a blessing may attend your efforts towards the restoration of peace."

This dangerous and secret undertaking does perhaps understandably, not appear in official accounts of the war, but is to be found in my Grandmother's account written for her children as well as in other tributes when he died and is alluded to in the memoirs of John Fry[61].

The next major initiative to confront Friends was how to deal with the 1916 Military Service Act. At the beginning of the war in 1914, the army was still made up of volunteers, but by spring 1915, despite Kitchener's recruitment campaign, it had become clear that the results of

---

[61] Memoirs of An American Quaker by Sir John Fry

voluntary enlistment were disappointing and were not going to provide the numbers of men required. So the Government decided to introduce a Military Service Act by which all voluntary enlistment would be ended and all British males between 18 and 41 were required to be conscripted.

From 1757 Quakers had been exempted on conscientious grounds, but unfortunately, the wording was left undefined and it would have been up to those implementing the Act to deal with it on a case by case basis. Many of those who sought exemption were Quakers who fully accepted the historic Quaker rejection of war; but there were those who belonged to other Christian denominations, accepting the 'Just War' tradition, but still wishing to stand out against it; still others were socialists and believed in a unity of fellow workers 'across the roar of the guns'; there were also humanists and anarchists, who rejected the ultimate control of the state over life and limb. Amongst Quakers, many felt that a total refusal to be involved in any work that could be said to be part of the war effort, was necessary to truly testify and demonstrate the conviction of the Society of Friends that all war was un-Christian.

All agreed, however, that participation in war was a matter for individual conscience, which overode all legal and social pressures and many of these came together in the 'No-Conscription Fellowship' formed in 1914 by John Henry, to oppose conscription and support the objectors. The group took on board views from all quarters, especially from many of the younger generation, some of whom came to pacifism from different religious convictions as well as a variety of political backgrounds. With Littleboy's experiences in prison in his mind, as recounted in letters to his parents[62] and reflecting his buoyant nature, John Henry was even more desperately keen to stand up and be counted and demonstrate his determination to live by and be a witness to the Quaker Peace Testimony.

Grandfather was by now already aged nearly 60, and too old for call-up, but at the risk of his own prosecution, he went out of his way to establish the Fellowship and to lead their members to the House of Commons where in due course and with the help of his MP cousin, Sir John Barlow, his advocacy successfully secured what became known as 'the conscience clause' in the 1916 Conscription Act, which enshrined in law the right to claim exemption from military service. And although there were still those who did not agree with his stance, nonetheless, the strength and honesty of his beliefs was respected on all sides.

I have discovered in my research concerning my Grandfather that he was not one to seek the limelight and so it is not always possible to find his name in the official reference books. As Henry Lloyd Wilson says in his obituary in The Friend[63]:

"He did not wish to be conspicuous, yet he was nearly always at the centre of events where often he was not noticed, but where his power and quiet assurance were the means of transmitting a steadiness and a confidence to all that he undertook. His ability, whether at Bournville or at Woodbrooke or in his great service to the Society of Friends throughout the war years both here and in America would long ago have gained him prestige. But that was not his way. Rather his quietness and confidence were his strength so that he became known and trusted as a wise guide and an inspiring prophet."

Thus very often it is behind the scenes that his presence can be detected and in so many tributes to him, is his influence in Quaker matters referred to and commented on, yet one can often search in vain for his name in the index of Quaker records. In no matter is this more apparent than in the setting up of The Friends Ambulance Unit which his close friends, all members of

---

[62] Interview given to the Imperial War Museum archives
[63] The Friend, August 22 1924

the FAU Committee such as fellow JPs John Henry Lloyd, Edward Cadbury and George Gillett mention in letters.

It was however, as a direct result of John Henry's securing of the exemption clause in the Military Service Act, that it became necessary to find outlets for those who had successfully come through their tribunals and so with Philip Noel-Baker, the fledgling FAU was established under the name of the Friends War Victims Relief Committee and later The Friends' Ambulance Unit, with the General Service Section of the FAU for those who could not be absorbed into the ambulance unit, and training took place at the old Quaker centre at Jordans.[64] in Buckinghamshire from where they were sent to serve at the Front.

It was as early as 1913 that John had taken over as Clerk of Yearly Meeting from Henry Brady Priestman and throughout the war years he brought a unique breadth of outlook, sympathy, patience and judgment to the post. He also displayed a deep spirituality and those present recall his devout introduction to the proceedings with its air of hope. As H G Wood[65] later remarked:

"John Henry Barlow possessed gifts of leadership to which others readily responded. His judgment inspired confidence, combining caution free from panic with a courage free from foolhardiness. He was one on whose insight and experience people relied the more they came to know him."

By the end of the war it could be said that almost single-handedly he had managed to hold the Society together, keeping the various factions together and people of differing views on side with equal skill. When eventually peace did come in 1918, John Henry was again ahead of his time, when after the signing of the Armistice, he made a much promoted plea at Warwickshire Monthly Meeting, with which Archbishop Desmond Tutu, one feels would have also concurred, speaking of the need:

"To express our profound thankfulness that the prolonged and terrible war is over. But we seek for Grace that we may regard with true Christian charity, those with whom our nation has recently been at war and that we may be preserved from cherishing feelings of revenge and bitterness. And may we face the future with wisdom, fearlessness, faith and humility."

By 1920 he was as busy as ever, being asked to act as Chairman of the great All Friends Conference in London and his quiet dignity and authority impressed itself deeply on all who attended. As an American Friends described it:

"We entered the conference and there we found a voice and through the days of the conference, that voice led us on, now gently restraining, now deeply inspiring, now boldly challenging — that voice which became the expression and the embodiment of the new unity for which he appealed."

Later the same year, he was the obvious leader to turn to when he was invited by the Society and the Government to head a deputation to Ireland with two other leading Quakers, Roger Clark and Peace worker, Edith Ellis[66], to report on the truth of the worsening conditions there, against the 'Black and Tans'. His report published in The Times on October 5 1920[67] was a model of judicial restraint and 'the more damning in consequence', wrote the Times correspondent.

---

[64] The Friends Ambulance Unit 1914-1919, Swarthmore Press
[65] Leading Quaker and Director of Studies at Woodbrooke
[66] Her convictions took her to Holloway for three months' imprisonment.
[67] The Times archives

"One whose insight and experience people relied on"

H G Wood, Director of Studies at Woodbrooke

Wilfrid Littleboy, imprisoned during WW1

Edith Ellis, Quaker Peace Worker, who was imprisoned as a Conscientious Objector. She later joined JHB on their visit to Ireland in 1920.

The Author writes:
"Many leading Quakers had great admiration for John Henry Barlow"

H G Wood said:
"His judgment inspired confidence, combining caution free from panic with a courage free from foolhardiness."

Wilfrid Littleboy (Chairman of Settlement Committee) wrote:
"If Friends in England and America now see their way to closer unity…we owe it, in no small measure to the faithfulness of John Henry Barlow, whom we all learnt to honour and love"

Henry Lloyd Wilson (Chairman of Woodbrooke Council):
"John Henry's…..great ability…would long ago have gained him prestige. But that was not his way. Rather his quietness and confidence were his strength so that he became known and trusted as a wise guide and an inspiring prophet."

Edith Ellis wrote:
"John Henry was a tower of strength in those difficult days of 1918 and his guidance was wonderful and later in prison gave me strength to go on."

Visiting the American Cousins 1922

Oliver Hayhurst Cash and his wife Eva with son Frederick

Herbert Cash 1922

The Author writes:

"In 1922 John Henry Barlow was the natural choice to attend the Five Year meeting at Richmond Indiana as London representative."

Mabel Barlow writes in her memoirs:

"We sailed from Liverpool on August 19th on board the White Star liner The Regina for Quebec and Montreal. We travelled through the Rockies to Portland and Oregon to see Aunt Sadie and Herbert and then down the Pacific Coast to Los Angeles and on to Riverside where we paid a fortnight's visit to Uncle Oliver and Aunt Eva.*"

*Herbert and Oliver Cash were Mabel's brothers, who emigrated to America – Herbert in 1887 and Oliver in 1894

The report ends:

"Broadly speaking, the courses before England seem to be limited to three: Repression and yet more repression, and all that this involves. The gift of a liberal measure of self-government, including fiscal and financial control. An independent Irish Republic. I am inclined to think England will rule out the first and third of these. What of the second? And what of the stopping of police reprisals, the withdrawal of the armed forces of the Crown as a pledge of good faith of the Government, whose good faith also stands in need of some guarantee of the kind? I believe there is hope in this direction. But action must be prompt and decisive. Tempers are hardening. The door of opportunity is closing. Will the government have the courage to act before it is too late?"

After he returned, he travelled widely across the country to bear witness to what he had seen, often '*suffering the audience's widely different views with courtesy and forbearance, so that meetings usually ended with a fairer feeling by the close*', as my Grandmother writes in her memoirs.

By the year 1922 John was also the natural choice to attend the Five Year meeting at Richmond Indiana as London representatives. He and Mabel sailed from Liverpool on August 19th on board the White Star liner The Regina[68] for Quebec and Montreal. Mabel writes of it:

"We were absent from home for three and half months....John received a wonderful welcome from American Friends. ....We travelled through the Rockies to Portland and Oregon to see Aunt Sadie[69] and her family, down the Pacific Coast to Los Angeles and on to Riverside where we paid a fortnight's visit to uncle Oliver and Aunt Eva.[70] Finally we stayed with kind friends near Philadelphia and a few days in Baltimore before sailing for England from New York on the Berengaria.[71] We wanted to be home for Jack's 21st birthday on December 10th 1922."

No English Friend was so warmly welcomed among all sections of Friends in the United States as JHB when he attended this conference. No other Friend was so clearly in the right place at the right time and so widely respected throughout the world. An extract from The American Friend:

"We present a Friend...his eye is sharp, escaping nothing within its vision. His features are clean-cut and strong. His words, chosen with rare precision flow readily and in his rich voice is a timbre that thrills and holds. When John Henry Barlow arose to speak, the benignity of his presence and the ring of his voice reminded us all of the panorama of the London Conference in 1920. His face in repose suggested a reticence bordering on austerity but which is effaced as soon as one comes into touch with his warm and genial personality. ....he is perhaps the outstanding preacher of his day."[72]

Mention should also be made of his exemplary work as a JP for more than twenty years which was remembered fondly by William Roberts, Chairman of the Birmingham Magistrates: *"Mr Barlow brought a cultured mind to all his work and his sweetness of nature was shown in the deep sympathy and careful wisdom with which he exercised his magisterial function."*

In 1923 he finally decided to retire by which time he was 65 and was glad to be able to do so, having been in business since the age of sixteen and he looked forward with great pleasure to

---

[68] Built in 1918 operated jointly by White star Dominion
[69] Herbert Cash and his wife Sadie
[70] Oliver Hayhurst Cash and his wife Eva
[71] The Berengaria was originally a German ship, The Imperator, later seized after WW1 and renamed
[72] The American Friend archives

spending more time with the family. He was presented with a beautiful writing desk[73] as well as Gibbons' *Decline and Fall of the Roman Empire*, which he had long wished to read. But as Friends learnt of his retirement, he began to be besieged by appeals for his help from all sides. He devoted time to visiting some of the Quaker schools, going to York to talk at Bootham and The Mount later that year and as one of the leading Quakers, he was asked to be the first member of the Society of Friends to speak on the Radio in 1924, a special honour.

This account of his life, firstly in Carlisle and later at Bournville, together with his work for The Society of Friends, leaves out his life as a Father. So I feel I should spend a little time on this, for he adored his children and having recently discovered some letters[74] he wrote to his daughter Millior, when she was away at the Quaker boarding school in Pinehurst in Sussex from the age of 13 from 1917 to 1922, they show precisely what a warm and loving man he was, far removed from the rather austere man often described by others and depicted in all the formal photographs. In her memoir, Grandmother too speaks of John's love for the children:

"John's joy in his children was great indeed. He prayed for great things for them and believed that they would achieve. He had a special tenderness for his two daughters[75] and his chivalry to all women was part of his nature.....as he looked at Millior, he had such a specially sweet smile as she went off into one of her wild moods."

John Henry's 'chivalry to all women' was also apparent in his attitude to women's suffrage and in a letter to his daughter after the passing of 'The Representation of the People Act' in 1918, he wrote:

"Isn't it fine women have the vote now? What centuries of unfairness and inequality there have been between men and women. It was splendid your Head Mistress took you all down to see her register her vote, hurrah!"

Our Grandmother also gives a lovely account of his relationship with the children, when they were very young:

"We loved to have a few moments with the children in the nursery before going downstairs in the evening. Then games of bricks on the floor or story-telling, or reading aloud......Home was to both of us the very centre of our lives.....and John used to love games with the children, especially charades in which he could so alter his face and voice and even figure, that he made a capital actor.... Saturday afternoons were invariably kept free for the children. He loved going walks with them, or when older for cycle rides or at home doing carpentry.....simple things. But he was not too lenient either. He could not tolerate acrimonious discussion or harshness towards each other in the family and the children knew at once when he expected obedience."

Amongst the cache left to Friends House[76] the following is typical of many:

July 11th 1917

"This week will be your 13th birthday. How quickly you grow up. Through all these years you have brought us so much joy and your Mother and I send all our love for your special day. Ralph had a great day at the High School sports on Saturday, high jumping and racing. He was first in the heat, but beaten unfortunately in the final.

---

[73] Now in the possession of my brother Nicholas Barlow
[74] Millior Braithwaite, Letters from her Father. Friends House collection
[75] Phyllis Deborah died in 1909 aged only 2
[76] Letters from JHB to Millior. Friends House archives

The growing family on holiday

On holiday. JHB, MCB, Basil Priestman, Millior, Ralph, John c. 1920

The Author writes:

"The above photograph, it seems to me, makes a wry comment on the family and the times. Even on holiday, my Grandfather is still wearing his hat, and the only one not smiling, solemnity being the default position; the rest are making an effort, though my Father, shutting his eyes is pretending he's not there! Millior is looking nervously at her Mother, who is giving half a smile back, while Jack is the only one really relaxing. Poor Basil Priestman, whose sister, Enid is shortly to marry Jack, is not quite sure whether he should be there at all, and is doing his best to hide. It is as though the photographer has cracked a dirty joke in an endeavour to get them to smile and nobody knows quite how to react. In a way it is a delightful picture and perhaps says more than it intends about the family.

"The photo on the left, on the other hand, though still posed and a little hazy, is rather more natural, with them all sitting amongst the hay. Jack is trying to look sportif, and Granny's got her best hat on, while Grandfather's gone for the flatcap look and my Father, as usual is pretending not to be there!"

On holiday 1919, (standing) Jack and Grandfather
(Sitting) Dad, Millior and Granny

Carol Saker's collection

The Times report on The Society's visit to Ireland 1920

Reprinted from

The Times

Tuesday, October 5, 1920.

IRELAND TO-DAY.

REPORT BY THE SOCIETY OF FRIENDS.

(FROM A CORRESPONDENT.)

At its September meeting the Executive Committee of the Society of Friends had before it the disturbed condition of Ireland. After serious consideration it was decided to send a deputation to visit the country to gather facts and impressions and report to a subsequent meeting as to the possibility of relief, reconstruction, and reconciliation. The deputation numbered three, of whom the writer was one. It may fairly be claimed that they went with open minds anxious to receive light from whatever quarter it might shine. It is thought that some account of what was seen and what impressions were received may be of general interest.

The chief centres visited were Dublin, Belfast, Limerick, Cork, visits being also made from these to places in the neighbourhood. Our interviews were with men of every shade of opinion—Unionists, Nationalists, Sinn Feiners, Protestants, Orangemen, Catholics, Labour leaders. They included members of Parliament, Bishops, business men, university professors, members of the Sinn Fein Cabinet, Sinn Fein judges, journalists, working men. Altogether we had about 60 interviews besides attending groups and conferences. Everywhere we were received with unfailing courtesy and kindness, and every facility was given for carrying out our commission.

First of all as to what we saw. On the surface Dublin was quiet, but while we were in the north Mr. Lynch was shot in a Dublin hotel and one or two encounters took place between the Irish Volunteers and the military. It was in Dublin that we had our first experience of the curfew, and received particulars of the burning of the 17 co-operative creameries. There, too, we found that there are two Governments in Ireland—that of the Crown and that of the Irish Republic. Each has its Cabinet, its Executive, its armed force, its Courts of justice.

It is no exaggeration to say that 80 per cent. of Ireland renders allegiance to the Irish Republic, whether willingly or unwillingly, and that in that area the authority of the British Government rests upon force and not upon consent.

In Belfast we saw something of the ruin caused by the recent outbreaks, but it was not until we

An extract from The Times report
The members of the committee were John Henry Barlow, Chairman of the Society of Friends 1913-1920, Roger Clark, the then Chairman and Edith Ellis

Mother has been in town today, preparing for a great Women's Peace procession with banners everywhere and an open air meeting in the Bull Ring. You asked me about poetry I could recommend....what about Shelley's 'Ode to a Skylark' or 'The Cloud'; perhaps Tennyson's 'St Agnes' Eve' or even Clough's 'Say not the Struggle Nought Availeth'. I've recently read 'The Ingoldsby Legends' which I found very amusing and clever. I shall be going to Leighton Park shortly to see Jack[77] and to talk at their Evening Meeting, so I will try and take the chance to come and see you too and bring the books with me.
Your loving Father"

There were summer holidays too which they all looked forward to, when their Father wasn't working and he could devote his time to the family. From his childhood in Carlisle, John had loved to go bathing with his school friends, as well as canoeing and skating and in the early days of his marriage he and Granny loved cycling round the Cumbrian countryside. These were all pastimes he passed on to his children and their holidays together in places such as Rockcliffe on the Solway or Llanbedrog on Cardigan Bay, were precious moments. Their last holiday together was in 1923 in Switzerland, when they went to visit Millior, who was studying at the finishing school at Chateau Mont-Choisi. This was beautifully situated above Lake Geneva, not far from the centre of Lausanne and they stayed nearby with a party of seven other friends. Switzerland was a country they had loved ever since my Grandparents had spent their honeymoon there, and it was also a place my Father adored, spending many birding holidays there with his great friend Duncan Wood and where in later years he took us children as well.

In the winter of 1923 John had, as usual, many engagements, speaking and helping Edward Cadbury with his candidature for election and visits to Newcastle. But Granny began to notice how thin he was getting and when the doctor visited he diagnosed a bad heart and ordered a complete rest. But sadly, not long afterwards, he suffered a severe heart attack and for the last five months of 1924 was very ill and in considerable pain, which he bore with great fortitude, echoing the suffering his own Father had endured nearly 70 years before. John and Millior were often at his bedside which brought him great joy. My Father, Ralph was still at Leighton Park and it was decided that it would be too distressing for him to see his Father's weakness and pain. Eventually after a long illness, born courageously, he died on August 8th 1924.

News went out on the Radio and the next day in all the national press commemorating a distinguished life...."*the leading Quaker of his generation.*"

The American Friend:
The Passing of a Quaker Statesman
....in the first shock of the news of the passing of John Henry Barlow, there comes back to us the sound of his voice...not of the addresses nor the many messages, nor even the fellowship....no we recall most that appealing, resonant voice. But not just that...it was the character behind the voice and the force and beauty of the message which it conveyed. In a life tireless of industry and distinguished service, John Henry Barlow was a living expression of Quakerism at its highest and best. His was the voice of conviction and courage. He was a world Friend – but ours as well England's, and his memory is dear to us all.

Lord Emmott:
I want to say how deeply I mourn the loss of one who essentially was a real Christian.

The Guardian:
"John Barlow was the outstanding member of the Society of Friends not only among the Quakers in this country but in America. His magnificent leadership during the war years made

---

[77] Jack refers to her brother John Cash Barlow

his choice as Chairman of the big All Friends Conference in London in 1920 almost inevitable. In this case, his chairmanship with its judicial fairness and its grasp of the meeting led to a unity which many had thought impossible. And his presence as an English delegate at the American 'Five Years' Meeting' was especially asked for. His voice and his manner held an audience as I have seen it influenced by no-one else. Grim and austere in bearing at first sight, John Barlow could be one of the most delightful of companions. The best ghost stories I ever heard were those he related in the twilight of Oriel College quadrangle after a busy day's conference. A Liberal to the end of his life, he had the fullest sympathy with schemes of reform of the most advanced character."

The Christian World:
A Great Quaker
"By the death of John Henry Barlow, the Society of Friends has lost one who may truly be looked upon as its outstanding member."

The Times:
'Balance without Compromise'
"This was perhaps the outstanding characteristic of John Henry Barlow, perhaps the most influential member of the Society of Friends.....He was a man of strong, deep-rooted conviction and no one would compromise less than he. His gift was to find where the roots of spiritual unity lay."

A short while later there was a memorial service held at Bournville Friends Meeting House with a large gathering of leading Quakers from all over the country. They had, explained William Littleboy, *"met for a form of worship as John Henry Barlow shrank from any ceremonial praise of the individual and it was his dearest wish that the occasion would be simply a meeting for fellowship in the Quaker manner. It was a joy and gratitude to us all that this man had lived amongst us and that we were here at such a time."* Rendel Harris[78] and Barrow Cadbury read from the scriptures and the meeting ended *"with solemn quietness as a fitting tribute to one who had served his fellow so well."* [79]

Obviously, JHB was a remarkable man whose social work in Carlisle at Willow Holme and his influence on the development of Bournville were outstanding achievements. No less important was his influence on Quakerism both in this country and abroad, especially during the war years. As a child I was very conscious of his presence: photos of him not only in the house but also in his memory at Selly Oak Meeting. And I can feel his influence very much through my Father – his strength of purpose and care for others less fortunate; his work ethic and belief in the Quaker principles of simplicity and lack of pomp; but by no means least, his love of the great English texts of the Bible, Milton and Bunyan which he passed onto my Father and he to me. And although my father said that his childhood was very evangelical and in some respects quite stifling, it is nonetheless a great regret to me that I was never able to know him. In one letter to my Grandmother after he died, a friend wrote: *"I think how thankful your children must be to have had such a father, one whom everyone loved, so good and true and always with such courtesy; he was a man who could not be ungracious."* Where it says 'to have had such a father', one could equally add 'or grandfather'.

---

[78] The First Director of Studies at Woodbrooke. "Woodbrooke was very largely Harris' creation and bears the impress of his personality to this day." *Woodbrooke 1903-1953 Edited by Robert Davis.*
[79] Birmingham News August 16th 1924

Grandparents at Jordans in 1923
Perhaps their last outing together before his illness

Grandfather and Mabel at Jordans in 1923, one of their last outings together.
Mabel centre, and JHB to her right behind the man standing centre picture.
Fellow Quakers not identified.

Family Barlow 1911

**1911 John Henry Barlow with his wife Mabel and family in the garden of 'Sunnybrae': John, Ralph, Millior.
Ralph was one year old. An elder daughter Phyllis had died when only two years old.**

Mabel Cash

Mabel Cash c 1873 aged 5

Mabel in 1879 aged 11 just before she went to Sidcot

1886 Holiday on the Norfolk Broads – Mabel (centre) aged 18
Back row:
Uncle George Barrow behind his wife Caroline Barrow, Elizabeth Taylor, Francis Brown
Far right: Cousin, Janet Taylor, sitting behind her husband to be, Joseph Clark.
Front row: left of Mabel is Charles Lean, great Uncle of film Director, David Lean

Chapter 16
Mabel Cash Barlow

My Grandmother, Mabel Cash was born at Radford House in Gloucester in 1868, the fifth of Frederick Goodall's and Martha's seven children. When FGC first moved to Gloucester to work in his father-in-law's cheese business, they lived in a pleasant little house in Brunswick Square in the town where the first two children, Gertrude and Louisa known as Lou were born. In 1863 they moved to a larger home known as Radford House, to accommodate the growing family.

Fred and Martha lived there for eleven years, where four more children were born, William, and Frederick, who both died young, and Mabel and Herbert. Their last child, Oliver Hayhurst was born at Churchdown, a little place midway between Gloucester and Cheltenham, to where they had moved in 1874. This was an old Manor house, believed to be Elizabethan with a large garden and an adjacent field where they were able to keep a small dairy farm. It was nearby a local beauty spot, 'Chosen Hill', from the top of which were spectacular views out over the Cotswolds. But sadly, due to financial disappointments in 1877, they had to move to a smaller house, Stroud Villas, Park End Road in Gloucester, which they came to love and where they remained for several years.

When the two elder children, Gertrude and Lou were old enough, they were initially sent to Woodhead's school in Scarborough, but neither of them was happy living away from home, and so Fred and Martha decided to get a tutor for them. This was an Irish lady, a Miss Grubb, who came to live with the family and who proved an excellent choice and a very good teacher. The children were all extremely fond of her, and kept in touch long after she had left their employ.

When it came to a choice of school for Mabel and Herbert, Sidcot seemed a natural selection. Fred had not only been on the Board there for some years but also acted as Clerk for seven years along with fellow members such as the Fry brothers, Richard, Albert and James. He writes how he *"often used to spend the Sunday staying overnight with Richard Fry and then driving the next day down to Sidcot in his carriage....I was on the best of terms with the boys and girls and the teachers and formed many lasting friendships."* Both the children loved the school, as their Father wrote in his diary: *"The parting of Mother from children was a sorrowful one, but their schooldays subsequently were very happy. Herbert stayed there for some 3½ years after Mabel had left."*

In 1883 when Mabel was 15 she advanced to Edgbaston High School and went to live in Birmingham with her Uncle and Aunt, George Barrow and his wife, Fred's sister, Caroline. She was extremely fond of them both and did very well at the school according to one school report, making *'excellent progress and pursuing her studies with industry and avidity,'* and made many friends there. Often Mabel and her sister Gertie would go on holiday with her uncle and Aunt which she always adored doing.

Meanwhile their Father continued on working in Gloucester with his father-in-law Samuel Bowly, which meant him taking on a lot more responsibility and when Sam eventually retired in 1878, FGC writes how: *"In partnership with George Bagg and George Aldridge, I carried on the business of wholesale cheese and provision merchants, English and foreign at High Orchard in Llanthony Road in Gloucester for the next seven years."*

When Gertie and Mabel were not with their Uncle and Aunt, all the children would go on holidays together, often to the West Country near Ilfracombe or to the Lorna Doone country in Exmoor. Sometimes other friends, such as Howard Sturge and his family, who were particularly close friends, would join them. There were several other outings too, and in 1889 Mabel writes an account of a visit to the Houses of Parliament in 1889:

"My first visit to the House of Commons! How my pulses thrilled with excitement at the thought of entering that grand old place; of hearing and seeing all those men of whom I had so often read, the men whose names resounded through the country and who formed our laws and were there representing the whole of England – except of course a considerable minority."

The minority she is referring to, of course, is women. Though it may seem surprising that my Grandmother should be an early feminist, it was a subject Quakers were later to take up, as witness her future husband's letters to Millior quoted earlier! Granny goes on to write:

"It seemed almost incredible that women were only allowed to listen to a debate, peering through aggravating bars, both perpendicular and horizontal, and shut up in a dark kind of cabin! There we were, caged in like dangerous creatures, looking through first one little aperture and then another of our cage, vainly trying to read our programme of the day's proceedings, by the few gleams of light that found their way into our prison."

Imbued with early feminism, she is plainly not impressed:

"How strangely far from uncommon, looked these representatives of the English people! It was necessary to recall that they had not been chosen for any outward appointments, but for some mental or moral capacity which their constituents had supposed them at one time to possess. There sat the Speaker (Mr Peel) with a ghastly green hue upon his face – thrown by the shade of the sounding board above him. Looking somewhat like a spectre as he rose, tall and thin to cry 'Order, Order'! Or to read some note. There surely on that further row, which was already crowded, a retired burly Publican has just squeezed himself. From behind the Speaker's chair enters a man who might be a paper hanger as he clutches a bundle of rolls closely to him, as he advances to take a seat. Is it Spring cleaning time?"

It is a wonderful account of the House of its day, and in many ways, could easily be a description of today's chamber:

"There are members in immaculate attire with dainty flower buttonholes, there are smooth, glossy top hats contrasting with others of a rumpled and crushed appearance. Keen eagerness and interest are here opposed to drowsiness and lackadaisical indifference. Others shuffle and lounge and lounge and shuffle as much as any schoolboy – until one longs for a schoolmaster to call them to order and forbid talking which often goes on in spite of the fact that some member is on his feet, delivering a speech.

Having seen enough of these everyday characters, the doors are anxiously watched – and at last, walking slowly – in comes the king of them all, W E Gladstone – and takes his seat on the front opposition bench. This is our first sight of the GOM [80], yet recognition is instantaneous. We in our cage lean eagerly forward, regardless of crushing feather and ribbons. We all peer through our peepholes and watch his every movement. He is about to speak……….See he half rises hands on knees, he essays twice or thrice – at last on his feet! Ears are now pressed close to the bars, we strain our faculties but only hear a few short sentences addressed to the Table in a rather low gruff voice. That is all – but we have seen him and heard him and for a while we are satisfied."

---

[80] Gladstone was known as The Grand old Man

Mabel Cash

Mabel in 1894 just engaged to John Henry Barlow

Gradually the elder children, now in their twenties began to get engaged. In 1883 when Lou was 22, she met Ernest Hutchinson, the son of Henry Hutchinson originally from Wellingborough, but now working in Gloucester for John Bellows and company. After a short engagement they were married in 1885 at Mercers' Road Meeting House in Holloway, London.

Not long after in 1884 when Gertie was 25 she met Joseph Henry Taylor of Middlesborough, the only surviving son of William Taylor and they too soon became engaged. Joseph Taylor was a leader in the Liberal cause and a strong worker for temperance. They were married on April 30 at Gloucester Friends meeting. The following year Ernest and Lou left Gloucester for Carlisle as Ernest had been offered a job working for Carrs and Co, where as I have already written, he largely took over the day to day running of the business after JD Carr had retired *"and with his great ingenuity and business capacity helped to double that large concern."*

Ernest and Lou soon became deeply involved in working with John Henry at Willow Holme, the poor slum area of Carlisle where they helped the down and outs and the alcoholics and set up reading classes. Mabel often used to go up to Carlisle to stay with her sister and Ernest and it was on these visits that she gradually got to know 'the Prophet' as she called JHB. In a letter she wrote to her Aunt Carrie (Caroline Barrow) in 1889 she described his effect on her:

"The man of the meeting ('The Prophet') is John Barlow, the only young man unmarried....I do so admire him, for he really is a splendid man and does such an immense amount of good work and he speaks so well. The friendship between John and myself was of slow growth. I was young and very shy when I first visited 'Glevum' (Ernest and Lou's house). *I used to pay a visit there every year and gradually 'Mr Barlow' and I became more acquainted and I grew less afraid of him. But he seemed so clever and so good and above me altogether!"*

That autumn Mabel paid another visit to 'Glevum' and discovered that John had already talked of his own love for Mabel to his sister and invited her stay at Murrell Hill Cottage. Later her father went to visit and John Henry asked him if he could marry his daughter.

"It was in the dear little drawing room of the cottage that John asked me to be his wife. What joy it brought into both our lives and what absolute happiness we have had in each other ever since."

One of the Carr family said: '*Mabel, you have chosen a Prince among men'*. Their marriage took place on 17th July 1895 at Holloway Meeting House and Fred writes how *'Martha was especially sad at the loss of their last cherished daughter from our home, though happy too for her future."*

After John and Mabel returned from their honeymoon at the Pension Kaufmann in Lucerne they joined Lou and Ernest with Mabel's parents near Ullswater, where they were holidaying with Joseph and Gertie. Their meeting and subsequent marriage came at a fortuitous time as the year before 1894 had been full of sadness and partings. Firstly in the Spring of that year, John's mother Eliza died, aged 81 which both John and his sister Mary felt very keenly, having been so close since their Father died. Then later that same year, Mabel's brother Oliver decided that he too would venture across the Atlantic to join his brother Herbert in Newberg, Oregon. It was a sorrowful parting for all, but especially for his mother, who as it turned out never saw him again. He sailed from Liverpool on the 'Lake Ontario' for Halifax and then on to Portland, Oregon over the Canadian Pacific Railway. For a time he worked with his brother on their small piece of land but then after moving around from place to place he settled in Chicago, where he met the twin Hunt sisters Eva and Iva, eventually marrying Eva.

Steam cars and family gatherings

1895 STEAM TRICAR

THE accompanying photograph of this 1895 steam tricar, together with a description of its initial drive in January, 1896, were discovered in an old bureau by Mrs. M. C. Barlow, who is the off-side passenger. It was built in 1895 at the works of Carr and Co., Carlisle, under the direction of the late Mr. Theodore Carr (Mrs. Barlow's cousin), who is shown at the tiller, the other passenger being his sister. It is from his description of the first drive, written more than 50 years ago, that particulars have been obtained.

The power unit was supplied by the Lancashire Steam Motor Co., which later became the Leyland Co., and was usually supplied for steam mowing machines; it was mounted in a wooden frame. Coils in the roof condensed the steam and led the water back to the boiler. The transmission was extremely simple, by a chain to the rear wheel.

It was claimed by Mr. Carr that this was the first attempt to use a steam engine of that kind on a small vehicle.

From The Carlisle Chronicle 1945

"The accompanying photograph of this 1895 steam tricar, together with a description of its trial drive in January 1896 were discovered in an old bureau by Mrs M C Barlow, who is the off-side passenger. It was built in 1895 at the works of Carr and Co., Carlisle under the direction of the late Mr Theodore Carr (Mrs Barlow's cousin) who is shown at the tiller. The power unit was supplied by the Lancashire Steam Motor Co., which later became the Leyland Company." Photo courtesy of Roger Barlow

Family gathering 1909
Back row: Ernest Hutchinson, Herbert Cash, Mabel and John Barlow
Front row: Joseph Taylor, Louisa Hutchinson, Gertrude Taylor, Eva and Oliver Cash

In 1898, Herbert married Sarah Lucile Bond, known as Sadie, who came from South California. Both of the brothers had a hard time of it initially, but they were full of courage and determination and with their wives, eventually built happy homes there. The two boys died quite young, Herbert in 1920 aged only 49 and Oliver in 1931 aged 56. Oliver's wife, Eva however, lived to the grand old age of 93, dying in 1971 in California. They had three children, Frederick (1906-1944), William (1911-1969) and Mary (1922 2003) and there are two grandchildren, Janet (b.1935) and Robert (b.1939) from Fred's marriage to Tressel Norman, who are still alive.

Meanwhile John and Mabel were building their home in Carlisle at Murrell Cottage as John's sister Mary had kindly moved out and went to live near their cousin Lizzie Carr at Coldale Hall. Mabel writes:

"I was shown all over the house. Loving hands had been busy and the house was exquisitely prepared for the Bride. Nothing seemed left unfinished. And when our guests had left and we were alone together, it was with hearts full of joy and delight that we looked around our sweet home, Murrell Hill Cottage."

They began life together with a maid Ann, a country girl of 19 *'who knew as little about housework and cooking as I did'* said my grandmother, asking a wage of £12 a year! My grandmother's account, shows what a different world the well-to-do Quakers inhabited then:

"I can see myself sitting down one morning in the sunny dining room with pen and paper, trying to make out a list of Ann's duties. When I thought of all the rooms and the staircase and the hall and the landings – to say nothing of the kitchen, scullery and back premises and beyond that, and all our wealth of silver to be polished – there did not seem to be a sufficient number of days in the week in which to get through all the work. But Aunt Mary gave me good advice and I abandoned the unwieldy list and Ann and I worked together most happily. But I had to receive lessons in jam and jelly making from Mag (their old faithful maid who had come from Edinburgh with them) *who insisted that it had to be just as 'the Mistress'(Eliza Barlow) had liked....I learnt many useful things from her."*

Their early married life was very happy and Grandmother and her sister Lou bought bicycles which Grandfather taught them to ride and they loved cycling around the beautiful countryside. It was quite daring for the time, as not many women cycled then, but she made quite sure that her riding costume was suitably decorous and wouldn't blow up, especially as they even went out on moonlight rides.

After their engagement, John Henry, in order to enjoy some home life, gave up a mumber of his many duties, though he still seemed to be incredibly busy, with Mabel often accompanying him on several of his visits, especially to the many Bible classes he took, and she obviously found it fulfilling: *"What joy there was in sharing everything,"* she writes.

To give some idea of a typical Sunday, the day began with the Adult School at Willow Holme, followed by Fisher Street morning meeting. At two o'clock a Men's Bible class and at three the Pleasant Sunday Afternoon Association. After tea, an open air meeting in Willow Holme, then the Mission Meeting or a service in one or other of the churches. During the week, of course, he worked long business hours at Carrs. No wonder they had no children during these first five years of their marriage!

Ernest Hutchinson, who became works manager of Carrs

Ernest Hutchinson and his young daughter Olive Margery 1887

The Author writes:
Ernest Hutchinson married my Grandmother, Mabel Cash's sister Louisa in 1885

I have already alluded to Mary's drawn-out illness and death in 1899, so I won't dwell on it again, except to say that she was nursed with great care and devotion by their cousin Ida Peile, who was later to nurse Grandfather during his last illness in 1924. Grandmother wrote the following description:

"Her room was like the gateway of Heaven. On the wall hung the text so beloved by their Mother 'When He giveth quietness, who then can make trouble.' And how true those words were. The Peace of God filled that room,"

During her later years Mary had left the Society and joined the Church of England, devoting her life to Christian service and was known as 'the angel of Carlisle' for her sweet nature and good works.[81] This was inevitably a hard time for John, as brother and sister and Mother had looked after each other, now the new unit was his marriage and friends and family such as the Carrs and Hutchinsons and his work. It is perhaps of note that in these early years of their marriage both John and Mabel were very much caught up in themselves and in the work at Willow Holme and all that that involved. So much so, that as I have hinted, no children were born until the major change in their life occurred, when they moved to Birmingham in 1900 with their first, John Cash being born on December 10th 1901.

As Granny describes: *"The years that followed were a very different life from that of the first six years in Carlisle. For four children[82] came to fill it with extra joy and gaiety and the home overflowed with young life."*

In 1904 Mary Millior was born and Grandfather wrote to Granny: *"Our little daughter is thy wedding anniversary gift to me. It is needless to say that thou could not have given me one more prized and welcome."* And in 1907 Phyllis Deborah was born and *'John's tender love and pride in his two daughters was beautiful."*

Tragically, Deborah Phyllis caught pneumonia and died suddenly aged only two when her parents were away for Mabel's Father's funeral in June of 1909. She was full of brightness and joy and her death was a bitter blow to them both. *"John's tenderness and care for me held me up through those terrible days."*

It was therefore, a great joy to them, when only a year later in 1910 my Father was born *"given us by God to help heal the sore hearts."* As my Father used to put it more prosaically, in his sometimes Eeyore-ish way *"I was a replacement child"*! But I think he was particularly loved for that very reason, as can be seen in letters Granny wrote to my Father during the war.[83]

They both revelled in the children and despite the many calls on his time at Bournville and travelling overseas, John always found time for the children - in the nursery, reading them stories, or playing games with them, especially on Saturday afternoons which were sacrosanct, as their time. And although there were the demands of work, the home was to both of them the centre of their lives, facing the difficulties of life through *"the peace and joy of our home. A peace and joy that came from God who had brought us together."*

It was something that they both handed down to their children, for when I was young, our house too was a happy and calm place and my Father would do everything to avoid an argument, bringing reconciliation through tolerance and understanding.

---

[81] Cumberland News 1899
[82] John Cash b. 1901, Mary Millior b. 1904, Phyllis Deborah b 1907 died 1909 aged just two, Frederick Ralph b. 1910
[83] See end of this chapter.

Louisa Cash

Mabel's sister, Louisa Cash (Lou for short) married Ernest Hutchinson in 1885

As the years passed, John Henry had more and more calls on his time, travelling up and down the country as well as abroad, both on behalf of Quakers and for the Bournville Village Trust. By now he was widely respected as one of the leading Quakers of his day, both for his oratory and wise council and as already alluded to in the previous chapter, he seemed never to stop; going to Holland for a Peace Conference, travelling to Ireland to look into the violence of The Black and Tans, being Clerk of Yearly Meeting for a record number of years and going to America for the Five Years Conference in 1923. No wonder he wore himself out!

The photograph, taken in 1915 (see p.116), of Cousin Nell's wedding, with my 5 year old Father looking typically, as though he's not enjoying the whole thing very much, shows how close Quaker circles still were at that time; to a large extent the social circle was a fairly narrow Quaker one and it's interesting to note that Millior's daughter, my late cousin Anna, was in turn bridesmaid to Cousin Nell's daughter Phyllida, such was the continuum.

When Granny and Grandfather first moved to Birmingham, they had various maids to help with the house and children and they obviously inspired considerable devotion, for they all became friends and stayed with them for many years. I know this too from my own childhood experience, as my Mother inherited a lady called Lydia Brookes from my Grandmother, when she moved down to London to live with my Aunt Millior. Lydia likewise, stayed with us for many, many years and was much loved by us children. The most faithful of all my Grandparent's maids was the indomitable Mag Carson[84] who had followed first Eliza Barlow when she moved to Carlisle after Professor John Barlow died in 1855, and then insisted on joining 'the young master', as she called John Henry, and his wife at 'Sunnybrae' in 1901. But two others also followed from Carlisle, Fanny Cowan and Jennie Hall, of whom my Father was particularly fond. She was described as 'a devoted and faithful friend for fourteen years and when she died they all felt her loss greatly.'

Both parents also loved the outdoors and Grandfather was fond of indoor pastimes such as carpentry, both of which delights they passed on to my Father and he to us, as he took us on many wonderful cycling holidays in Wales or the Cotswolds, and always walking or climbing wherever we happened to be. I also remember our poor Mother recounting how on her honeymoon in the Lake District, Father had taken her across the dangerous 'Striding Edge' near Helvellyn, much to her fright! But as well as outdoor pursuits my Father also passed on to me the pleasures of carpentry, which I developed at both the Downs School and Leighton Park, where such hobbies were well taught and I even nearly took it up as a career, when my Father suggested that I go to Ruskin Hall, now Bournville Centre for Visual Arts to study professionally. So my Grandfather's loves passed down through his son to his grandchildren.

I have already covered their children's early school days in the chapter on Quaker schools but after his time at Leighton Park, Jack began work almost immediately; Millior left Edgbaston High School to study abroad in Lausanne, before becoming a teacher herself at Mrs Grice's, a Primary in Harborne; whereas my Father continued his studies at Birmingham University,[85] where he read History

In July 1920 our Grandparents celebrated their Silver Wedding, although only my father was at home, but many cousins joined them including 'dear Aunt Carrie' (Caroline Barrow) and afterwards they joined William and Maria Darby for supper[86]. (see family tree p 267).

---

[84] Mag was buried near the family plot at Lodge Hill cemetery in Birmingham when she died.
[85] He got a 2i
[86] W & M Darby, descended from Deborah Barlow, who married John Thistlethwaite, whose daughter married a Darby!

As discussed in the chapter on Grandfather, in 1922, the year before John Henry retired from the BVT, he and Grandmother attended the Five Years Meeting at Richmond Indiana, leaving the children behind, though by this time John (Jack) was nearly 21 and had already worked at Kalamazoo before starting at Cadburys, Millior was 18 and studying French in Switzerland and my Father was 12 and just beginning at Leighton Park.

John Henry and Mabel left for America on 'The Regina', embarking from Liverpool, first for Quebec and Montreal just enjoying travelling and being together and later meeting up with Barrow and Geraldine Cadbury as they went to Indiana. John had become very well-known through his Clerkship of Yearly Meeting and the All Friends' Conference so that everywhere they went in America, they were among friends and John was greeted enthusiastically and given a wonderful welcome.

The extended visit to America, also gave them a chance to see Granny's two brothers Herbert and Oliver and their families, staying in Portland Oregon with Herbert and his wife Sadie and family and then down the Pacific Coast to Los Angeles to Riverside where they spent a fortnight with Oliver and Eva. They ended their stay with friends in Philadelphia and a few days in Baltimore before returning to England on the 'Berengaria' in time for John's 21st on December 10th 1922.

My Grandparents were not pompous people in any way but my Mother always thought Granny Barlow a bit of a snob, so sailing on the smartest of the Cunard's liners might have appealed to her! 'The Berengaria' was built in 1913, but being launched only a few weeks after 'Titanic', was able to incorporate considerable safety improvements before making her maiden voyage to New York in 1913. After the war she became the pride of the Cunard fleet and along with the 'Aquitania' and the 'Mauretania' was among their most famous and luxurious transatlantic liners.

The ship was beautifully designed not only in the first class areas but throughout the ship. All accommodation was similar to that found in the latest hotels. For instance, all the rooms were provided with electric connections for lighting, and heating and there was a ventilation system for each room. In addition to the large main stairways between decks there were also elevators providing communication to the five decks and at all levels there were small shops to meet passengers' needs. They were away some three and half months, a time Granny records *'of extraordinary happiness. We were free to travel, which we both loved and we were together.'*

In 1923 they both attended Yearly Meeting in London and John stood in as Clerk again as Roger Clark had to be unavoidably absent. *"How wonderful it was to have John Henry Barlow at the table again"* wrote The Friend. The following year 1924 John retired from business, glad in many ways to be able to do so, having been in business life since the age of sixteen. *"How he looked forward after our holiday to returning home without being obliged to go to work the next day"* wrote Grandmother.

However, he was not idle, as Friends, learning of his retirement, began to ask for his help in all sorts of engagements and he started to be as busy as ever again. But even by the Christmas of 1923 when they were at Aunt Carrie's, Grandmother writes:

"I was feeling anxious about John, he was getting very thin and had a troubling cough. I had a strange presentiment that the coming year was bringing sorrow."

Family at 'Sunnybrae'

John and Mabel at 'Sunnybrae' in 1909 with their two children John and Millior and their cousin Oliver Hayhurst Cash, over from America

By the New Year he was frailer and later complications meant having an operation. He stayed in the Nursing Home for a couple of months rallying sometimes, especially when he was allowed back home. But not long after his return, he had a bad heart attack, though he hung on for a few more weeks. Cousin Ida Peile who had nursed Grandfather's sister Mary at the end of her life, came down to help look after him, as well as a Nurse. The three eldest children were constantly by his bedside and gave him great pleasure but it was decided that my Father, '*his dear Ralph*' should not be brought home from school, for fear of paining him too much seeing his father's weakness. The next day he said farewell to the children "*Show great and constant love one to another and give God the best of your lives.*" My grandmother wrote of his unfailing courage during the last months and of his unfailing courtesy which others had remarked on all his life. Then on August 8th 1924 he died.

My Grandmother received literally hundreds of letters from all over the world speaking of the passing of a great man. Summing up the many messages, perhaps the words of one of the leading Quaker writers J Edward Hodgkin, spoke for many when he wrote:

"*The Society of Friends can seldom have possessed a man so wonderfully gifted and prepared to lead it as he was; and withal so humble and self-forgetful in the service he gave. None of us who went through those war Yearly Meetings will ever forget the way in which he was enabled to handle difficult and trying matters that inevitably came up. It seemed to me that his judgment and tact were never at fault. I feel as though the death of so great a man has left us with a tremendous responsibility as well as a great and inspiring memory.*"

Apart from all the work he had done in the early years in Carlisle, the pioneering work at Bournville, the Peace work on behalf of Friends everywhere, he was also one of those who helped to get Woodbrooke off the ground in the beginning[87]. The Woodbrooke Committee noted in their minute:

"*John Henry Barlow perhaps did more than anyone to make the opening of Woodbrooke a success. His secretaryship for over fifteen years, his years of Trusteeship and his chairmanship of the Settlement Committee was vital. Particularly during the difficult years of the war (1914-18) we came to appreciate the value of the discerning and weighty judgment which he brought to the service of the College.*"

After John Henry died in 1924, my Grandmother stayed on at 'Sunnybrae' for a number of years until she eventually moved with my Father and his sister Millior together with her maid Lydia Brookes, to No 6 Swarthmore Road in Selly Oak, Birmingham in 1932, taking the name of 'Sunnybrae' with her. Her eldest son, John Cash Barlow, had got married in 1926 to Enid Priestman, who came from another large Quaker family from Edgbaston and so had already moved away. There was an odd quirk with the Priestman family, in that all the boy's names had five letters such as Enid's brothers, Basil, Miles and Ralph, while all the girl's names had four letters like Enid and Lois!

John worked for Cadbury's for over 40 years, ending up as Manager of the Contract sales, though their son Roger suggested to me that it was not a job he really enjoyed. In their early married life, they lived near Stratford-on-Avon, when he was Sales Manager for Cadbury's. They used to take in lodgers, one of whom was the famous actor, Donald Wolfit, then appearing at the Stratford Memorial Theatre with his wife Rosalind Iden, for whom they would often baby-sit their daughter Margaret.

---

[87] Thomas C Kennedy notes in his book 'British Quakerism 1960-1920' "Cadbury's closest confidants were his wife, Elizabeth, his sons George Jnr and Edward, together with his friends Henry Lloyd Wilson. Joseph Hoyland and John Henry and Mabel Barlow."

A family wedding and young children

The wedding in 1915 of Eleanor Taylor, known as Cousin Nell. She was one of two children of Mabel's eldest sister Gertrude Cash and Joseph H Taylor and is here marrying W E Frank Woodall from Bromsgrove, son of William and Caroline Woodall.

The family Barlow is out in force:
3rd from left: Grandfather, JHB; in front of him, Uncle John; to the left of the bride, Millior; to the right of the bride, my Father wishing as usual that he was elsewhere! ; back row 2nd from right in feather hat: Granny Barlow.
Standing on left with walrus moustache is Edward Cadbury and behind Millior and the bride is Elizabeth Cadbury (née Taylor). In later years my cousin Anna was bridesmaid to the Woodall's daughter Phyllida.

Ralph, John and Millior 1916

The Author writes:
"Good little children all…….butter wouldn't melt…….How my Father would have hated the frill round his neck"!

Ralph aged c. 2 with Millior aged c. 8 1912

116

During the war John was in the Home Guard, being seconded from Cadbury's to the Ministry of National Service Hostels organisation[88]. In 1945 he moved back to Cadbury's as head of the Trader's Advisory Bureau and they bought a house in Innage Road, Northfield, Birmingham, where we often used to visit as children.

John was quite a shy man, but always wonderful with children and loved playing games with us. They only had one child, Roger (b.1930) who married Mary Biddle and they had a daughter Annabel (b.1963)[89]. John retired in 1963 and the Bournville Works magazine wrote: *"JCB was a modest man but a meticulous worker with a wide understanding of the trade. Outside his work, one of his many interests was motoring and his cars were always immaculately kept. He also had a deep interest in social work and for many years was a prison visitor."* Roger told me recently that in all, his father had 19 different cars, though when he acquired a Jaguar, Cadbury's told him they thought 'it was a little flash'! He sadly died quite young at the age of 73 in 1972, but Enid lived on into a ripe old age, moving to live at the sheltered housing development, Queen Mother Court in Bournville, where my Mother's sister Winifred and her husband Llewellyn also lived. She later died at the age of 91 in 1991.

Our Aunt, Mary Millior, known as Millie had been to Switzerland to study French but had returned by the time her Father had died and she began to teach at Mrs Grice's Primary school in Harborne, where much later I and my brothers and sister went. Millior married Alfred Braithwaite in 1939, from yet another old Quaker family. He was the son of the eminent Quaker historian, William Charles Braithwaite and his wife Margaret Masterman,[90] known for her pioneering work in the field of computational linguistics. Alfred and Millior's youngest child, my cousin Carol, recently told me that her two distinguished grandparents, William Charles Braithwaite and John Henry Barlow in fact knew each other well, through London Yearly Meeting, long before their respective son and daughter met in the 1930's!

After they married, they moved away from Birmingham to live firstly in Gower Street, London, near Alfred's firm of Solicitors, Waterhouse & Co, and later at a lovely house in Golders Green, where they made a wonderfully welcoming home, at which we often stayed as children on family visits to London, as well as on many occasions in later years. I recall one occasion in particular, when we came down for my 16th birthday and we had been offered the use of the house as my Uncle and Aunt were away in the States. My parents had arranged as a special treat, to take us to Covent Garden one night to see Margot Fonteyn, but on our return, to our dismay, we discovered the house in a terrible mess as burglars had got in, in our absence. Some years later, when I was doing some social work in the East End of London, together with my school friend Tom Lowenstein, who lived opposite, I also stayed there very happily for some weeks. Millior had something of the intimidating nature of her Mother when I first remember her, but in later years she mellowed and she and Alfred were all that an Aunt and Uncle should be; wise, welcoming and loving. I miss them both greatly.

Alfred's family were all very bright intellectually. His eldest brother Richard was Professor of Moral Philosophy at Kings College, Cambridge and their children Catherine and Lewis were equally clever. His eccentric sister Connie, was a lecturer in Social Studies at Birmingham and Newcastle Universities and used to delight us children as she broke all the rules, by wearing trousers and smoking heavily. Alfred and Millior had two children, Anna Millior[91], born in

---

[88] Letter from Roger Barlow to Antony 14.07.14
[89] Annabel works for Princess Cruises, part of the Cunard group as a Casino supervisor!
[90] Alfred's Father, William was the author of one of the most authoritative histories of Quakerism.
[91] Anna sadly died of cancer in 2011. She married twice, firstly Jimmy Kerr by whom she had two children Abby, who also sadly died aged 36 and Jane. Anna later married Callaghan OHerlihy.

The new 'Sunnybrae' and Uncle John's wedding

The 2nd 'Sunnybrae' at 6 Swarthmore Road

John Barlow's and Enid Priestman's wedding 1926.
Back Row: Ralph Barlow and Charles Gillett and right, Ralph Priestman.
Seated: Mabel Barlow, Lois Priestman, Millior Barlow, Marian Priestman and
seated on the ground Pat.

1942 and Carol May[92] born in 1948 with whom we grew up, as we often stayed with each other's families and went on holidays together. My sister Rosemary who is of an age with Carol, has remained close to her and her family and David and I to Anna and her family, whom we miss greatly, since her early death in 2011. Alfred died in 1975 aged 74 and Millior in 1993 aged 89, both buried at Jordans.

More of my Father in a later chapter, but after he left Birmingham University, he was apprenticed to the Bournville Trust in 1932 and he married my Mother in 1936, moving into 26 Linden Road, Bournville, where my brother David was born in 1937. With war imminent, my Father joined the Auxiliary Fire Service in 1939, before joining the Friends Ambulance Unit in 1940. I was born in 1941 at 'Beaconwood', the home of their close friends, Honor and Christopher Cadbury (George's grandson), as it was thought safer to be up on the Lickey Hills, near Rednal, than nearer the City, especially with Dad away. There was also a great deal of pressure from Quaker elders such as Paul Cadbury, for other Quakers to take in refugees, and my parents decided that they would let Linden Road to a Polish family, the Tritsch's[93].

My Mother's sister Winifred and her husband Dr Llewellyn Rutter, had reluctantly opted to send their two eldest children, Michael and Priscilla to live in America for the duration of the war to be safely away from the bombing. They therefore had spare rooms, and very kindly offered a home to my Mother and brother David and I, and so for three or four years we lived in Wolverhampton, where our Granny Barber was already living. How we all got along together is a mystery and it is a great tribute to the temperament of my Aunt and Uncle that we did, for life was surely full of difficult emotions. They were inevitably missing their own children while simultaneously two other noisy youngsters were banging around the house and my Aunt was busy trying to help Uncle run his surgery. My Mother, not long married and not in her own home, was worried sick about my Father, especially when he became so ill,[94] with only occasional news filtering through from abroad.

My Father reluctantly left the FAU following his illness in 1944/5 but it was not until the end of the war in 1945 that we were able to move back to Birmingham, firstly, after the Tritsch's had moved back home, to Linden Road and then to Swarthmore Road, which was now empty following Granny Barlow's move to London to live with Alfred and Millior in Golders Green in 1943. Granny remained living with them for most of the rest of her life, returning to the Midlands only when she was ill, to be in The Woodlands[95], where she died in 1956.

I remember Granny Barlow as a tall, rather austere person, but she came from such a different era and outlook, when Quaker families did devote their lives to good works, as she and Grandfather had done. She also had a long widowhood of over thirty years, living with her daughter and family in London, which in itself can't have been easy for anyone. But for many years she continued to be involved with Quaker life in London, including Hampstead Meeting and London Yearly Meeting and looking after the legacy of her husband. On the other hand, I remember happy holidays at Burnham-on-Sea, where Alfred's relatives owned a large house called 'Blencathra', right by the sea and where Granny together with my Uncle Alfred and Aunt Millior, along with our cousins Anna and Carol, and our Mother and Father and we children, would all go around Easter time.

---

[92] Carol married Moussa Saker and had two children Adam and Sami
[93] My parents left all their belongings at Linden Road during the war and they were not especially happy on their return at the way some things had been treated.
[94] My Father contracted Epidemic Encephalitis in Ethiopia in 1943
[95] A Quaker home for the elderly, where my maternal Grandmother also died in 1965

Millior with Alfred and her Mother

Left:
Alfred and Millior at 'Blencathra' 1956
The Author writes:

"The Braithwaite family had a family house, 'Blencathra' at Burnham-on-Sea in Somerset, where our family often used to stay with Uncle Alfred, Aunt Millior and our cousins Anna and Carol along with Granny Barlow. The house was named after the northern peak of the Lake District, a familiar haunt of old Quaker families. It was a rather forbidding Victorian seaside house, with a large stuffed owl in the hallway. It was only a few minutes' walk from the beach, where there was a paddling pool, in which we loved to paddle as children."

Below:
Millior and Granny shortly before her death
The Author writes:

"Granny Barlow in the garden at 17 The Park, in Golders Green, where she lived for the last 13 years of her life with her daughter and their family, after she moved to London from Birmingham in 1943. She had a long widowhood of over 30 years, which she bore with fortitude and though sometimes forbidding, she was a distinguished lady of grace and elegance."

It was a rather forbidding, Victorian house with a large stuffed owl in the hallway, which used to scare us as children and upstairs were old style beds with brass knobs at each corner, which we loved to unscrew. Granny was very fond of us children and used to take us into nearby Weston-Super-Mare, to buy Knickerbocker Glories[96] I recall, and sometimes we would accompany her on walks alongside the railway, where we could pick cowslips, not yet protected flowers, so that we could take some back to put in a vase with other wild flowers.

Later when I was away at boarding school, she would always write to me and quite often enclose a little money to supplement our pocket money, which was always welcome as our Father's small allowance to us was a meagre 10/- each half term! She was also very generous to my Father, helping out financially, as with four children[97], he often found himself overstretched. To us, our maternal Grandmother, Granny Barber seemed much more approachable. Indeed from my earliest days at Wolverhampton, I can just remember going into her room in the mornings and sharing her cup of tea in bed! Granny Barlow would never have suggested that!

When my parents were courting, to use an old fashioned expression, Granny Barlow thought my Mother's family was very 'below the salt' and hardly suitable for the so-called Quaker royalty from which she was descended! My Father would always reassure my Mother, that he would win his Mother round eventually, which of course he did. In later years, when Granny was living in London, my cousins Anna and Carol were somewhat undisciplined children as Alfred, a lovely person in so many ways, was not a strong disciplinarian and the two girls would often tease their Grandmother.

I remember once Granny telling Anna off, only to be told that if she ticked her off again, she'd 'kick her in the bum'! A sentiment not inclined to endear her to Grandmama! So in comparison, the Barlow children were 'models of good behaviour' and she reluctantly conceded in later years that Joan was a very good mother, as the following letter amply demonstrates, which my Grandmother wrote to my Mother during the war, from which you get quite another sense of this remarkable lady and of the family closeness and maternal love she had for her children and their families, which perhaps she found it hard to express openly; a generational trait perhaps, which my Father and his sister also possessed. The following is typical of many written to my Father during the war years (June 17th 1943):

"My beloved Son, Your lovely letter this morning has rejoiced my heart. Thank you so much for writing. Father and I felt that you were given to us to comfort us after the loss of little Phyllis and you have certainly brought us unbounded joy. You have been such a dear and helpful son and since you left Birmingham, I have missed you dreadfully and the closing of your home, has cut out a large part of the happiness of my life....You have a beloved wife and two adorable sons, to help you stand firm and steadfast and to help you remake a happy home on your return.....Do not think you have disappointed me dear. I am profoundly thankful for the stand you are making and for all your love. You have been a joy and comfort to me all your life even though we may have differed at times, it has never severed our love[98]....To take the stand you are doing needs grit and much grace and you may be sure I love you all the more for it....I will gladly help Joan all I can, you can rely on that and hope indeed to see her here tomorrow for lunch....Good bye my precious boy. My love and prayers companion you. Ever your loving Mother."

---

[96] Large scoops of ice cream with fruit and juice
[97] Nicholas was born in 1958, some 13 years later.
[98] This is a reference to the concerns she had over his marriage to Joan, but already you sense her attitude has completely altered with references to 'a loving wife' and 'helping Joan all I can'.

Not only is it a most heartfelt letter, but whatever animosity may have existed between my Mother and my Grandmother, had also been forgotten. So reality is often quite at odds from what are, after all, my childhood recollections. How we saw her and how her contemporaries saw her are, as the following tribute shows, completely different.

Writing in The Friend, Miriam Carter[99] gave this tribute:

"John and Mabel Barlow's married life was supremely happy and in their beautiful home, visitors found peace and refreshment which seemed to embody the answer to the prayer 'Take from our souls the strain and stress, and let our ordered lives confess, the beauty of thy peace.' Despite the claims of her young family, Mabel entered intimately into the life of the neighbourhood. She helped Theodore Wilson to start the Infant Welfare Centre in Birmingham, worked ceaselessly for Temperance causes, Women's Activities and aided her husband in his work for Peace. Her first allegiance, however was to Selly Oak meeting and she was seldom absent on Sunday mornings, not infrequently taking vocal part. She had a personal concern for every member and a sympathetic understanding of young people. Beauty of character was mirrored in the gracious charm of her personality."

Among Quaker circles she was widely respected and loved and she maintained a happy home both in Carlisle and in Birmingham and the personality revealed in letters, shows a lady not only of moral strength and Quaker values, but of deep maternal instincts. She was undoubtedly a lady of strong personality and yet graciousness who had been an ideal companion for my Grandfather and who had adored him from the start. Their shared Quaker background and beliefs complemented each other and she was the perfect foil to everything he did. The memoir she wrote of John Henry for their children is inevitably a paean of praise but none the worse for that and all the praise is certainly echoed in other's appraisal of him in letters and journals. As so often with the younger generation, one's memories are of course of the person in later years. So from the memories of others of her generation who knew her and the respect the Society showed her, she emerges as a fine lady whose influence I can see very clearly in the lives of my Father and my Aunt and I feel sure much of what she stood for has been handed down.

The view from Chosen Hill, looking out over The Cotswolds where Mabel grew up

---

[99] Miriam Carter, a leading Quaker in Birmingham and a lady we often visited as children in her house in Witherford Way.

Mabel Cash Barlow

The last picture of Granny Barlow in 1956, the year she died, as I remember her

Ellen Barber

**Ellen Eyre in 1900 aged 21 at the time of her marriage to William Ernest Barber
"Her eyes could fetch ducks off the water" said young Mr Barber**

Chapter 17
The Barbers and Eyres

We will now leave the Barlows for a while, to examine my Mother's family origins more closely. My Mother, Joan Barber, was born in June 1914, the youngest of four children of William and Ellen Barber, then living in Bournville. Both her parents - her Mother's family the Eyres and her Father's family the Barber's - were from very humble backgrounds and distinctly on the wrong side of poverty. My Mother's sister, Aunt Winifred talking in later life of her Mother said:

"My mother had a very hard life. Her parents had died when she was young and soon after she married my father, they found out that he had a weak heart. It was an awful blow to her that he wasn't strong but I never heard her grumble. No Insurance Company would insure father because of this and so we really were quite poor after he died. Mother would never let anyone say that we were, but we were poor. Mother used to take in paying guests to earn extra money." [100]

But my maternal grandmother, known to us as Granny Barber, was a very ambitious lady, determined that her children should better themselves and not remain in this same poverty that she had been born into. Indeed within a very short time, not only did her own children do well, going to good schools, but they married well and their children continued to prosper. I made brief mention in Chapter 14 of the Cadbury influence, and how Quaker philosophy and generosity had helped to raise my Grandmother out of poverty. But it is worth emphasising the huge social mobility that this demonstrates for within only a hundred years, her great hopes for her family had been vindicated, when as mentioned in Chapter 14, not only was her grandson, Michael Rutter knighted in 1992 for services to psychiatry but my elder brother David, acceded to one of the top positions at the BBC. How proud she would have been.

My Grandmother wrote her maiden name as 'Eyre', which was more relevant than it might initially appear, when it came to tracing her forebears. She and her siblings had been left as orphans, when first her Mother, Susannah (née Amos) died in childbirth in 1883, and then her Father, William died in a terrible industrial accident only two years later. Their family background had been difficult to unravel, and it was only with the help of a professional genealogist Anthony Adolph[101], that her background was eventually revealed. Much of the difficulty of tracing their name, was due in no small measure to the illiteracy that was still pervasive amongst the nineteenth century poor. But also, the spellings were still fairly fluid at this period, and the name Eyre appears in many different forms, from Hair or Hare to Ayre and Eyre. And so it was that my Grandmother's paternal Grandfather, named John, was eventually tracked down under the spelling of Hair, not Eyre at all. Little wonder, my own attempts met a buffer!

Great, great Grandfather John Hair (1825-1895) was born in Overseal, a town then in Leicestershire, but which was later to come under the aegis of Derbyshire. He was registered as a 'labourer' and sometime about 1845 he married Martha Upton (1833 – 1889) from Horton Street in nearby Darlaston in the Black Country. They had a large family of at least eight children, the eldest, Thomas, being also born in Overseal in 1846, followed by Hannah in 1851 and then William in 1854 who, along with the rest of the family (Alice, Ann, Joseph and Barnabas) were all Darlaston born. William Hair is discovered in the register initially as Mr W Hair then, a few years later as Mr W Ayre and only finally as Mr William Eyre.

---

[100] From 'The Life and Times of Llewellyn and Winifred Rutter' in interviews with Michael and Marjorie Rutter 1997
[101] Anthony Adolph is a consultant on 'Who Do You Think You Are?' on BBC Television.

Quite what brought about this change, is difficult to say, but in the History of British Surnames[102], it states that this old Derbyshire name was, *'from very ancient times, often listed as variously as Le Here, Le Heyr, Le Eyr and finally just Eyre, without the French prefix'*. Oddly enough, many of the male members of families with this surname, had been christened William!

My Mother thought that her Grandfather, William had possibly got his first job with the Hydraulic manufacturing business, 'James Tangye and Bros', in Mount Street, Birmingham, founded by the Quaker family of Tangye[103] - Richard and his brothers James and Joseph - in March 1857. Richard Tangye had been a pupil at Sidcot School, one of the oldest Quaker Schools in the country, though the present school was only built in 1808. Whether there was truth in that, I cannot ascertain, but I do know that in later in life William worked at the Jones' Iron Foundry in Regent Street, Darlaston and by 1874 he had met a young seventeen year old girl, Susannah Amos, the daughter of a miner, John Amos and his wife Mary, also from Darlaston, whom he married at St Peter's Church in Walsall in 1874.

Granny Barber, however, wished to move on, and in later life, she hardly mentioned her brothers and sisters, and even though her elder sister Emily, was to be her bridesmaid in 1900, the family more or less disappear from her story after that. The truth is, however, that Ellen Eyre was the second of five children born to William and Susannah. Her elder sister, Emily was born in 1875, followed by Ellen herself in 1877, then William Joseph in 1880, James Alfred in 1882 and finally Susannah in 1883. But this is where tragedy intervenes, as sadly their Mother died in childbirth with Susannah, with pelvic cellutisis, an infection of the uterus, and though the baby lived, she too was to die only two years later. Worse was to follow, as only two years after the death of his wife and child, William died as well, aged just 30, in an explosion at Jones, Ironmasters, who had by then moved to Walsall. The rather gruesome details of this were recorded in the Tamworth Herald of July[104] 18 1885.

The Tamworth Herald, July 18 1885

SERIOUS DYNAMITE EXPLOSION

William Ayre (30) labourer, of St Patrick's Square, Short Acre, has been killed along with John Agers, another labourer, being dreadfully injured by an explosion of Dynamite at the works of Messrs Jones, ironmasters, the Birchills, Walsall. The two men were engaged in blowing to pieces an old 'bear' of iron which had been discovered in the earth. They had drilled a hole in the metal and charged it with dynamite, when the latter, from some cause unknown, exploded and the two men were riddled with fragments of the metal, one of which completely passed through Ayre, destroying his eyes. When others arrived Ayre was already dead, though Agers was alive and taken to the Cottage Hospital.

This left the five children orphans, with the girls being taken in by Crowley's Orphanage for Poor Girls in Edgbaston[105] and the boys, William and James, going to Josiah Mason's Orphanage in Erdington[106], (photo overleaf) though by 1891 James turns up living in Walsall, having been adopted by the family of John and Ann Causer.

---

[102] The History of British Surnames by Richard McKinley 1990
[103] Richard Tangye's niece Helena married Francis William Lean, whose son was the film Director David Lean, at Leighton Park with my Father.
[104] The Tamworth Herald, July 18 1885
[105] Founded by Thomas Crowley in 1871, who was a Quaker and the father of Aleister Crowley.
[106] Mason's orphanage was built in 1869 by Josiah Mason, the Birmingham philanthropist who had made his fortune in pen Nibs and invented EPNS, itself an anagram of Pens! The orphanage opened in 1871.

Sir Josiah Mason and his Orphanage

SIR JOSIAH MASON'S ORPHANAGE AND PLAYING FIELDS.

SIR JOSIAH MASON.

Entered at Stationer's Hall.] [H. Penn, Photographer to THE QUEEN, 8, Cannon-st., Birmingham.

Sir Josiah Mason, maker of pens and pioneer of Electroplating, leading him to the acronym EPNS.

The Author writes:

Josiah Mason made his fortune from making pen nibs in central Birmingham, and then gave most of his fortune to building and running an Orphanage in Erdington in North Birmingham. It was a massive building and could house nearly 400 children and included a school that was one of the best in the area. It opened in 1868 eventually closing nearly a hundred years later in 1964 to make way for new housing. This is where Ellen Eyre's two brothers William and James went after 1885, when their Father died in an industrial explosion and as their Mother, Susannah had died in childbirth two years' earlier, they were left homeless.

Ellen and her elder sister were taken in by Crowley's Orphanage in Icknield Street in Birmingham's Jewellery Quarter. This was founded by Thomas Crowley, a Quaker timber merchant in 1871. Smaller than Mason's, it was renowned for how it cared for its children.

© Reproduced by kind permission of the National Portrait gallery

Crowley's Orphanage for Poor Girls, was established using funds from the estate of Thomas Crowley, after his death in 1869. Born in 1799, Thomas Crowley, a Quaker, was a local timber merchant, who had prospered and in his will endowed an orphanage, which opened only two years after his death, on 25 March 1871 at Icknield House, in old Icknield Street in the Jewellery Quarter of Birmingham. A Ladies' Committee was formed to oversee the daily running of the orphanage and the first minute book of this Committee, records the aims of the orphanage, in which it will noted, their charity only extends to those born legitimately!

"Firstly, the spirit of the charity is to maintain and educate poor orphan girls, who were born in wedlock, and who have lost both parents: and afterwards to place them out in situations where they may maintain themselves. The education shall be specially directed to the perpetuation of the girls for domestic services, including plain sewing. Girls are accepted into the orphanage between the ages of 6 and 13 and the person who nominated them for admission was to provide a set of clothing. In 1889 and 1894 funds provided by the estate of Mr. William Middlemore were used to purchase property at 43 and 45 Lee Crescent where a new orphanage was created."

In 1940, the orphanage at Lee Crescent was evacuated because of the proximity of the bombing and all the girls from the Orphanage, were transferred to other institutions, including the Blue Coat School and the Middlemore Homes. The Orphanage did not re-open after the war and in 1948 the funds of the charity were transferred on to the Middlemore Homes. Eventually the whole Orphanage was converted into flats by the Middlemore Homes, and opened in 1957 as a residential centre, for families in need of 'temporary accommodation and rehabilitation', and coincidentally, my Mother Joan was, many years after, on the Committee of the Middlemore Homes for several years.

This connection with The Middlemore Homes, maybe the reason my Mother was under the impression that her Uncle William had been sent to Australia, under one of the many schemes set up by John Middlemore, to give such children a better life there. But I have found no evidence for this. In fact quite the contrary, as I discovered William settled happily in Darlaston, where, as we shall see later, he ends up marrying twice. What is more of a mystery though, is why none of their immediate family helped out, rather than let the children go into an Orphanage. William's parents John and Martha Hair were still only in their 60s and didn't die until 1895 and 1889 respectively; William's many brothers and sisters, who all lived in Darlaston, were young and had homes; indeed Susannah's parents, John and Mary Amos lived till 1901. For some reason none of them helped out in looking after the orphaned children. Maybe, with growing families, they had no spare room, or there were family rifts. Who knows? An unsolvable mystery. But counter-intuitively, by going to a caring Orphanage, she and her sister, possibly did better than they would have done living with impoverished family members, as will soon become apparent.

Returning to Great Grandfather William, it is interesting to note that Tangye's, being a Quaker firm, had offered George Cadbury a great deal of engineering and practical building help in the initial construction of Bournville, so 'by indirect and crooked ways,' it is possible to speculate that my great Grandfather might have been involved in the building of the houses, in which his daughters Ellen and Emily, later eventually came to live! On firmer ground, however, the later Quaker influence was direct and very specific, for at some point in their early childhood, Emmeline Wilson, a member of the Quaker family, the Edward Wilson's, used to visit the Orphanage and take the children on days out into the country and these visits were often to a farm in Coleshill near Meriden, very close to where my youngest brother, Nicholas now lives with his family and where she met a young William Barber who was probably moonlighting, earning a few extra bob as a farm hand, possibly on a farm where one of his Uncle's worked.

Grandfather, William Ernest Barber

William Ernest Barber c.1899

When my Grandmother and her sister finished at the Orphanage, she turns up in the 1891 census, aged 16 at the Training Home for servants at 66 and 67 Summerhill Road, Birmingham. Quite how long she spent there I am not certain, but on completion of the training, probably around 1892, she and her sister began working as live-in-maids at adjacent addresses, 42 and 43 Frederick Road in well-to-do Edgbaston, the home of the Quaker family of Walter and Agnes Barrow, members of the family that owned the big grocery store on the corner of Bull Street and Corporation Street in Birmingham, known as Barrow's Stores. Their cousins, Geraldine and Barrow Cadbury, also by coincidence, first cousins of my paternal Grandmother Mabel, were on the Board of the Orphanage, so I presume that they helped to find a place for my Granny and her sister to work.

When John Cadbury first expanded his chocolate manufacturing in the 1850's he passed the retail side of the original tea and coffee warehouse in the centre of Birmingham, to his nephew Richard Cadbury Barrow and as Barrow's Stores, they continued to flourish as a shop for general provisions, first in Bull Street and then, following the redevelopment of the City centre, on the corner of Bull Street and Corporation street until the 1960's. They were so much part of my childhood; how well I remember the Barrow's rep visiting us on a Tuesday to take our order and then on a Thursday, the big blue Barrow's vans arriving with their wicker baskets piled high on the roof, to bring our weeks' stores. Walter Barrow was the family and company's Solicitor and also Vice Chancellor of Birmingham University, so it was a good family to be working for and I suspect that Emmeline had quite a lot to do with organising for my Grandmother and her sister to obtain such posts and lodgings.

Emmeline continued to keep an eye on them both and undoubtedly helped to encourage the friendship my grandmother had formed with William Barber, for by 1899 when she was 21 and he was 24, they had become engaged and were subsequently married in September 1900 at the Congregational Chapel in Frances Road, Edgbaston, now no longer there. And as Emmeline Wilson was a guest at the wedding, it is not difficult to surmise that she had certainly had a helping hand in the process, for not long afterwards Ellen became a Quaker!

Of Granny Ellen's siblings, her sister Emily – or Aunt Em as she was known - married John Patrick Wylde and they lived at 94 Gristhorpe Road in Selly Oak not far from where Ellen and William ended up living at 124 in the 1920's. They had three children, Leslie, a handsome man according to my Mother and very musical, as well as Rowland and Thelma. My Mother writes that she was 'never very close to them as they were older than I was' but she also said that Granny Barber often told her 'not to bother to keep in touch with my sister and family', indeed she didn't appear to want to keep in touch with any of her siblings. This was, I suspect all part of her fairly ruthless plan to reinvent herself; by cutting off her past there would be no record of her humble origins.

Another sibling of my Grandmother's, William Joseph Eyre (b1880), far from moving to Australia, as hearsay would have had it, married twice, firstly a Harriet Wilday in 1906, who was also an orphan and whom he had met at Sir Josiah Mason's Orphanage, from which there were two children, William born 1907 and Daisy Lois born in 1909. Sadly, Harriet died about 1910, and in 1916 William remarried a Florence Kimberley and they had several more children, two of whom, John 1918 and Harry Leslie 1920 sadly died at birth; Marguerite born in 1919 died at the age of 10 in 1929, and only Olga, born in 1926 survived, dying eventually in 1970 aged 44.

James Alfred Eyre
Ellen Eyre's brother

James Alfred Eyre/Ayre/Hair b.1882.

Finally, her youngest brother, James Alfred Eyre, (see the only known photograph of one of my Grandmother's siblings[107]) then aged 39, married Alice King (née Baker) in 1921, a widow at a Registry Office in Walsall[108]

By his marriage to Alice he had one child, Ellen, who according to her Granddaughter, Pauline Lines, was named after James Alfred's sister, my Grandmother, Ellen Eyre. If this is true and I see no reason why it should not be, it suggests that possibly Granny and her siblings were a deal closer than some family legends would have one believe. James apparently told his daughter that he was the Manager of the Deepmore Colliery, but on the Census form he is listed simply as a miner, and I would think it more likely that he was a workaday Collier. The Deepmore Colliery was one of the many coal mines dotted around the area that contributed to that part of the Midlands being known as the Black Country.

The Barber family into which my maternal Grandfather, married in 1900 also came from a relatively poor background. William Ernest Barber was born in 1875 the son of James Barber (b.1827), a lowly warehouseman and his wife Thirza[109], (b.1836) who was the daughter of Edward and Sarah Dudley from Tipton in Staffordshire. Both his parents were illiterate as the marriage certificate is signed with a cross by both husband and wife. James' father had been an agricultural labourer when he married Thirza Dudley in about 1856 in Tipton[110] Parish Church in the heart of the Black Country, though by the time of the birth of their youngest child, William in 1875, James was a grocer's porter or Warehouseman. After they were married, they went to live in Blythe Road in Coleshill which crosses the river Blyth, where their six children - four boys, Edward, Albert and William, and two girls, Sarah and Lydia - were all born. James may well have changed from being a labourer to that of a grocer's boy for more money in order to look after his large family. It is noteworthy that on the 1891 census many of the family are still living in the same house in Blyth Road probably to save money, as well as to help with the finances.

My Mother used to tell me that she well recalled her father's eldest brother Edward, or Uncle Ted as he was known, living only a few doors away in Bournville at 21 Willow Road, when they lived at No 1, with his wife Annie and their four girls, Phoebe, Jessie, Elsie and Ellen. She also recounted how her Mother had said, that if it hadn't been for Ted, she didn't know how they would have managed, as her husband William often gambled the money away. But as my Mother was born in 1914 and therefore, only a child at the time, it would appear that she actually remembered incorrectly, as it wasn't her Uncle Ted who lived at 21 at all, but her Father's brother, Uncle James Barber with his wife Annie and the four girls! This was unusual for my Mother, whose memory was usually excellent.

It is, of course, possible that despite him not living opposite, it was nonetheless Uncle Ted who helped them out financially. In fact he lived with his wife, the widow, Mary Smith and their three step children in Coventry Road, Coleshill! But as Edward was nearly 50 by the time he married in 1907, maybe being the eldest and not marrying earlier, he was better placed than the other brothers with their large families, to help out in money matters. Another mystery that is probably unresolvable!

---

[107] Photograph provided by courtesy of James Alfred's Granddaughter, Pauline Lines.
[108] She had three children by her first husband, Thomas King – Thomas, Leonard and Alice
[109] Tirzah (my delight) found in the Book of Numbers, was the origin of the name Thirza, the name of Abel's
    wife in Solomon Gessner's idyll of the *Death of Abel*, a great favourite among the poorer classes in England.
[110] Tipton is between Wolverhampton and Birmingham

Barrow's Stores and Black Country pits

Young Ellen Eyre was found a home in the Edgbaston house of Walter Barrow of Barrow's stores

Deepmore Colliery in the Black Country, where Ellen's brother Alfred was a miner.

The Hair/Eyre family seemed to have all worked in the colliery business, whereas all the Barber boys went into printing. My Grandfather, William, I believe worked with a company called The Birmingham Print Works, eventually becoming a Master Printer. I suspect that the company may have been in the Coleshill district, as they were then living in that area as printers and wouldn't have wanted to travel too far for their work, in those days.

When William and Ellen married in 1900 they went to live first in Smethwick in Weston Road, where the first child Dorothy May was born in 1901. Dorothy was always known as Bobby, because as my mother told me, she found her surname Barber, difficult to say and it came out as Barbie or familiarly Bobby! A few years later they had moved round the corner to Three Shires Oak Road, where Winifred Olive (known as Win) was born in 1904. In later years, with a sense of having moved up in the world, Win never cared to be reminded that she had been born in Smethwick, which she considered to be rather working class! By 1906 when William Reginald (known as Reg) was born, they had moved back to Coleshill, possibly to be near the rest of the Barber family. Then for some reason, whether because times were hard and they decided they couldn't afford more than three children; or maybe because there were some miscarriages, they didn't have any more children for eight years.

It may of course, also have had something to do with the fact, that they discovered that Grandfather Barber had a valvular disease of the heart, from which he was later to die in 1922; or possibly, as already mentioned, Grandfather was gambling large amounts of his money away. Whatever the reason, sometime between Reg's birth and my mother Joan Mary's birth in 1914, they had moved to 1 Willow Road, Bournville, as also had William Barber's brother, James Albert to number 21, and here again we can sense the help of Emmeline Wilson. So maybe things were looking up, and another child seemed alright, or perhaps it was just one of 'those accidents'! Before too long, perhaps because they needed a bigger house with an extra child, around 1917/18, they moved off the Bournville Estate, not far away to 124 Gristhorpe Road, Selly Oak, followed a few years later in 1924/25 by Granny's sister Emily, who moved to No 94, with her husband, John Patrick Wylde, whom she had married in 1902 and their three children.

My Grandfather died in 1922 which must have been a terrible shock for Granny with four children and no insurance or pension and hence no income. My Mother, who was only 7 when he died, told me she was taken out for the day by her eldest sister Bobby, so that she wouldn't be unduly upset and she never subsequently recalled much about her Father. It meant that all of the children had to start earning money as soon as they were able, in order to keep the family.

Interestingly my Aunt Win, recalling her childhood to her son Michael[111], said that:

"We had a resident maid right up to the time Father died, though goodness knows how they could afford it, but most people did in those days. Her name was Dora and she had a bit of a lisp, which I found peculiar." Winifred also recalls that they had a piano, writing *"that entertainment in those days was very much home-made, and my sister Bobby used to play the piano, which she was always very good at. We used to bring our friends over for tea and we would all group round the piano singing."*

I am led to speculate whether some benefit from a Quaker Trust was perhaps helping them out. When they were living in Smethwick and Coleshill, the elder children must have gone to local schools in the area, but later, when they moved to Bournville, my Mother went to Bournville Infants School, and was taught by Miss Hilda Pumphrey, the same Headmistress who had been there since it opened in 1910, and which is illustrated in the photograph on page 75.

---

[111] Life and Times of Llewellyn and Winifred Rutter 1995/6

The Barber family

Grandfather, William Ernest Barber and Granny Barber with their eldest three children c. 1908 all dressed up!: l to r: Winifred aged 4, Reginald aged 2 and Dorothy aged 7. My mother Joan was not born till 1914.

As they grew up, Quaker assistance continued to help Ellen's children as Win, Reg and later my Mother, Joan all went to the Quaker boarding school Sibford, near Banbury in Oxfordshire. Their eldest child Bobby, didn't want to go away, telling her Mother she would run a way if she was sent, so in the end it was thought better not to, if she was likely to be unhappy. But the rest of the children did, and after an initial period, seemed to have settled in very well.

Win's memories are again telling, as she recounts how to begin with, as it was her first time away from home, she was quite unhappy and the matron *"sensed that I was unhappy and used to come and sit on my bed and put my hair in curlers, something that I would have never have done at home. Actually, it was quite uncomfortable to sleep with my hair like that, but she thought it would make me happy."*

In another story concerning her first impressions, she remembered: *"Soon after I started at Sibford, a prefect asked me to put her bath water on. I thought it was a most peculiar thing to ask me to do and I said: 'Why? Have you got something wrong with your hands?' She said 'You cocky little new kid'. But I certainly didn't go and put her bath water on! I had never come across anything like that before and I found it all very different and I was very miserable for the first few weeks, but after that I was happy."* Win always had a great sense of humour and told a good story. My Mother also told me that she had been happy there, but in one letter home to her Mother she did reveal one glaring omission, confessing how she *"greatly missed not having mint sauce!"*

When their father died in 1922 the family had to rally round. Win again: *"We were a close knit family, perhaps because Father died young. I remember a cousin telling my brother Reg, after Father had died, that he was now the head of the family. I thought that was a bit hard on him because he was only 14 and it suggested that he had a load to carry. But Reg took it well and was always very good."*

After William died, Ellen longed to move back onto the Bournville Estate, and helped again by the Wilsons, they eventually moved to number 47 Witherford Way with the children, which was a big enough house for her to take in lodgers, usually from Woodbrooke College, the other side of the Bristol Road, which greatly supplemented the income. It is an interesting phenomenon, that unlike most people today, my Mother was born, went to school, married and lived within a very small area of South West Birmingham. Born in Willow Road, Bournville to the West of the village Green, she moved half a mile further East to Linden Road when she first married, overlooking the Green; then after the war to Swarthmore Road, in middle age on to a larger family house in Weoley Hill, the other side of the Bristol Road; then when the children had left home, they moved back again to Acacia Road in Bournville, and finally after Dad died, Mum moved to a bungalow in Westholme Croft, which was itself only a short distance again from Bournville Green!

I am not going to go extensively into the lives of my Uncle's and Aunt's families, outline details of which can be found at the end of this book, but it is important to give them some space, because we were a very close family group, with Granny as the physical and emotional centre. We constantly visited each other's families, often went to stay with each other as we grew up, and many of the cousins went to the same Quaker schools together.

Once our Grandmother's children had left school, from necessity, they soon set about obtaining jobs, so that they could help with the family finances. The eldest, Bobby got a job over in Erdington and moved into digs there, where she was soon to meet Leslie Hazel of the well-known firm of Sutton Coldfield undertakers. My Mother would often amuse us by telling how Uncle Les had driven over to Witherford Way, in order to ask my Grandmother's permission to marry her daughter.

Joan Barber

Joan Barber aged 5 in 1919

Coming straight from work, however he arrived of course, in the company car, which was inevitably a hearse. He proceeded to park in the road outside Gran's house, which caused some consternation in Witherford Way and didn't initially amuse his prospective Mother-in-law very much! But matters were smoothed over and Bobs and Les married in 1930, setting up home in Sutton, where they remained all their working life. Their eldest child, Barbara[112] was born in 1931 and then they adopted Susan in 1942. We used to visit them frequently, and I remember that they used to keep pigs for a time, and we would often take food scraps over for them. Both Uncle Les and Aunty Bobby had a great sense of fun and we always enjoyed visiting them. Les in particular was a great comedian and always made us children laugh with his jokes and old Black Country stories about Enoch, though I'm afraid we probably made fun of his broad Brummy accent! In 1962 they retired to Sheldon in Devon, near to where Sue and her husband Clive Boyce lived, but tragically Bobby died in 1965 from lung cancer. Les stayed living there until he died in 1976 and Sue and Clive still live at New Barn Farm in Shillingford St George, near Exeter.

Winifred, like my Mother went for secretarial training, though she didn't really enjoy it very much and later took a job as a librarian for a while, but as this involved staying out late, often until 9.0 o'clock in the evening, her Mother wasn't too keen for her to continue, so she gave that up too. But a little while after this, having decided that what she would most like to do was to work at Cadbury's, she set about it in a typically forthright manner, which she describes in her own inimitable style:

"I had met Mr Cadbury at Quaker Meeting,[113] so I stopped him one day, when Mother was away on holiday with Joan, and asked him if he could find me a job in one of his offices, saying that I was very good at figures. He said 'What would your Mother think about this?' I said 'I don't know, I haven't asked her, but it is what I want to do.' He said 'When your Mother comes back from holiday, I'll go and see her.' So when Mother came back from Llandudno, he came round with his chauffeur and had a cup of tea and discussed whether I should go to his works or not. Mother said 'If Winifred wants to do that, I'll certainly back her.' So he asked what kind of work I could do. Because I had said I was very good with figures, he thought that the men's wages office might be a very good place and that's how I first got to work at Cadbury's!'"

Both Winifred and Reg were keen sports players, especially hockey, often playing with their good friends, the local Holding children,[114] whose family were builders on the Bournville Estate. They were all sports mad, which is how she came to meet the young trainee Dr Llewellyn Rutter, the son of the eminent Quaker, Dr Hubert Rutter. They married in 1932 and took up a post at the Quaker Hospital in Brummana in the Lebanon, moving there immediately after the wedding, without a honeymoon, as they were required to begin work straight away!

The two eldest children, Michael and Priscilla were born out there in in 1933 and 1935 and during their four years there, all the members of their close family visited them including Granny. My Mother visited twice, becoming involved with a young man there named Eddie Rizak, to whom she was nearly engaged. As she was already nearly engaged to my Father, however, wiser heads prevailed, which is just as well, as otherwise I wouldn't be telling this tale!

---

[112] Barbara married Scott Stuart, a sports equipment manufacturer and they had had two boys, Matthew and Robert.
113 This would have been George Cadbury junior at Bournville Meeting House. So they must have started going to Quaker Meeting soon after they moved to Bournville in 1917. Win says she was 15, so that would have been 1919.
[114] The Holding family owned a large building company in Bournville and were all friendly with the family and we children grew up with their children, who were all very sporty and competitive.

Willow Road, Bournville,

No 1 Willow Road today where Joan was born

Joan aged 3 and her brother Reg aged 10 in 1917

Win and Llew returned to this country and bought a practice in Lea Road, Wolverhampton where they lived for many years[115] and where the two younger children George and Richard were born in 1942 and 1945. In 1940 Win and Llew took the difficult decision that Mike and Prill should go to live in America, as there seemed to be a real possibility that this country would be invaded. They went to live with a Quaker family called the Rhoads, who were friends of a family they had known in the Lebanon, the Nickoleys. As mentioned in the previous chapter, my Mother stayed for a while with Honor and Christopher Cadbury, out at Beaconwood in the Lickey Hills, where I was born, but for two years from 1942 to 1944, she and my elder brother David and I lived with Win and Llew, together with Granny, in the house in Lea Road, Wolverhampton, that Win and Llew had had built for their home and surgery. My Father had joined the Friend's Ambulance Unit and was away abroad for the duration. It was an immensely difficult time for all, as most were not in their own home; news was hard to come by concerning the children in America, or my Father either in India, China or North Africa; and Win and Llew had to cope with others living with them and it is worth repeating what a tribute it is to both my Uncle and Aunt, that everyone managed to get on with each other.

But somehow we all did manage and grew up very fond of each other. David and I and Win and Llew's younger two children, George and Richard all went to the Quaker prep school, The Downs in Colwall, near Malvern and then later on to Leighton Park School in Reading. Mike and Priscilla went to the Quaker schools in York, Bootham and The Mount. Mike became one of the leading child psychiatrists of his generation working at the Maudsley Hospital in South London. Prill married George Sidrak and moved to Jamaica where both she and George taught physics and mathematics; George became head of Physics at Eton and Richard worked very successfully for a variety of leading companies.

Reg, Granny's only boy, left Sibford when he was 16 in 1922, and he too started working at Cadbury's. His younger son Christopher Barber,[116] later told me that the firm had paid for his Father to go to Manchester University to study Economics, where he stayed at Dalton Hall, the same hall of residence as I was later to go to in 1962. Unfortunately, Reg wasn't finally able to get a degree, as at that time, Cadbury's were only able to finance him for two years and his Mother couldn't afford to supplement the fees. But Reg continued to work for the firm for the rest of his life, first as Sales Rep, based in Canterbury, where they moved to after he married Vera Lunt in 1935, and where they lived for the rest of their married lives, with the two boys Graham and Christopher being born there. By the time he retired, although he was eventually made Export Manager for Cadbury/Fry's in London, Reg often surmised that his decision to go into the Airforce during the war, rather than the FAU, prejudiced his promotion at Cadbury's. The two boys both went to Canterbury's famous King's School, with Graham becoming a pilot for British Airways and Christopher going into Banking.

Uncle Reg was perhaps our favourite Uncle, always jolly and full of laughter and inevitably endearing himself to young children, as the bringer of gifts in the shape of special, grand presentation boxes of Cadbury's chocolates, with beautiful designs on the lid. Sometimes we would go and stay in Canterbury, which was a special treat as it seemed such a different City to Birmingham. This seemed - unfairly of course - to be a really historic city with a splendid old Cathedral, surrounded by fine green sward, not stuck on an island in a dirty industrial city like Birmingham! I recall a special holiday when my cousin Susan Hazel and I went to stay in Canterbury and as Graham was away learning to fly, Sue and I and Chris had great fun messing around and generally annoying our Aunt and Uncle, by making too much noise!

---

[115] In 1963 they moved to Nottingham when Llew was made Regional Medical Officer. Granny had lived with them since the war but then moved to the Woodlands, a Quaker home for old people in Northfield, B'ham until she died in 1966.
[116] His eldest son Graham, a pilot with British Airways, died in a plane crash in 1980 in Alaska.

Les Hazel and Dorothy Barber

Dorothy Barber always known as Bobby and her husband Leslie, 'Les' Hazel c. 1945
Photo courtesy of Sue Boyce (née Hazel)

Graham was initially in the RAF and then joined British Airways with whom he flew for many years, before tragically dying in a plane crash in 1979 in the Gulf of Alaska where he was on holiday with his friend, the successful television script writer Ian Mackintosh and his girlfriend Sue Insole[117], researching Ian's next drama. Ian had worked for MI5 and his TV dramas *Warship* and *The Sandbaggers,* had focused on espionage work which had resulted in him being cautioned under the official secrets Act, which he had ignored. Because of the speed with which the accident was hushed up, the lack of an official enquiry, and the haste on the part of British Airways to compensate Vera, I will always remain suspicious as to the nature of the 'accident'. But that's a story for another place.[118] Vera never really fully recovered from Graham's death, especially having already lost Reg at the age of 59, when he died from cancer of the throat in 1965. She sold up the Canterbury home and moved into Graham's house in Hampton where she felt at home, surrounded by memories of him. It was also very difficult for his brother Chris, who had to shoulder filling the gap left by his brother's death. Chris worked for Barclays Bank in Sutton where he still lives with his second wife Cheryl[119].

My Mother left Sibford in 1932 at the age of 18 and then, following secretarial training, worked for three years for the two King Edward's Schools at Five Ways and Camp Hill. She left in 1936 when she married my Father, Ralph at Selly Oak Meeting House, and settled in Bournville, where my Father had taken over as Head of the Bournville Village Trust, in the position his Father had previously held. They had five children, of which more in the next chapter!

The photograph taken in 1950 at the Rutter's house in Wolverhampton, shows the Barber family and their children and grandchildren, gathered around the family centre, our Grandmother, though everyone is looking particularly glum, with not many smiles, and my Cousin Graham, sporting a black eye, for a reason now long forgotten! Perhaps we had all been re-arranged once too often, or just that quite a few, like my Father, just hated having their photographs taken!

Granny Barber remained living with Win and Llew in Wolverhampton and for many years worked part time in Hatchards book shop, which she enjoyed enormously as she loved reading. Win and Llew were very accommodating and generous and even though Granny helped both to look after the children and about the house, it can't have been easy. But they both attest in Mike's recorded interviews how well she fitted in: *"Granny was very much part of the family and never a problem. She was always very careful not to intrude on us, often saying she would go to bed early 'because she was tired', when she just wanted us to have the evening alone."*

They remained at Lea Road for many years and my Father and one of us children would go over most weekends to Wolverhampton to bring Granny to spend Sunday with us in Bournville. So frequently did we make the journey that I used to think the car would probably be able to find its own way along the Wolverhampton New Road! After a while, Win and Llew moved from Lea Road to a lovely house in Tinnacre Hill on the outskirts of Wolverhampton. Granny was at first reluctant to move, but in the event she did and often said it was the happiest five years of her life as it was such a beautiful place. But then Llew was appointed as Regional Medical Officer, which meant moving to Nottingham and leaving Tinnacre Hill, which after some debate they did in 1963.

---

[117] Sue Insole was the daughter of leading English batsman Doug Insole
[118] Of many unexplained facts, it would be unusual to fly a fixed undercarriage light aircraft over open water and not to have checked the oil pump.
[119] Chris married Bridget first in 1965 and they had 3 children - Katharine, and twins Andrew and Edward

Winifred Barber marries Llewellyn Rutter

QUAKER WEDDING

Mr. Llewellyn C. Rutter and Miss Winifred O. Barber, married on Tuesday at the Friends' Meeting House, Bournville.
[Photo : Midland Press Agency.

Win and Llew's wedding 1932 . Birmingham Post
l to r: Llew's sister Janet, Llew, Win, Pam Cotterill (cousin) and Win's sister Joan

Reg Barber and Vera Lunt

Reg and Vera Barber 1961

'Warship' scriptwriter feared lost in crash

By GUY RAIS

THE eldest daughter of Mr Douglas Insole, the former England cricketer and Test selector; Mr Ian Mackintosh, a television scripwriter whose series included " Warship "; and a British Airways captain are missing, presumed dead, after a plane crash in the Gulf of Alaska.

The Author writes:

"News of the crash that killed my cousin Graham with his friend Ian Mackintosh and his girlfriend Sue Insole in *The Daily Mail* 1979.

There were many inconsistencies in the accounts of what happened, particularly regarding 'running out of oil', an unlikely event for an experienced pilot, and against all correct advice, flying a fixed undercarriage plane over open water, which Graham always told me 'one never did'.

Finally, the hastiness with which the whole affair was hushed up and compensation paid, never added up to me. Ironically, I received a postcard from Graham some days after he died."

144

Granny Barber and her children and Grandchildren

Family gathering of the Barber clan c.1950.
Back Row l. to r. Graham Barber (with Black eye!), David Barlow, Priscilla Rutter.
2nd row: Vera Barber, Christopher Barber, Michael Rutter, Llewellyn Rutter, Ralph Barlow, Barbara Hazel, Leslie Hazel, Susan Hazel.
3rd row: Reg Barber, George Rutter, Richard Rutter (on his knee), Winifred Rutter, Stephen Barlow, Granny Barlow, Antony Barlow, Bobby Hazel, Rosemary Barlow, Joan Barlow

Above - Granny Barber with Win and Llew in 1950s at their home in Wolverhampton

Right – Reg and Vera with their children Graham and Christopher in 1944.

They were very happy to have Granny continue living with them, but she finally decided not to make the move and went instead to live in The Woodlands, a Quaker residential home for the elderly in Wolverhampton, which Llew's Father had helped to establish. It was a very difficult time for her, as both Bobby and then Reg died from cancer in 1965 and she lamented 'Why couldn't I have died instead?' She did settle down, but was never entirely happy there, lamenting I remember, that everyone was so old! Dad continued to bring her over to lunch every Sunday and then every month she would also spend a week in Nottingham. She stayed in The Woodlands for about three years until she died in 1966 at the age of 89. Granny was one of the kindest, most loving and generous of people, who lived for her family and always took an interest in their careers. When we were children she would take us out for a treat and always brought a little present for us. There was nothing she loved more than to hear from us and we all missed her tremendously when she died, especially Mum, who had, as the youngest, perhaps been the closest of the children to her.

Win and Llew remained in Nottingham for about twelve years altogether, until they retired, and after my Father died in 1980, they both came back to live in Bournville to be near my Mother. First they lived in their own flat back in Witherford Way, not far from where she had lived as a child with her mother, and then later they moved to a semi-care home, Queen Mother Court, where they still had some independence. They enjoyed their lives there and were great companions for my Mother with whom they did so much. They would often go around for coffee or sherry mornings, made frequent visits to the Birmingham Repertory Theatre, which they all enjoyed tremendously, were members of the Quaker Book Club, the QQ[120], which circulated a number of books to each member to read each month, and they were keen members of the 'Fifties Club' an old Quaker social group limited to fifty members, which as Llew later remarked said something about the size of the early Quaker houses! Llew lived well into his nineties dying in 2003 and Win died at the great age of 103 in 2007.

Much as I have enormous respect for the many distinguished and eminent members of our old Quaker forebears, from James Lancaster onwards, recounted in this history, I can't help owning to a feeling of wonderment and awe at the sheer courage and determination that brought Granny Barber from being orphaned in the Black Country, and having to work as a servant girl in Birmingham, through to a happy marriage, only to suffer the loss of her husband in early married life, to nonetheless producing four bright children, who took advantage of opportunities offered them, and succeeded beyond their Mother's wildest dreams. This really is some achievement and though one can see clearly a guiding Quaker hand, it owes most to the indomitable spirit of one remarkable lady.

1908

1950s

1965

[120] Quaker Quindecim – 15 Quaker members

Granny Barber

Granny Barber aged about 80 in 1957

Two remarkable headmasters and a Quaker play

Thomas Rogers of KE Camp Hill

Charles Dobinson of KE Five Ways

My Mother dressed as a boy in one of the plays with Selly Oak Friends at The George Cadbury Hall.

Chapter 18
Joan and Ralph - early married life

Joan Barber was not only the youngest child of William and Ellen, but was born nearly eight years after her brother Reg, the next oldest and so in some ways was almost brought up separately. As a result her siblings, particularly Reg were very protective towards her, especially after her Father died from a heart disease when she was only eight years old. Similar to my Father, Ralph whose own Father, John Henry had also died when Ralph was still a young twelve year old schoolboy and who had been looked after at Leighton Park, rather than be allowed to go home to be with his dying parent, my Mother remembers her sister Dorothy, taking her into Birmingham the day her Father died, to distract her from the sadness of the occasion. I don't recall either my Mother or my Father ever talking a great deal about their own Fathers and quite likely at those young ages they didn't recall that much anyway. Although there are several pictures of my father with his parents, I have not come across any pictures of Mum with her Father, but nor on the other hand are there pictures of her with her Mother; in fact apart from a lovely photo of her aged three with her brother Reg, most of the pictures of her as a child, she is on her own.

My Mother went first to Bournville Infants School before going on to the Quaker School, Sibford near Banbury, with the help of a scholarship. After Sibford, she went on to train at a secretarial college and in 1934 got a job working for two remarkable Quaker Headmasters, Charles Dobinson and Tom Rogers of the two King Edward's schools at Five Ways, to the West of the City and Camp Hill, close to the City centre[121] respectively, which I remember her telling me, involved several bus and tram journeys to the City centre[122].

They were both extremely kind to her and took an interest in her life and indeed it says a lot about Joan's nature and gift for friendship that she remained friends with both them all their lives and Mr Dobinson[123] came to her wedding when she married my Father, in 1936. My Mother was a very outgoing person playing tennis and joining the Quaker dramatic society at Woodbrooke College, where she first met my Father. They were in several plays together including 'The Quaker', though my Mother often seemed to get the best reviews!

A review in The Birmingham Post praising the production of 'The Quaker' lauds Miss Joan Barber over Mr Ralph Barlow!

"Miss Joan Barber gave a very polished and accurate portrayal of her role and Mr Frank Westlake too interpreted the part of Nathaniel with sincerity.....Mr Ralph Barlow could, with advantage have put more fire and reckless spirit into his part. He did not completely sink his own personality....Other parts were played by Miriam J Carter, Edwin O Ransome and Hilda B Jenks. Miss Barlow was responsible for the costumes.[124]

My Mother adored the theatre all her life and would, I think, have loved to have been an actress herself. My Father also loved the theatre and wrote many plays for us to enact as children. Some were adaptations of famous books such as Winnie the Pooh, in which as a chubby child, I inevitably ended up being cast as Pooh, and some original pieces such as one, imagining

---

[121] Both schools eventually moved. Camp Hill to King's Heath in 1956 and Five Ways to Bartley Green in 1958.
[122] Joan's Diary memoirs
[123] Mr Dobinson's son Humphrey, was at Leighton Park with David and I
[124] All familiar Quaker names of families we grew up with. The Ransomes, Edwin and Hildah and their children Robert and Dinah, were particularly close friends. Frank Westlake, a local Headmaster and Miriam Carter were close neighbours in Witherford Way and good Quaker friends of my parents. Miss Barlow, was my Father's sister, Millior.

characters on a billboard coming to life! They often took us children to the theatre, especially the old Birmingham Repertory Theatre, then still under its founder Sir Barry Jackson or to what was then known as The Shakespeare Memorial Theatre in Stratford run by Glen Byam Shaw, and they later encouraged me when I decided to go into the theatre.

Although my Mother and Father were already seeing a lot of each other, in fact Joan had a number of boyfriends before my Father, including Allen Maw, whose parents were Quaker missionaries and whose brothers were at school with my Father. I recall my Mother describing one of their first outings together, to see a film at the local cinema, only to find that it was so full, that they were unable to sit together! The relationship didn't develop, but they remained good friends all their lives and I am now close friends with Allen's widow Ruby.

Her next boyfriend was Eddie Rizak, whom she had met in the Lebanon when she went out there with Granny Barber to see her sister Win, after she and Llew moved there to work at the Quaker Hospital in Brummana.

According to Llew:

"Every member of my family and Win's family came out. Joan went out twice" and Win writes, *"Joan had a great time with the boys in the village. Mother felt very responsible for her"*!

This relationship was obviously a bit more serious, as Eddie came over to England in 1935 and she seems to have been quite smitten. However, obviously, she decided to stay with Ralph, with whom, as is perfectly evident from letters she wrote from the Lebanon, she was very much in love. Occasionally she would drop such casual asides as -"If I'd married Eddie, I'd have been very well off!" - a reference to my Father's often precarious struggle with money, but it was to be a supremely happy marriage and one she never regretted. A letter my Mother wrote home from the Lebanon as early as 1933, is admonishing my Father for not having written to her:

'Roisee', Brummana, Lebanon 8.8.33
My dear One
No letter again for nearly a fortnight – have you forsaken me dear? ....It seems such ages, absolutely years since I saw thee[125] *- I do so long to talk to you and see how you are – if you have changed and to hear all about your dear self. It gives me lots of joy to just think about you and picture all you are doing – but it gives me greater happiness to be with you – sharing the same things together and talking over all our little joys and sorrows. I do so long for the time we shall meet – when you will hold me tightly in your arms and kiss me – I want you dearest Ralph. Are you still missing me, I wonder, or am I merely Joan of the past, so to speak, just a memory? It will be so thrilling getting to know one another again. – at least getting to know each other in the flesh as in the spirit. I strongly feel we are 'one'. I marvel at the way we seem bound together and God does guide us my darling.*

A little further on, written three days later:
At last a letter from you – it arrived yesterday, exactly a fortnight since the previous one. Now look here Mr Barlow! I'm beginning to think you are forsaking me, you have written such a short letter and hardly a love letter. I think I must be fading from your thoughts. You just write me a nice long letter next time and tell me all about your thoughts and yourself....Goodbye now my darling own Ralph. God bless thee and keep thee. All loving wishes and constant thoughts.

Ever thine, Joan

---

[125] It's interesting that in several letters of this period, my Mother adopts the Quaker form of address.

My mother's first boy friends

Two of my Mother's first boyfriends before she married my Father.

Eddie Rizak, (left) who my Mother met in the Lebanon on two visits there to join her sister Win and husband Llewellyn in Brummana.

(Right) Allen Maw whom my Mother had known through Quaker circles in Birmingham. His parents, Geoffrey and Mildred Maw were Quaker missionaries in India and Mildred remained a great friend of the family, with Mildred only dying in 1987 at the great age of 102.

The Author writes:
Quite how my Mother arranged for her two suitors to meet and be photographed, I never asked her! Allen subsequently married first a Lebanese lady, Nahia and later Ruby Momber who were both friends of my Mother's and Ruby (now Ruby Maw) is still a great friend of mine.

Joan Barber

Joan Barber at the time of her engagement in 1934

Ralph Barlow

My Father, in the 1930's when he first met my Mother and decided to propose to her.

The Author writes:
"Dad had a birthmark, which his Mother always had removed from his childhood photos, which probably wasn't easy for him at school, but he learnt to live with it and his children came not to notice it either."

None of that sounds as though there was ever anyone else but my Father as far as she was concerned and that everything else was mere flirtation. There is a letter that she wrote to her Mother and sister Bobby from Jerusalem about her time on the boat going out to the Lebanon, which confirms this, where she clearly relishes the attention she has been getting!

American School of Oriental Research
Jerusalem, Palestine

15.5.33
My very dear Mother and All
Thank you so much for your letter. I was thirsting for news from you, especially as I have been in bed feeling wretched as could be. But don't worry, I'm practically myself again now.....

Now for a little back news. I was loathe to leave the dear old ship when we got to Port Said as I had such a wonderful trip and made so many jolly friends.....It's all stamped on my memory so vividly: swimming, dances, walks round the decks, watching the moon and sunsets across the sea, being shown over the ship by the Officers and the whole life in general aboard ship. I so enjoyed being on the Dutch ship...so many nationalities around one and I got thoroughly spoilt. I must say without conceit that I was the centre of attraction and didn't I enjoy it!!....

Dorothy and Edward Cadbury[126] have looked after me admirably – they are dears. Dear love to you all – Bobs and Les and Barbara and a big hug and kiss for you dear Mums. God bless and keep you.

Your loving daughter, Joan

As mentioned in a previous chapter, my Father had been an early pupil at the Quaker preparatory school The Downs in the Malvern Hills before going on to Leighton Park, a Quaker Public school near Reading, schools to which he sent his sons and he was later a long standing member of the Board of Governors at The Downs. He went on to Birmingham University in 1929, as according to him, his Mother thought Oxford or Cambridge were probably dens of iniquity, whereas at Birmingham, he could live at home. He draws attention to this in his wartime memoirs stating how he wished he had been more worldly wise when he joined the FAU! Having read History at Birmingham one of his former masters at LP, Tom Elliott thought he might take up teaching:

"I hear from Duncan that you had thoughts of teaching....this gave me a sudden glow of pleasure. The need in Friend's Schools particularly, for the right sort of man is so great and the opportunities, so vast. I think we are on the eve of a great new era in education with scope for new ideas and enthusiasms. And I think you are exactly the right sort of person, as you have enthusiasms, wide interests and ability. Above all, you know already that schoolmastering is not class room teaching only and that the spirit of man needs fostering and feeding as well as the intellect."

However, although his great friend Duncan Wood did initially go into teaching[127], subsequently indeed at Leighton Park, whatever ideas my Father had himself contemplated of taking up teaching, it was not long after he graduated in 1932, that he decided to join the Bournville Village Trust. Whether his Mother put pressure on him to work there and to follow his Father, I have of course, no means of knowing, but in a letter dated March 16th 1932 engaging him, from Elizabeth Cadbury, who it will be recalled was his Mother's first cousin, she says:

---

[126] Edward and Dorothy Cadbury accompanied her out there and treated her like the daughter they never had.
[127] Duncan later worked for Friends, becoming Head of the Geneva Summer School which I later attended after leaving LP.

Dear Ralph
I reported to the Trustees the conversation which I had yesterday with you and your Mother…and they are very pleased that you would like to come to the Estate Office in the summer.
Affectionately, Cousin Elsie

So I suspect the initiative may well have emanated from the family, but my Father seems happy enough to have acquiesced and by the autumn of '32, on the Trust's initiative and with some additional financing, he is busy travelling through Europe, including a visit to Russia, looking at various housing projects. The engagement letter offers £25 towards the travelling and a remuneration of £1250 for the initial training period under his Father's successor Leonard Appleton. My Father always acknowledged the great help LPA gave him in those early days and often paid tribute to him.

"I began at the Estate Office for the BVT in 1932, latterly as Assistant Secretary to Leonard P Appleton. My debt to him is great; he taught me to work hard and thoroughly; he taught me too what I know of administration; and taught me above all that the man in charge was responsible. Never say 'well it's not my fault'; everything should be known or foreseen. Bournville, I felt had outlived its usefulness and much of its reputation as a housing experiment. We attended housing conferences and meetings but we had less to give. But under LPA the Estate was well run and the assets grew."[128]

It is not quite clear exactly in what year my parents first met, but my Mother's letters quoted above dated 1933, clearly show that they had known each other for a while and they were acting together in plays at The Midland Arts Club in 1934 and 1935. My Father's Mother put up a lot of opposition to the marriage, probably on the grounds that my Mother didn't come from what she would regard as 'Quaker royalty'! But my Father always reassured my Mother by telling her *"to have patience; you'll see, it will be alright in the end."* So some of my Mother's flirtations were, I suspect, to apply gentle pressure on my Father to sort things out. So although by this time there had obviously been an understanding, they were not in fact, formerly engaged until the beginning of 1936.

For a lot of the detail of the early years of their marriage and the period of the war, I am indebted to my Father's memoirs, that he wrote for the benefit of his children and so I shall quote freely from these in the account of this period. They were married in September 1936 at Selly Oak Meeting House which was a big affair with many of my Father's Quaker cousins and his close friend Duncan Wood as his best man and John and Enid's son Roger as a page. My Mother used to say how difficult Enid was over Roger's outfit, which drove her mad!

George Cadbury's son Edward and his wife Dorothy, were particularly kind to my parents. Having no children themselves they treated them and my parents' life-long friends Jeff and Margaret Gillett, as the children they never had and my parents' first house 26 Linden Road, was a wedding gift from them. It was designed by the architect William A Harvey[129] and was a house of character both within and without. As my Father wrote:

"Both dining and drawing rooms were of unusual shape and the view from the windows out over the then open country of the estate and the slopes of Frankley Beeches, was a fine one, with a glorious beech in the foreground. We had bought some nice furniture and we shall not quickly forget the first sight of that house, filled with our own belongings, the sun streaming in through the windows, when we returned from our honeymoon."

---

[128] Ralph's FAU 'Memoirs for his children'.
[129] William Alexander Harvey was the principal architect of the BVT, strongly influenced by the Arts and Crafts movement.

My parents' wedding

My parent's marriage 1936 at Selly Oak Meeting House

The reference to their own belongings, would have included a considerable amount of Brynmawr Furniture, which came from a manufacturing company in Wales, set up by local Quakers to relieve the economic depression in the 1930s. They were designed by Paul Matt, whose Father had worked for Charles Rennie Mackintosh and he was much influenced by the simple lines of the Arts and Crafts movement, that appealed to Quaker philosophy. Many Quaker families, setting up home at this time, bought Brynmawr.

They spent their honeymoon in the Lake District, near Kendal and my Mother's memories of having to negotiate the vertiginous dangers of Striding Edge, was something she never forgot! But they both enjoyed walking and climbing throughout their lives and took us children on many such holidays to Wales, the Lakes and to Switzerland, which we all came to love as much as they did.

My Father, who in later life, often preferred just the company of his family, rather than to be disturbed by visitors, here recalls with fondness, the Keens next door:

"We became very attached to our neighbours, the Keens[130], an elderly couple, whose deep knowledge of books and pictures, of which he had a good collection, fired our interest and we learnt much from Mr Keen. They both played several instruments including the violin and piano and were very fond of musical evenings, but neighbours had strict instructions not to disturb them on such occasions!

The garden was a great joy, rather narrow but long and sloping away from the house. A wilderness when we took it over, we created something which we thought rather beautiful. We grubbed up two big syringa trees from the top of the lawn and with infinite labour made two herbaceous borders. We also made two rose beds where there had been a tangle of pergolas and smaller walks and we made steps down to the lawn and built a wall to provide a proper bed in front of the house. One year petunias were especially successful, another year, yellow antirrhinums. Below the wall and in it we had rock plants which made a brave show from the time that the first aubretia, alyssum and arabis came out.

There was normally colour in the aconites and snowdrops and daffodils round our fruit trees which grew in a grass patch at the bottom of the garden. We always got lovely bowls of flowers from the garden and I shall never feel for any other garden as I felt for this one. Just after the war had broken out I also rented and worked an allotment; there are few satisfactions like growing your own vegetables.

In 1937 we spent our holidays in Galloway. We hired an Austin 7 and drove all the way up there and back – the return journey I remember was 250 miles, which Joan did not enjoy very much as she was expecting David, but it was a lovely coast and I shall always remember the beauty of the flowers along the coast."

My brother, David was born in 1937 in the Linden Road house:

"Poor Joan had a bad time delivering David and I remember sitting up all night, reading a book of American poetry, though I remember little of it now. David was and still is, a great joy to us and his long illness[131] was an enormous worry to me."

---

[130] Dolly and Ernest Keen from whom they bought some astute acquisitions including some Turner prints and a Thomas Collier, now in my possession.
[131] David had Pink Disease, caused by exposure to Mercury, a common component of baby products at this time. David was ill for several months and it sadly affected his fertility in later life.

26 Linden Road, my parents' first home and neighbours

A wedding present from Edward and Dorothy Cadbury.

My Father wrote:

"We had a fine view out over Frankley Beeches and the garden was a great joy to us. I shall never feel for any other garden as I felt for this one."

My Father wrote:

"Our next door neighbours, Dolly and Ernest Keen, whose keen knowledge of books and pictures, fired our interest."

Friends and influences

Leonard P Appleton

Duncan Wood

Horace G Alexander

The Author writes:

"Leonard P Appleton, known as LPA, had succeeded John Henry Barlow at the BVT and as my Father recounts: *'My debt to him is great.'*

Duncan Wood was his great friend from the time they were at The Downs together, where they both had a consuming interest in ornithology, which continued throughout their lives. They were both taken under the wing of Horace Alexander, one of the leading ornithologists of his time.

Horace was also a distinguished and influential Quaker, becoming Ghandi's right hand in the years leading up to independence. Duncan was also my Father's best man at his wedding."

In the early years of their marriage, as my Father writes, they did not have a great circle of friends:

"Both of us had less self-confidence then than we have now. But there were Duncan Wood[132] and Horace Alexander[133]; friends of Joan's, the Cortas's from Syria and others from Woodbrooke, who stayed with us, and Frank Westlake. There was also a couple in charge of a refugee hostel in Maple Road, of whom we were fond. After we were first married, we had many people in to supper and Joan excelled herself in the provision of excellent and well-served meals. Some of the time we looked after ourselves but we also had then an Austrian girl who was a good cook and a great worker, but quite unprincipled and later still we had a French girl, Suzanne, who was a good Christian, but oh so lazy! Latterly we had a maid called Bertha of only moderate talent! For a while too, Joan's mother lived with us."

Duncan Wood and Horace Alexander were lifelong friends of my Father's, especially through their shared love of birds. Indeed, Duncan's book about Horace's love of ornithology[134] was dedicated for *"Ralph Barlow, my first birdwatching companion"*. Duncan's parents Herbert G (known as HG) and his wife Dorothea, also lived in Linden Road at No 22 and were very influential Quakers, both in thought and deed. HG was Director of Studies at Woodbrooke and his many books on Quakerism and Quaker teachings were and are, highly regarded. Horace joined the staff of Woodbrooke in the early twenties to lecture on International Affairs and eventually succeeded HG as Director of Studies and my Father writes of him in his history of Woodbrooke, typically evoking a memory combining Quakerism and birding!:

"I remember visiting Berlin with Horace to see Corder Catchpool at the Quaker Centre. It was in the course of an ornithological trip to East Prussia shortly before the war (one of the best bird trips I have ever enjoyed) and we wondered if we should get out before the Germans occupied Memel."

HG and Dorothea had four children, Audrey, Duncan, Ross and Margaret, but Duncan was my Father's especial friend and from their school days at The Downs, were very keen birdwatchers. There is a letter from Duncan to my Father dated 1927 which is just signed 'Love From Me' and though I had it authenticated by Duncan's daughter Rachel[135], it could only be from Duncan to my Father, as in five pages, he only discusses how many birds each has seen and is very miffed that my Father has seen a Serin,[136] and he hasn't! Their friendship was a deep and enduring one and it might be appropriate here to quote from a note that Rachel found in her Father's collection, that my Father had sent in 1941 just before Duncan left for China :

"In memory of a friendship which has been one of the best things in my life. In gratitude for this and all that it has meant. In remembrance of so many good times – of laughter and birds and walking. With the most sincere good wishes for the success of your venture. Success which I know you will achieve because you so richly deserve it. With the most sincere and heartfelt prayers for your safety and looking forward eagerly to your return. Whatever may have come by 1943, Joan and I will be overjoyed to see you and there will be a home and welcome for you in our house wherever it may be and whenever you may need it. If there is anything I can do for you, however small, do not hesitate to ask. I shall miss you more than I can say. God bless you. Yours ever Ralph."

---

[132] Duncan Wood was at school with Ralph, both at The Downs and Leighton Park, where their joint interest in Birds began, and later was his best man.

[133] Horace G Alexander (1889-1989) a very influential Quaker, member of the FAU, close friend of Ghandi and Nehru. Also one of the great ornithologists of his generation.

[134] Horace Alexander 1889 to 1989, 'Birds and Binoculars' Sessions of York, 2003

[135] Now Rachel Malloch

[136] Serins are small finches with short stubby bills and forked tails.

It might also be apposite to cite a section of Duncan's Foreword to his own book on Horace:

"Ralph and I met in the early twenties at The Downs School....Horace had been at school there twenty years before us....Every Wednesday afternoon was devoted to a 'hobby' which was compulsory in that you had to choose which branch of Natural History you would study. When I went to The Downs....I had no interest whatever in any branch of natural history...until by chance, I saw a Nuthatch. I had no idea that there existed a bird capable of coming down a tree-trunk head first. I was fascinated...but I needed a true companion who shared my suddenly new-found interest. So at the beginning of the next term Ralph Barlow – bless him - took me on. He was already a budding birdwatcher and recognised that by signing up for birds, we would have the freedom to explore the countryside on our own and unsupervised. We used that freedom productively...thus we began a close partnership in the pursuit of what became a lifelong absorbing interest....and it was our good fortune to be members of the large Quaker community in south Birmingham and thus neighbours of Horace...who invited us two to join him in birdwatching....From then on Horace became our mentor and a much cherished companion in birdwatching expeditions."

After The Downs, they both went to Leighton Park and as he says, were taken under the wing of Horace Alexander who apart from being the *éminence grise* of Quakerism, was undoubtedly the leading ornithologist of his time and started the West Midland Bird Club, with which my brother Nicholas is now very involved. I can also recall many birding outings in our childhood, with my Father and Horace and, as my brother David often remarked, a rare bird, ever hidden to humbler watchers, would always appear for Horace!

"As always birds were my chief hobby – next to gardening! I visited Bittell[137] and Belvide[138] on many occasions often with Horace and Duncan and Celia James[139]. These were both magnificent stretches of water and we saw many rare birds there, in particular it remains in my memory as a place where vast numbers of waterfowl could always be seen in winter. Belvide was a particularly lovely place, a great sheet of water with woods on either side.

The ducks, among them many goosanders, swimming out on the water and vast flocks of lapwing, passing gulls and many leisurely Herons. There were always many bird outings. Every winter we made an expedition to the Severn Estuary to see the great flocks of wild geese; once we went to the Chilterns and had a glorious day seeing Stone Curlew; another memorable expedition was to the moors near Buxton, where we saw nesting Twites, Ring Ousels, Grouse and Blackcock; and twice at least we went down to mid Wales to see Kites. Oh those days of unlimited petrol!"

Before the war my parents enjoyed several holidays abroad including in 1938, when they had a wonderful fortnight in Switzerland, while Granny Barber kindly looked after David. They stayed in Grindelwald, Wengen and Kandersteg, where I also remember going, with my Scout group, to the International Scout Centre, when I was about twelve or thirteen. My Father had told me to look out for Wall Creepers, and I shall never forget seeing these exquisite birds with their bright crimson wings, up in the high mountain area just below the Blüemlisalp and proudly being able to tell my Father, that I had indeed seen them, with photographs to prove it.

---

[137] The Bittell Reservoirs are located in Worcestershire between Barnt Green to the south and Longbridge to the north and famous for their bird life.
[138] Belvide Reservoir Nature Reserve is situated near Brewood, Staffordshire, seven miles north-west of Wolverhampton. H.G. Alexander was largely responsible for putting Belvide on the bird-watching map and the reservoir was soon established as one of the most important ornithological sites in the Midlands. It is now scheduled as a Site of Special Scientific Interest.
[139] Another great birding friend of my Father's.

"Mountains always fascinate me, - writes my Father – with their incredible height and snowy purity. Up in the high Alps we found gentians and soldanellas and I shall never forget Joan's delight at finding them. As always she had an overpowering temptation to pick them and often we had wonderful bowls in our rooms. We walked over from Grindelwald to Wengen and down to Interlaken and then up from there to Kandersteg by train. On our return we had two days in Paris and saw some of the French housing at Suresnes[140] *and we visited the Louvre, a great highlight of our trip.*

In 1939 we attended a Housing Conference in Stockholm, travelling over there in a luxurious boat from Svenska Lloyd[141]. *We were both thrilled with Stockholm, a city beautifully situated and containing so many lovely modern buildings. We shall both of us remember the reception given to members attending the conference in the Town Hall. The beautiful rooms were filled with people in evening dress and the lights glittered on the water outside. The light nights and the wonderfully dressed shop windows also linger in my memory."*

My Father had been to the Baltic twice before, once with Horace to Stockholm when he had gone by boat across the Riga, then by train to East Sweden where they had had a marvellous birding holiday and in 1936, in his early years at the Bournville Village Trust as mentioned, he had been to Leningrad and Moscow as part of his initial training to look at the most recent housing developments there.

"We were intimately concerned with the question of preservation of the countryside. In those years, the BVT acquired and managed large agricultural estates just outside the city. We saw a good deal of and worked closely with the National Trust and we were behind an exhibition on development of the countryside in Birmingham. It was tragic that so much of this effort was to be interrupted by the war. There were also many social problems presented by the huge municipal estates in Birmingham and this was a concern to us. Joan and I worked for a time with little success in a mixed club we started on the Weoley Castle Estate[142]*."*

My parents were at that time very loyal members of Selly Oak Quaker Meeting, with my Father as both Clerk of the Meeting and Chairman of Birmingham Young Friends.

"With Dr Rutter's help, I did a good deal of work for Young Friends. I was also Secretary of the Woodbrooke settlement committee. Initially Joan and I did a lot of pacifist propaganda and generally gave our time to a number of good causes. We read gloomy prognostications in the New Statesman and News Chronicle,[143] *but hoped that our little comfortable world would not be shattered. We could not wholeheartedly disapprove of Munich, because it gave us a year's respite. How little we understood of world politics then and how much more do we now."*

Thus the early years of the marriage had been wonderfully happy and secure; a lovely home and garden, a young son, and a job my Father enjoyed doing; a small group of friends, mostly Quaker whom they had known, often since childhood and pastimes they both relished. Then, as my Father recalls, it all ended:

"Such was our world, when the war came and shattered it; how bitterly we resented its going. Would we have it back now if we could? In essentials, it is all we wanted back, but how different we are now."

---

[140] Suresnes is a housing commune in the western suburbs of Paris.
[141] Svenska Lloyd (Swedish Lloyd), one of Sweden's oldest shipping companies.
[142] A housing estate to the North of Bournville.
[143] A well-known Liberal paper of the time, owned by the Cadbury family which closed, controversially, in 1960.

Chapter 19
Ralph and Joan - the war years

Still drawing on my Father's memoirs, this chapter recounts the difficult years of the war. In some ways the first months of the 'phoney war'[144] meant little change, except that my Mother and brother David, along with Granny Barber, Aunt Win and cousins Michael and Priscilla[145] were all evacuated to 'Birdrop Farm' near Sibford,[146] which belonged to an eccentric couple, a Mr and Mrs Poulter, leaving my Father behind. Many families were evacuated at this time, because of the perceived danger of a German invasion and it was widely considered possible that they would be there for some time. My Mother and Win often used to recount how they had taken vast quantities of belongings with them, including their potted bulbs!

My Father writes:

"My Mother still got petrol for her car at that time, before the days of rationing and I drove them all over there. They shared a dirty, inconvenient, old fashioned farm house with an outside toilet. I later visited them out there some weekends and though I quite enjoyed my weekends in the country, I don't know how they stood it for three months."

The farm was apparently quite primitive and six year old Mike is supposed to have commented to Mr Poulter – "Why have you only got one lavatory? My Father has two!" To which Mr Poulter replied – "Maybe your Father needs two"!

My Uncle John's wife, Enid had been evacuated too and John moved in with my Father along with their Mother, who came to look after them. Dad recounts how:

"The break-up of everything that seemed to matter was shattering. I shall never forget the misery of those weeks, nor the hopelessness of hearing the Prime Minister announce that they were calculating a three years' war."

When the War eventually started, my Father initially joined the Fire Service:

"At the time of Munich[147] I had joined the Auxiliary Fire Service (AFS)[148] and by September 1939 was supposed to be trained. In those last tense days when war was expected and the street lamps started to go out, we were given respirators and tin hats. All that autumn we were on duty three or four nights a week. Comfort increased from the early days when we slept on a bare concrete floor to the time when beds were provided some long time later. We were at a post under Ward's shop on the Green.[149] I remember those early nights when the future seemed utterly and impossibly black and the company hopelessly uncongenial. Later however, I came to enjoy it and a sense of camaraderie grew up. We turned out to various practices in cars that might or might not start. Once early on the telephone rang in the small hours and we all leapt up expecting a call –but it was a wrong number! There were rumours of raids, rumours of everything, but my time at that post and later at another in Raddlebarn Road, were undisturbed by fires.

---

144 The period from September 1939 – April 1940

145 Mike and Priscilla later moved to America in early 1940 to live with a family called Mr and Mrs Rhoades and Joan and Antony and David went to live with the Rutters in Wolverhampton away from the worst of the bombing.

146 Sibford, near Banbury in Oxfordshire. There is a Quaker school there where Win, Reg and Joan had all gone.

147 The Munich Agreement in 1938 signed by Neville Chamberlain conceding the Sudetenland region of Czechoslovakia to Germany. When Adolf Hitler continued his aggression by invading Poland, Britain declared war on Germany on 3 September 1939, and Chamberlain led Britain through the first eight months of the Second World War, prior to Churchill taking over.

148 The Auxiliary Fire Service (AFS) was first formed in 1938 as part of Civil Defence Air raid precautions.

149 Wards was the electrical shop on Bournville Green.

The Friends Ambulance Unit

Leaving South Africa for Egypt 1942 with my Father front right

In January, still not much seemed to be happening in the war and Joan and David returned from Sibford and life became more normal again. We went to Dunster[150] for a week in May. We walked everywhere. The country was unbelievably lovely; the trees all in fresh green with bluebells, primroses and cowslips everywhere. While we were there, Germany invaded the low countries and the calling up of my class was foreshadowed. It was a rude shock in that lovely rural calm. We returned home."

It was not an easy time, as he had begun to enjoy his time in the AFS:

"I came to enjoy the camaraderie of my fellow firemen. They were a mixed lot, mostly working class or clerks, but on acquaintance they were likeable and we had our jobs and our gossip. On one day we had a flower show and were at home to our wives and friends. It was with considerable satisfaction that I won some prizes. At that time I think the AFS was inefficiently organised. There were too many people in responsible positions who had got there because they knew the right man. Many were inefficient and few Station Officers knew how to command. Our own S/O was however a happy exception, he was very keen, very efficient, conscientious and hardworking.

In many ways it was a narrow restricted life and chances of promotion or increased responsibility were very vague but I enjoyed it. I was not initially a leading fireman but I worked hard and was anxious to be promoted and I remember with pride my name going up on the board in charge of the big 700 gallon pump and I remember one day we had to go to a 'do' in Cotteridge Park and I experienced a boyish thrill, driving on it with the bell ringing!"

My parents and David were still living at Linden Road and my Father was able to indulge his other great passion, gardening and cultivating his allotment. Looking back, he wrote:

"I am surprised that I was so satisfied, but I was. I remember, just after the outbreak of war I talked with Joan outside the station and she said that in one way she was glad we had declared war as it was at least decisive but events soon escalated with the disturbing news of Dunkirk[151] and then the air raids. At first came the warnings which got us all out of bed at night and I had to see Joan and David into the cellar that we had adapted. I then bicycled down to the Station and we would stand by for a time and then go home when there was the 'all clear'. In August, raids became worse and the Market Hall[152] was burnt out and though not engaged in that particular fire, my crew was standing by on an adjacent station. A few nights later high explosives and incendiaries were dropped round the centre of the City. The crew I was in went to a fire in Great Charles Street in the centre of Birmingham. We were towing our pump behind an old Austin which would not go properly and I wondered if we should ever get up Suffolk Street (by the Post Office). I remember the glow of the fire against the sky. Eventually we arrived, I ran out our hose and we fought a large fire in a partially gutted factory building. Although we were in no great danger, bits of the glass roof kept falling and on one occasion the full force of the hose was directed into my face when the man holding the branch[153] fell over."

Before long however, official feeling was against conscientious objection and the City Council decided to dismiss the CO's from the Fire Service, including my Father. But for a while, as the Trust were paying him a half salary, he stayed on as a volunteer.

---

[150] Dunster Yarn Market in Somerset, had been a model for the Rest House on Bournville Green

[151] The Dunkirk evacuation, was the evacuation of Allied soldiers from the beaches and harbour of Dunkirk, France, between 27 May and 4 June 1940, because the British, French, and Belgian troops were cut off by the German army during the Battle of Dunkirk.

[152] The Bull Ring Market Hall clock in Birmingham, was completely destroyed in 1940, during a bombing raid.

[153] The purpose of the 'branch' was to provide the velocity at the end of the hose to project the water/foam where it is required.

CITY OF
BIRMINGHAM
A.F.S

AUXILIARY FIRE SERVICE

THIS IS TO CERTIFY THAT

F. R. BARLOW

HAS COMPLETED IN A

SATISFACTORY MANNER A

COURSE OF FIRE TRAINING

9th May 1939.

OFFICER COMMANDING THE
AUXILIARY FIRE SERVICE

My Father writes:
"At the time of Munich I had joined the Auxiliary Service and by 1939 was supposed to be trained." (see left)

As a Quaker, born of many generations, strictly brought up, I could not believe that war could be right........so I eventually officially registered as a CO and joined the FAU."

The Author writes:
Eventually, in early 1940, the City Council dismissed CO's from the AFS and so my Father took the difficult decision to join the FAU in October 1940.

(Below) my Father on leave in 1942, wearing his FAU uniform, with my Mother and David aged 3 and myself aged 1 in the garden at Lea Road, Wolverhampton

Eventually, however, despite being short of personnel, the City decided to get rid of all 'Conchies', but by then my Father had decided that he would definitely apply to join the Friends Ambulance Unit. This though, as he remarks, was "*a cruel blow, having to leave home and part from Joan and David and give up our home and beloved garden.*"

My Father's original decision to register as a Conscientious Objector had not been an easy one, coming as he did from a very old Quaker family. Here my Father writes of the inner struggles he had at this time:

"*My AFS Station Officer, Mr Stacey, and Section Officer Mr Burman, were both very kind and got up a petition, asking that I should be retained. I was very tempted to do so, but Horace (Alexander) persuaded me not to, I think on the whole rightly. I then had a fortnight's break followed by my tribunal. I have never been a very rabid pacifist. I have seen so clearly the belief of most men, that Germany represented a power of evil, which if not stopped, would have dire effects for the world. I realised that hard as it was, this country was bound by treaties to help Poland. I understood and was grateful for the protection from the armed forces and I did not want to shirk or have an easy time. Yet I was a Quaker, born of many generations, strictly brought up and I could not believe that for me, war could be right. I believed war to be so utterly wrong that even though short term results seemed to justify it, it would be very wrong in the long term. So I eventually registered as a CO and I do not regret it.*"

I should expand a little on the circumstances surrounding my birth. As the raids were becoming ever more severe and beginning to worry my Mother, then pregnant with me, and as my Father was about to leave to join the Unit in London, late in 1940 Honor and Christopher Cadbury, kindly asked my Mother, to stay, together with my brother David, at their home 'Beaconwood', in the Lickey Hills near Longbridge, north Birmingham, where it was thought it would be safer for us all, as it was well away from German bombing. So it came about, in one of the hardest winters on record, with snow drifts several feet deep, that in January 1941, I was born. In later life, my Father told me how he had to hire a pair of skis to get up Monument Lane to 'Beaconwood', not knowing sometimes, whether he was progressing up the road or on top of the hedges, so deep was the snow everywhere.

When my Father joined the FAU it was still very much finding its feet. The chief architect of the new Unit was Paul Cadbury, the son of Barrow Cadbury, who was a Trustee of the BVT and became a key figure in the reconstruction of Birmingham after the War[154]. Paul and Arnold Rowntree (both members of the Friends Ambulance Unit during the First World War) re-formed the Unit with the intention of again enabling conscientious objectors to undertake civilian service in a military context.

One of the aims of the Unit was to assist those conscientious objectors who were not members of the Society, and thus less likely to be granted exemption from military service. Paul had been encouraged by Rowntree to set things in motion once again and for vigour, tireless energy and sheer determination to get things done, Paul was the ideal man. Paul wrote a letter to *The Friend*[155] in September 1939 putting forward details of procedure:

"*We are concerned that young Friends and others who wish to undertake civilian service shall be able to do so.....There are a number of our members of military age who wish to give proof that although they register as CO's they have no wish to be exempt...*"

---

[154] 'Birmingham Fifty Years On' by Paul S Cadbury published by the BVT
[155] The Friend archives

Paul Cadbury and Hubert Rutter

The Author writes:
"The person most responsible for the re-formation of the FAU, was Paul Cadbury (left), son of Barrow Cadbury and a Trustee of the BVT."

Paul Cadbury wrote:
"The Unit's purpose is one of actions and not of words. Its aim is to go wherever the need is greatest, and to give disinterested service in the relief of suffering, wherever it may be found."

The Author writes:
"The first volunteers turned up at the Manor Farm in 1940 and were soon receiving lectures in first-aid from Dr Hubert Rutter (below), whose son Dr Llewellyn Rutter, was my Father's brother-in-law, in whose house in Wolverhampton, we lived after 1941."

Not long after that first letter appeared, volunteers began turning up at the Manor Farm[156] to convert Farm buildings into a camp and many local Friends gave invaluable help as well as The Village Trust, led by my Father. This first camp became the model for others that followed and those pioneers began to receive training such as lectures in first-aid from Dr Rutter, who was by then also connected to our family as the Father of his brother-in-law!

As we have seen, the FAU existed in the 1914-18 war, first as the Anglo Belgian Ambulance Unit and then later as the FAU. Training at that time took place at Jordans, the quiet Buckinghamshire village, which as Tegla Davies says[157] is 'the Canterbury of Friends'. It worked on ambulance convoys and ambulance trains with the French and British armies and numbered over a thousand men in France and Belgium. By 1919 it had broken up and by 1939 its members were approaching middle age and had become prominent in politics or in letters, in industry or other professions. There had been occasional reunions and it was at one such in 1938 that under their inspiration, the new FAU was formed. But as Tegla Davies says:

"The new Unit was in many ways different. No doubt those who came together at Manor Farm in 1939, thought they would largely repeat the pattern of the previous war, but that was not to be. France fell and the war spread to the ends of the earth and to the ends of the earth, the Unit took its work. It started off with a short-lived expedition to Finland and Norway. Gradually, in 1941, it gathered strength and confidence and built up work which took in all over eight hundred of its members to see service in twenty-five different countries in Europe, Africa and Asia."

In the front of the FAU Annual report 1939 – 1943, it boldly states its credentials: *"A venture in faith, in the midst of war, in Britain, India and throughout free China,"* and in many respects it was that idealism that imbued those early recruits. My Father records his first memory as a member of the Unit as turning up at Manor Farm, Northfield for the Camp and being introduced to other members gathered round the mess table.

"Anyone who arrived then must think with affection of the people he met there and throughout my time in the Unit I have been glad to think that amongst those potential section leaders were John Burt, Harold Kempster and Duncan Wood. The camp was full of enthusiasm…in fact we were all imbued with the general enthusiasm of those days and the Unit was still very much our unit. At that time the FAU was in a very formative stage and had not by any means resolved in its own mind, if it was to become an efficient relief organisation or whether it wanted to be some sort of religious order."

From the Camp, my Father moved in late 1941 to London, where he was based for a while at Poplar Hospital near the East India Dock Road, helping in the Outpatients Department or Firewatching:

"Regularly every night the warning sounded and we would hear the thunder of the guns and see the bombs falling across the river with the glow, smell and smoke everywhere. The next day I saw the terrible damage, with the ruins still smoking and the tired firemen amid a whole tangle of hose. Then the Air raid casualties would come in and we would help deal with them. Two soldiers, I remember, dead from the 'Ack Ack' battery and a badly wounded Policeman. A poor woman came in to find her husband and we had to tell her that he was dead and I escorted her home. Another time a man came in, badly injured and concussed by bomb splinters and paralysed down one side. I used to dread my turn on duty as he lay bloody and unconscious, snoring dreadfully. Down at the far end the ward wireless was turned up loud, blaring out jazz

---

[156] Manor Farm in Northfield had been lent by Dame Elizabeth Cadbury as an initial camp.
[157] 'The Friends Ambulance Unit' by A Tegla Davies George Allen and Unwin 1947

David and Antony at Wolverhampton 1941-1943

Antony aged 3 months at Beaconwood

David and Antony in Lea Road garden 1943

Granny Barber with Priscilla, Michael and David in 1941

music. Eventually, he died with his wife by his side and the screens around his bed. I was immensely impressed by the courage of the injured and the devotion of the staff."

But after some time in Poplar, he remarks that:

"Curiously we became attached to the district. The wide straight roads. Whitechapel and the East India Dock. The Jewish shops. The rare grimy parks and the streets of Wapping with their towering warehouses. The prospect with its view of the river and the passing ships. It was altogether an odd life but I learnt a lot."

Then in July he was appointed Head of the London Relief Section, based in a cold and inhospitable Hostel behind the London Hospital, which involved long days and being available all hours. My Mother meanwhile, had moved to Wolverhampton with my brother and I to stay with Uncle Llew and Aunty Win. He writes frequently of these difficult times:

"Unit members, like everyone else in this war, know what separation means. Often, although away from home, the husband has the more interesting job, seeing people and getting about, whereas the wife has the harder job of looking after the children and a dull daily round. I saw many relationships grow apart. But Joan was wonderful. She kept her courage, brought the children up marvellously and thank God, we did not grow apart. For a time, I think she thought I was growing away from her, but she was quite mistaken.[158]"

He then goes on to talk about the experience of FAU life:

"I am grateful for the friends I made and the life that existed in the hostel. It gave me something new, something that I might have got had I gone to a University away from home. A chance to talk about everything from books, films and plays to history and religion, Quakerism and war. And what a fantastic world I had to deal with, ranging from homosexuality and birth control to the problems of the war such as protection from gas or the mundanity of beetles in the kitchen. And such a mixture, with Anglicans, Methodists and Quakers from State schools and Public schools; snobs and democrats. And a day might start with my interviewing an Italian refugee, followed by a Quaker Committee meeting at Friends House and ending with supper with two high-ranking BBC officials......I boasted in a letter to Joan, that after the war I felt I could run anything!"

As the year 1941 drew to an end he had to go down to Bournemouth for a high level conference about the future of the Unit and personnel, which by his description, he didn't much enjoy!

"Bournemouth in that dull November weather was a deadly place. An ugly town, ugly cliffs, with a deserted and barbed wire beach. Bournemouth is the most God awful place anyone ever went to. Frightful, nightmarish hotels, pseudo Gothic churches, formal, ugly gardens, and dreadful rows of endless shops. Houses of every style except good – ugly and vulgar. Even the scaffolding and barbed wire along the shore were beautiful by comparison."

As a result, the two parts of the Relief work (FWVRC and CRS[159]) were amalgamated into the Friends War Relief Service and much of my Father's work was handed over to a Committee of Meeting for Sufferings, though neither the Society nor the Unit were entirely happy about the outcome. But the long term result was that he was appointed IC of the Middle East Section

---

[158] He refers to one of the staff in Gordon Square called Angela de Renzi Martin, now Sinclair-Loutit, to whom he was very close and about whom my Father dropped several hints in later life. She herself told me recently (2014) that they had had a 'relationship' but she was to become a close friend of all the family and I stayed with her and her husband, Kenneth in Paris. In 2013 we met up again at the inauguration of the FAU Memorial at the National Memorial Arboretum at Alrewas, Staffs and I arranged for her to talk on the Today programme about her time in the FAU.

[159] Friends War Victim Relief Committee and Civilian Relief Section

My Father with FAU colleagues

Ralph, with pipe, centre back, Tom Tanner to his right and John Bailey 3rd left and other Unit colleagues

FAU Executive 1941 at Gordon Square
Back Row: FRB, Peter Gibson, Freddy Temple, Dick Symonds
Front Row: Richey Mounsey, Peter Hume, Tom Tanner, Brandon Cadbury, John Bailey

Photos courtesy of Friends House archive

and by June 1942 he was sent abroad and remained so for much of the next three years until he was invalided out in 1944:

As Tegla Davies[160] writes:

"It was becoming increasingly clear, as unit sections were now at work with the British and French armies and in Syria, while another section was due for Ethiopia, that a Senior Unit Officer was needed in the Middle East, who would be responsible for the whole field. Already there had been difficulties in arranging loans or transfers of personnel between the Hadfield Spears Hospital[161] and the British Army work. The Syria clinics were expanding and further workers would have to be transferred to them. In general with possibilities of further work afoot, there would be great advantages in pursuing a correlated policy. So it was agreed that a senior officer, or as he came to be called, an O.C.M.E (Officer-in-Charge-Middle-East) should be sent out. The choice fell on Ralph Barlow, who was in charge of relief work in London and Deputy Chairman of the Executive Committee. Arrangements were made for Ralph and thirty-three men to sail."

But as my father wrote at the time, it was one of the most difficult times of his life.

"I shall always look back on the days preceding my departure as among the most unpleasant I have ever spent. I felt that I ought to go, but I went with a heavy heart. The parting with Joan was dreadful. I shall not ever forget my farewell telephone talk with her. In many ways they were the worst days I have ever lived through; sorrow at parting and dread of the future."

My Father makes various comments about this period of the FAU and about his fellow Unit members:

"I do not know if it was right to try and combine the Relief Officer's job with that of the Chairman's, while Tom Tanner was away. Anyhow, I did it and overworked, going up to Gordon Square each day. The Unit then was at a difficult time. Relief was finished and we were desperately in need of overseas work. Richard Symonds was a great help to me, both with ideas and sympathy and Brandon Cadbury[162], who might have been Deputy Chairman, was very loyal and his influence on the right, for caution and conservative values, balanced Richard on the left. Both were most valuable. Brandon was twice the man with Tom away. I was very reluctant to do the job, but Tom determined that he was going to go to America and he left very suddenly."

It was, however the figure of Tom Tanner, who dominated the Unit from 1940 to 1942[163] and who undoubtedly laid the grounds for its future success. Here my Father has some words to say about him:

"Perhaps I might say a word here about Tom. He was addicted to the sins of the flesh, liked to keep things in his own hands and he liked celebrities. He boasted that he was not in any way cultured, but he had an immense capacity for work, self-confidence, good judgment and flair. He was a natural leader and administrator. He was able to size up a situation quickly and seize an opportunity. He inspired amazing devotion and in every sense, was a really big man; perhaps the only one that the Unit produced and it was he that put the Unit on the map. None

[160] The Friends Ambulance Unit, George Allen and Unwin 1947

[161] The Hadfield-Spears Ambulance Unit was an Anglo-French volunteer mobile medical unit, financed by Sir Robert Hadfield, the British steel tycoon and later by Mary Spears. Vehicles came mostly from the war office, drivers from the American Field Service and hospital orderlies from the FAU in London.

[162] Brandon Cadbury (1915-2011) son of William Cadbury, the 2nd son of co-founder of Cadbury Brothers, Richard Cadbury

[163] Tom Tanner made a visit to China in 1942 with Peter Hume and their boat was torpedoed in the South Atlantic and all but one lost. A cruel blow for the Unit.

Ambulances outside Gordon Square, London
Hadfield Spears hospital, Egypt

Ambulances and FAU members ready for an expedition in Gordon Square, London

The Hadfield Spears Hospital in Egypt

of us could have done for the Unit what Tom did. He liked company, going places and doing things. We had little in common, but I think we liked each other."

On Tom's return from America, my Father wrote:

"Tom's American trip produced little, but, and it is a big but, it achieved better understanding of each other's point of view. He had made a wonderfully good impression. Brandon and I went to meet him and in his long absence (nearly two months, including a bad 21 day, stormy, sea voyage home in a small boat with inches of snow and ice in the cabins) we might have forgotten a little of what manner of man he was. But his power and ascendancy soon made themselves felt. He had become hugely respected by the American Friends Service Council, helped the American Friends to take the war seriously following Pearl Harbour, and he straightened out the Americans about what was going on in China. He is a big man, Tom, no doubt about it. It's odd having him back and I hope I shall behave properly. When one has been boss, it's strange having to take second place and I can't quite adjust myself!"

My Father was first put on the Executive Committee in June 1941 and, he commented:

"I remained on the Executive until December 1944 and I thought it was one of the best things the Unit produced. On Tom's return it was decided that I should go abroad and he gave me a letter of appointment as OCME, which instructed that I was to co-ordinate the various sections; to set up an HQ in Cairo, to visit and report into Relief possibilities and everyone seemed to be of the opinion that it was a job that only I could do, though I am not so sure about that.

At the end of May 1942, I had two weeks' leave, and then, after several delays I was suddenly told that we were due to leave the following Tuesday. I had an agonised weekend with Joan in Wolverhampton, during which she was wonderful and then finally, before I left, I had dinner with Tom and as I was driven to catch the boat, we passed through Westminster and to the other sadnesses, was added the sadness of leaving London that I had come to love so well."

With my Father's family connections, he had access to many leading Quakers, including, of course, Horace Alexander. At the end of 1941 the Japanese had entered into the war, and as Geoffrey Carnall writes in his 'Life of Horace Alexander'[164], *"with their rapid conquest of a great part of south-east Asia, it seemed only a question of time before an attack was mounted on India itself"* and the FAU felt immediately that it was important that they should establish themselves there, and in January of '42, my Father wrote to Horace inviting him to the London FAU hostel where he was staying, with a view of sounding out his thoughts:

"Although it was barely a week since his wife's death, Alexander was exhilarated by his talk with Barlow and the possibilities and....an offer was made to the Viceroy to send an experienced FAU group to India to help advise on civil defence matters and the offer was accepted……Horace agreed to act as leader....which also gave (him) an opportunity to 'keep the way open for negotiations between Mahatma Gandhi and the Government'."

This was also significant for Horace, as after he returned from India in '43, he was much taken up with thoughts about life after the war and during a visit to America to talk about his work in India and China, and to consult American Friends about the shape of further Quaker initiatives in Asia, he wrote to my Father on the subject. As Geoffrey Carnall puts it in his book:

"He set down his reflections on life after the war in a long letter to Ralph Barlow, a sympathetic and knowledgeable listener whose judgment he respected....about a possible return to India to involve himself in and to advise on the development of Quaker work there."

---

[164] Gandhi's Interpreter, A life of Horace Alexander Edinburgh University Press Ltd 2010

It was of course his work in India with Gandhi, during the struggle for independence, which would consume Horace in the immediate post war years leading to the establishment of an independent India in 1947 and which would be one of his abiding legacies.

Of the next period in my Father's life, he described it well in an article for The Leightonian magazine,[165] :

"I went out to the Middle East in June 1942 with a Unit section which was going to reinforce the Unit section already working in that theatre. We went out as was the custom in those days, round the Cape, spent five weeks in Durban and reached Egypt about twelve weeks after we left this country."

In Durban they were put up in a transit camp and as he recounts:

"I think all of us will remember the wonderful hospitality of Durban Quakers[166], who gave us meals in their homes, took us out into the country to see the valley of the Thousand Hills. We were fortunate in being able to arrange work for a large number of the party in the King Edward VII Hospital."

After their time in South Africa, the party moved on up, first to Syria in the Middle East, where they were to become part of the Unit already embedded with the 8th Army, before going on to Cairo. My Father writes: *"On arrival in the Middle East, I was in charge of the Unit's work in that area for nine months"* and Tegla Davies, writing in his history of the FAU, gives a more detailed summary of my Father's duties:

"Ralph Barlow was in charge of all sections of the Middle East and responsible to him were Peter Gibson for British Army work, Michael Rowntree for The Hadfield Spears Hospital and John Gough for the Syrian clinics. Ralph also visited Ethiopia and Teheran. His function was to develop unified policy based on an assessment of the work that was being done in the various fields, to balance conflicting claims for extra personnel, to pay regular visits to sections, to represent the FAU to military HQ and to keep the Executive Committee at home abreast of developments and areas for new work in the area."

Not much then! My Father takes up the narrative again:

"In Cairo, I made trips into the Desert to visit Unit Sections working with The Royal Army Medical Corps (RAMC). I went on with John Bailey[167] to Capuzzo[168] and then onto Tobruk[169]. This was quite soon after Alamein and there were German vehicles scattered in various stages of wreckage all along the road and our transport was going up in a continual stream."

Even in the middle of a war area, my Father typically, ever nature loving, recorded the flowers and of course, the birds:

"My last visit to Tobruk remains in my memory because of the flowers. All along the road and in the wadi below the camp, the bare limestone sides were like an enormous rock garden with groups of anemones, rock roses and geraniums; in the bottom a stray growth of barley, rough bushes, drifts of yellow daisies and scarlet poppies, all blowing gently in the hot afternoon sun. A lark tried to sing and a fine cock Black Redstart flew from bush to bush."

---

[165] The Leightonian is the magazine of his old school, Leighton Park. LP archives
[166] One of the most remarkable of the SA Friends was Florence Bayman, who after the war, came to England and settled near us in Birmingham and became a dear friend of the family.
[167] John Bailey was second Officer of the Middle East Convoy
[168] Fort Capuzzo was taken and retaken by the British Army and Rommel between 1940 and 1941
[169] At the beginning of WW2, Libya was an Italian colony and Tobruk became the site of important battles between the Allies and Axis powers.

He made two trips to Syria, passing through Palestine, visiting the work the Unit was doing with the Polish refugees with Michael Rowntree:

"I shall always think of Palestine as one of the loveliest of countries which I visited. Jerusalem I liked particularly. I called on some friends in a small house in the Russian garden of Gethsemane, which looks straight across to the terraced slops of the old city and the walls beyond and it was here that I read in a Palestinian paper of the death of Tom Tanner and Peter Hume and I remember with what heavy hearts we drove back to Cairo."

During this extended time abroad, my parents wrote to each other constantly and their correspondence will undoubtedly form the basis of another book as they chronicle in considerable detail both my Father's work in different parts of the world as well as his thoughts on the value of it all and on how much he misses my Mother. And from her, they tell of living in Wolverhampton with her sister and family and bringing up David and I and of the concomitant difficulties that entailed, but also reciprocally of how worried she is about my Father and how she misses him equally. I have already cited extracts from my Mother's pre-marriage letters from Syria to my Father, so I shall now quote briefly from a letter of my Father's from Cairo to her. Here's my Father in one of his typically introspective moods:

FAU Cairo
"....the Unit is an exacting mistress, occupying most of one's waking hours. The great thing is never to let oneself get an idea of one's own importance. To remember how inadequate one is, how pitifully inadequate and insignificant a thing the Unit is compared with the forces that are in conflict. Is it all worthwhile and what does it all mean?

Do we stand for anything worthwhile? One tries to testify against war but one shares in other manifestations and activities of the Society which produces it. We are outside the army, but we have many of its privileges. I especially as an Officer. Ah well, perhaps it's no good being introspective. We have chosen our way and must make the best of it. Sometimes I wonder what I would do in another war. And yet the more I see and know of war, the worse it seems. On balance I think I am more a pacifist now than ever......

.....Darling, I'll end this now and start again tomorrow. Always you are in my thoughts. I love you so and find more and more what indeed I always knew, that thought of you and home is my anchor on life. Dear heart I love you, what more can I say, except say it again. I LOVE YOU.

My dear love to both the children
God bless you my dear
All my love Ralph"

Or a week later, slightly less gloomy:

"My own dear Joan
I wonder if you received my previous letters. If you did you will have gathered I was in a black mood. But today I am rather more cheerful, but in consequence find I miss you even more.....
I do think of you always and love you most dearly. You are ever in my thoughts and prayers. God keep you and give you strength. My only desire is to be with you again and to hold you and kiss you and be in your arms. I ache for you my dear, dear wife. My Joan, the best Joan in all the world.

Dearest and everlasting love, Ralph"

Tom Tanner

Tom Tanner
"The figure who dominated the Unit from 1940 to 1942 and laid the foundation for its future success."

It is this strength of feeling expressed constantly in letters between them that maintained their love for each other amidst all the welter of events going on in their lives; for him abroad in often traumatic circumstances and for her in England but not in her own home. It is also a relationship of complete equals who can both express thoughts and discuss issues, happy in the knowledge that they will be reciprocated. There is an intensity of love that does not subside when they are reunited but only grows with the years and his letters on my Mother's birthdays, each one preserved over a lifetime are as lovelorn and heartfelt after forty years as they were in their courtship.

On a lighter level, I should of course also mention Bird watching, which was never far from his mind and most letters comment on them:

From Cairo again:

"At Luxor I was very interested to see hundreds of storks in migration resting in the desert and when disturbed, slowly rising and after circling in the air, continuing their journey North.......
....Yesterday we took the early train down the line to see the Clinic which is situated near a lake and we had a couple of hours to spare. What birds! Just below us was a tree which contained Ravens, Blue Starlings, whose wings are a most wonderful glossy, metallic blue, red-winged Starlings, Bulbuls[170], Cormorants, Ibis - beautiful in flight, white dark skin along the back of the wing and black head and long curved beak. There were lovely Bee-Eaters, Hornbill and Doves in the trees. Suddenly we saw the birds in the water – Pelicans, real live Pelicans! There were also brilliant Yellow Wagtails on the bank and Redshanks and Dunlin and a Bittern flew past...Joy!"

My Father and Horace also sent regular articles back home to The Birmingham Post of 'Birds in Egypt' or 'Birds in India':

The Birmingham Post April 30th 1943

"Most of this morning I have sat on a rock rising steeply from the Nile, watching the bird life....always there are Kites, flapping to and fro and wheeling high up in the sky; their shrill mewing cry, so common a sound in Egypt, goes on from dawn till dusk. These are African Kites: once, I suppose, the red Kite was as common over London......England is a thousand miles away but some of the Warblers, Sandpipers and Martins may well make the journey in the coming weeks. Those of us who are here will not see them in England this year, save in memory. But perhaps in the future we shall again hear the first Chiff-Chaff in the usual corner of the Lickey Woods. Or see the first party of Sand-Martins flitting over a sheltered corner of Bittell reservoir.....then we shall remember that we saw them once on their journey under the hot winter sun of Egypt. Perhaps we shall remember too, the Kites and Egrets and Vultures; but I, at any rate, shall not miss them much; though it would be good to see a Bee-Eater in Worcestershire!

From our Correspondent FRB"

And in a delightful letter from Cairo to my brother David, on his 5th birthday (see p. 185), he draws little sketches of the camels and donkeys, so much a part of Egyptian life. Then on the reverse side he talks of Cairo and the birds and adds a fairly approximate sketch of a Kite! I suspect my dear Father wasn't ever going to be a great artist, but for a child, how they must have enhanced a letter!

---

[170] Passerine song birds found in Asia and the Middle East

"My dear David,
This is a very noisy town with donkeys braying, trams, trains; it never seems quiet, The trams and buses are all single deckers.[171] The river Nile runs through it, a great, wide river, full of silt and the Egyptians depend on it for water for their fields, as little rain falls here. Egyptian Kites, a large sort of Hawk, are common in the town and one can see them everywhere. Please give my love to Mummy and Antony and both Grannies,

Love Daddy"

Meanwhile, in Teheran just prior to Christmas 1943, he flew to see the Polish refugee camps for himself:

"Mountains as far as the eye could see, covered in what seemed like seas of white, woolly cloud and as the sun began to go down, it caught the snow and rock, bringing out a rainbow of wonderful colours. Finally, we dropped down to a brightly lit Teheran, which was a somewhat bleak and squalid town, but delightfully cool after Cairo. This was one of the most important routes of the war with supplies continually passing to and from Russia. I was impressed by the standard of the refugee camps and full of admiration for the tremendous courage of these refugees who had suffered and lost so much. But it was clear that they were still thinking and planning for a future in which they would again be able to be a great military power one day."

As a result of the deaths of Tom Tanner and Peter Hume my Father was asked to be Deputy Chairman again and to complete the visit they had been planning to India and China, where he was joined by Brandon Cadbury. But before leaving the Middle East, he made a last visit to Ethiopia, to Addis and on to Jiddah:

"This was the nearest I ever got to Mecca. On my arrival in Addis, I was met by Harold Waller with a small car and holding a monkey, who had inconsiderately just made a mess on the driving seat and I have always admired the way in which Harold sat in it! And as in Syria, I was immensely impressed by the steady hard work the Unit was undertaking. I think the best trip I made was to Fiche[172] with Jack Frazer. When we arrived, it was assumed that we knew something about medicine, as we were called in to advise on the son-in-law of the Ras[173]. In fact two people who knew less about medicine than Jack and I, it would have been hard to find! But I hope that we emerged without entirely giving the game away!"

Ethiopia had been the scene of two military campaigns in the previous seven years and when Haile Selassie[174] returned in 1941, he found the country ravaged by war, the administration completely disrupted and the Italian officials displaced. In an effort to introduce reforms, establish social services and rebuild the national life, the Ethiopian government accepted the offer of the FAU to send men to assist with medical work and the development of medical services. Initially a party of forty was assembled with men who had undergone special training in British hospitals in tropical medicine and in basic Amharic.

Eventually, the British Army was largely withdrawn and only a small military mission remained, so that the Unit's work was quite different to that originally envisaged. They had to act much more independently and accept a far greater responsibility than planned. By the time my Father arrived things were getting underway and he writes:

---

[171] David became fond of the buses in Wolverhampton, which, like the trams, were all double deckers, and used to stand at the bus stop outside 31 Lea Road in Wolverhampton and talk to the Drivers when they stopped! Imagine that today!
[172] Fiche is a town in central Ethiopia
[173] Ethiopian aristocratic and court title, as in Ras Tafari
[174] Emperor of Ethiopia from 1930 to 1974.

"I met Hailie Selassie who was very complimentary of the work of the Unit and I saw for myself how it had increased since 1941. Now the section consisted of seven doctors and some 39 others assisting with public health administration, in hospitals and provincial clinics, in leprosy camps and in schools."

Some eleven hospitals were established in addition to the main hospital in Addis and Unit members supervised eight provincial clinics, often with men who had no medical experience before the war. One of these was the successful actor Patrick Barr[175], whom I remember visiting back stage with my Father, on several occasions after the war, when he had resumed his career. Here he writes of his time in Ethiopia :

"My job here is bigger than I ever imagined. In addition to the 70-100 out-patients a day and getting the ward to run smoothly, I have under my care the health of 300 schoolchildren, 650 soldiers and about 130 police. It is also expected that I shall do malaria surveys of the Awarb river valley, supposedly the worst place in Ethiopia. A survey of the schoolchildren's health revealed that out of the first 100, only 12 were free of diseases such as trachoma, scabies, tropical ulcers and scurvy."

Unsurprisingly, it was during his time in Ethiopia that my Father picked up an undiagnosed fever and on his return to Egypt in 1943, he was hospitalised. He also managed to pick up Jaundice *"one of the more depressing diseases that I have had."* But he was determined to continue on down to India and by the time he arrived in Calcutta he was, as he says *"in a pathetic state",* and it took about two months in hospital in there, before he was well again *"which was something of a bad dream"* he writes. This is about as near as he comes to admitting how ill he was. My Father hardly ever talked about this period and skips quickly over it in his memoirs. I do remember, however, him telling me many years later that at one point, he had terrible hiccups for about two days and had he not stopped, he might well have died. But for a true account of his illness, I have found the record made by a remarkable Polish doctor, Dr Budzislawski, who was the only person to correctly diagnose what was wrong with him.

He wrote this medical report for the FAU:

"Mr Barlow arrived in Bombay from Egypt at the beginning of May and when leaving the ship he complained of severe rheumatic pains in his limbs and his body and a fever. But despite this he had taken the train on to Calcutta, by which time he could barely stand on his feet. He also had difficulties with his food due to a clumsiness of his left hand. He had a temperature of 101.71 and a severe hiccough which prevented him from eating or drinking. He had difficulty in speaking. From all these signs I made the diagnosis of Epidemic-Encephalitis and sent the patient to hospital. After nearly two weeks he was greatly improved but still very weak, though the hiccough had subsided. By the 30th May I found his speech improved and though he could get up, his walk was staggering and uneasy. He had difficulties with concentration and became quickly irritable."

At the beginning of June he was seen by a Dr Love and Lt Col Seaward, who both confirmed Dr Budzislawski's original diagnosis but unbelievably, both of them agreed, that despite his weakness, he could proceed to China. The fact that he had been close to death's door was seemingly ignored in the demands of war, though knowing my Father's tendency to brush illness aside and pretend it wasn't happening, I suspect he would also have had a hand in persuading them to let him continue with Tom Tanner's mission to China. Later, his sister

---

[175] Patrick Barr was a star of stage and screen, appearing in such films as *The Dam Busters* and *The Longest Day*

Millior, often used to say that some ill-advised decisions were taken and thought that as a result, he was never as strong a person again after the war.

My Father again takes up the story:

"Things that stick in my mind of my time in China, was first of all the extraordinary feeling of isolation of China from the rest of the world. I recall hearing on the wireless of the fall of Mussolini, but it seemed like a happening almost from another world. But I was impressed by the generally friendly atmosphere, especially in the section at Kutsing and once Brandon arrived from Chungking we had a complete orgy of meetings, which on the whole, did, I think achieve something. I also recall with pleasure meeting up again with Duncan Wood and the day we spent bird watching above the lake outside Kunming."

Regarding China, it might be relevant to quote Horace Alexander, who was then leader of the FAU section in Calcutta, on his visit to China for Friends Yearly Meeting in Szechuan. Friends had been in China for sixty years, working devotedly as doctors, teachers and evangelists. During a lecture Horace gave in America[176], he said:

"The picture to-day after sixty years, is disappointing. The Society as it is seen in west China today, is still an alien growth with no roots in the soil. Then comes the FAU, followed by the American Friends Service Council – a hundred or so western men and a handful of women, giving their services to China for the period of the war, striving in a number of ways to fill in the great vacuum of medical skill for the soldiers and civilians of China. Though some fundamentalist missionaries look on the FAU as a sub-Christian organisation yet its members seem to be more sure than are members of the FAU in some other parts of the world, that they have a Christian motive....Will this great undertaking, then, just withdraw in another year or two, leaving no sign?"

That was the question. If the work was to be followed into a post-war world, the future lay with the permanent American Friends Service Committee, not with the temporary FAU. And so the balance of responsibility began to shift from London to Philadelphia. And when in 1946 the decision was made that the FAU was going to wind up its commitments overseas, the AFSC came forward to take the lead.

My Father returned to Calcutta by air and from thence to Cairo which involved a night in Karachi, calling in on the coast of Baluchistan and a flight up the Persian Gulf to Basra, where he spent a night, meeting up with Horace and:

"sitting out in the garden in front of the hotel beside the Shatt-al-Arab[177] and watching some terns and bee-eaters while eating some of the delicious first dates of the season."

He stayed in Cairo for about three weeks and met up again with colleagues Michael Rowntree back from North Africa, Jack Frazer from Ethiopia and John Gough from Syria and writes:

"I discovered I was beginning to have a very warm feeling for Cairo, which was, surprising as it may seem, a comparatively clean city after some I had seen. He then returned home from Cairo, on three months' sick leave, by sea and he describes *"seeing the search lights of Malta and passing through Gibraltar. But I shall never forget the thrill of coming in and docking at the same quay from which we had left and the excitement of really being back in the UK again, which has never left me."*

---

[176] Friends Ambulance Unit by A Tegla Davies 1947
[177] A river in Southwest Asia near Basra, formed by the confluence of the Tigris and the Euphrates

The China Convoy

My Father's Unit lorry in China, with the 'wicked twenty four bends' near Annan in the West of Taiwan

When my Father was initially given sick leave, my Mother and David and I left Wolverhampton and gradually we all moved into 6 Swarthmore Road, as Granny Barlow had by then moved down to London to live with my Father's sister, Millior and her husband Alfred. My Father's initial reaction was of relief:

"It was more than pleasant at being home again, but I couldn't help feeling that it still might only be temporary."

The rest of 1944 my Father spent at Gordon Square, where he ended his career with the Unit as Officer for Overseas Work as well as continuing as Deputy Chairman of the Executive Committee, a function which eventually engaged him full-time as Chairman for the latter part of 1944, when Christopher Taylor was away visiting the Mediterranean.

"After a job in the field, it was difficult to avoid a feeling of uselessness. But actually I think the Unit Office was well run and well informed. I was responsible for all overseas work and worked happily with Ronald Joynes, whose long experience of the Overseas Office was invaluable. On Doctor's orders I was supposed to be going slow, but I got very tired and cannot imagine that I was 100% effective. I made it my business to build up confidence between London and China and on the whole, I think succeeded. The China section under Duncan Wood and Ken Bennet successfully consolidated previous undertakings. Altogether it was an interesting job."

Finally in December he left the Unit on Doctor's orders, though with much misgiving, and some of his thoughts at the end are worth quoting as they reflect on his Christian beliefs as well as the value of the work of the FAU in which he had so honourably served.

"I was brought up in strict Quaker surroundings. These must have affected me more than I realised. My debt to them is tremendous...............In my time in the Unit my beliefs have changed considerably. Beginning perhaps as a more orthodox Quaker, I shared in and derived much benefit from devotionals. I began to feel however that while sometimes held in the spirit, they were more often a dry formality. We had not enough of "that of God" in us; were too much equal in age and experience.

On the boat and for some months after leaving home they seemed to have much more meaning. They seemed to bring me close to home and to Joan. In alien surroundings they had meaning. I remember them on the boat and in camp at Durban. I remember too Anglican services on board, in the Cairo cathedral and one in a little Nestorian church in Tel Tamar. From the time of my illness my interest has waned. At Darjeeling I acquired new interest and respect in Quakerism from reading Rufus Jones and William Charles Braithwaite, but my religious life such as it was atrophied.

In this mood I returned home. My whole self was submerged in the delight of getting home again and I wanted nothing more. I found myself on the one hand convinced of the importance of the Quaker message and methods and certain that it should be given to the world as a way of life through worship and service, but on the other critical of committee methods, traditional phraseology, bad choice of personnel, woolliness and isolation from the world. I still feel this very strongly and I wonder too how far the meeting for worship really "speaks to my condition". Here I know the remedy is partly in my own hands but I have not the spiritual depth to give the sort of ministry that is required, and too many doubts to give anything at all. Yet I think that in future my service will be with Friends. Of religion I have little certainty but of the need and demand for service I am quite certain.........

Horace Alexander and a letter from daddy

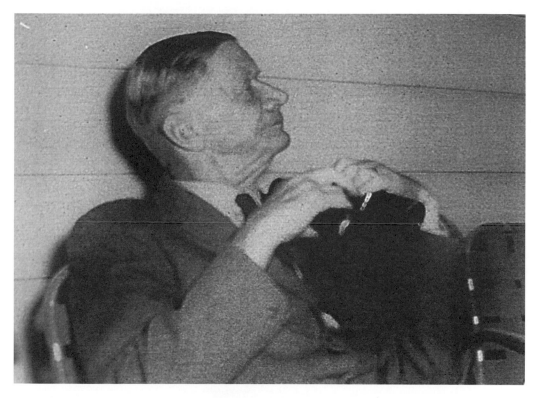

Horace Alexander, bird watching, which like my Father he could always manage to fit in whatever the situation.

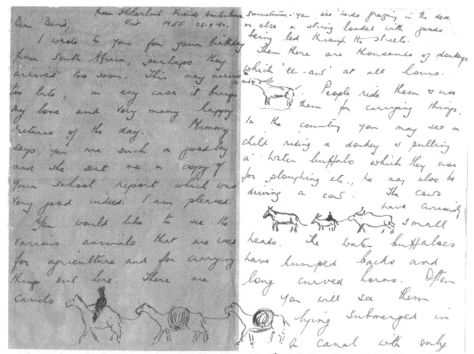

A letter from Daddy to my brother David on his 5th birthday, from Cairo (See p.179)

My father invalided out of the FAU and brothers grow up

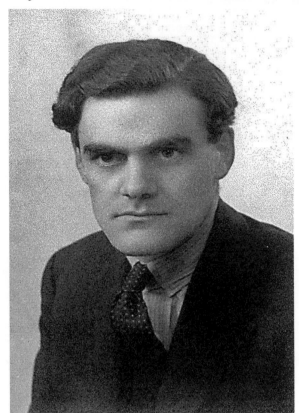

The Author writes:

"My Father was invalided out of the FAU on his return from Ethiopia in 1944 after suffering from Epidemic Encephalitis, from which he nearly died.

He was determined to complete the mission to China, he undertook on Tom Tanner's behalf, but he was eventually given sick leave and spent the rest of '44 till the end of the war in Gordon Square.

Meanwhile David and I were growing up!"

Yet I believe Christ meant pacifism and I cannot square war with his teaching. I find it too hard to break away from my traditional Quakerism. I cannot believe that so great an evil as war can bring lasting good. After 5 years of war the world must be a worse place. The inhumanity and callousness of war grows……

I owe much to the Unit. I got on in it on my own merit and it has given me experience and self-confidence. I have made my way, stood on my own feet and done a job. I have gained knowledge of all sorts of people and places. Why did I get on? I was not a pioneer, I did not create. I came to the fore to administer, run and in a small way develop a going concern. The answers are partly seniority, partly Quakerism, conscientiousness, and some administrative ability. What more I know not. This experience has made a different man of me. It came almost too late, I should have had it at University or directly after.

Coming when it did into a happy married life it nearly broke me. It must nearly have broken Joan, but she stood up to it in face of all sorts of difficulties, kept her courage, did not let me who had a much more interesting and varied life grow away from her, brought David and Antony up wonderfully. And now for a time at least we are reunited again and our marriage survived the storms and is as wonderful as ever. But this is not the end, only a breathing space. The world will terribly need our services. What form it will take and how it will come I do not know."

He expanded his views on the need for service in an article which he wrote for The Friend[178] in 1945 which he concludes by saying:

"The outsider's view of the Society of Friends is embarrassingly high and in all respects we should do what we can to see that this view is justified. I think too that the Society should, as far as possible, try to provide some channel for the very strong urge for service which so many people share and which has perhaps been intensified by the war years. For many it will be right to live in their own homes and carry on with their normal jobs, but there will be plenty of scope for local service. A minority may wish to serve abroad and again, I feel that the Society should make this possible, as I am sure that it has something to give to the world through service."

I have described the period of the war in some detail as it was a crucial and difficult time in both my parents' lives. A time of extended separation not long after their marriage, was testing for both of them. For my Father it was simultaneously a time of unknown danger and uncertainty, as well as a time to prove himself with his colleagues, many of whom were Quaker friends and relatives whom he had known since childhood such as Michael and Brandon Cadbury, Duncan Wood and Michael Rowntree. It provided leadership opportunities in many different theatres of war and in the event, despite as his great friend Duncan Wood said on reading his memoirs 'typical Barlow understatement', he made an immense contribution to the success of the Unit in the Middle East, Ethiopia and China as well as in London. This is well attested by everyone in a stream of letters, when he was invalided out, from all with whom he had worked from Paul Cadbury to the humblest in the Unit. I will quote from a few of them which clearly show how much he underrated his own achievements:

From Paul Cadbury, Gordon Square, December 1944
Dear Ralph
I am so sorry that you are leaving the Unit on medical grounds, though I feel sure it is the right decision, despite my certain knowledge that you are one of the few men in the Unit that cannot be replaced….. Yours ever Paul

---

[178] The Friend archives

From John Fleming, December 7 1944[179]

Dear Ralph
You are probably tired of hearing it said that you are irreplaceable, but I must say I feel that too. Of all the leaders of the Unit, you are the one in whom I have always had the completest confidence and with whose eminently balanced viewpoint, I think I have never disagreed.
With very best wishes
John

From Tegla Davies, Gordon Square December 3 1944

My dear Ralph
You know how I feel about your going and I have sensed over the last few days how you in turn have felt about having to go. The Unit gets hold of one....Most of all I want to thank you for your loyalty. You must know that we feel you to have so many admirable qualities for Unit administration; but what I have appreciated most of all is your old fashioned loyalty to the Unit as an idea and to me personally. You have been a tremendous and irreplaceable help to me over the last year.
Take care of yourself Ralph
Ever yours,
Tegla

From Harold Watts, Failand House (A Training Centre, near Bristol) January 8 1945

Dear Ralph
I can't help saying that I for one am going to miss you in the affairs of the Unit. It is all very evident to those with some knowledge of Gordon Square, what good sound sense you brought. And those in the body of the Unit will always remember you as someone in whom they had supreme confidence.
All the best, Harold

Finally, to quote another letter from Tegla, though this time to my Mother:

4 Gordon Square December 3 1944
Dear Joan
I am writing a note to you because I want to thank you for the way in which you have co-operated with us over the last year and let us keep Ralph, although many a time you must have felt very inclined to make a fuss. In the case of married members of the Unit it is only too easy to forget that it is the wives at home who have very much the thin end of the stick. You must have felt constant worry and anxiety over the last year, but (if I may say without sounding patronising) you have been so very good about it and we do appreciate your attitude.

Heaven knows Ralph is the last man we can spare from the Unit and that is why we have hung on to him for so long. I have always known that the confidence of the Unit and particularly of overseas sections is greater when he is there. But on coming back and seeing him certainly no worse, but not much better either, I came to agree that it was only fair to himself and his family to encourage him to go. I have particular cause to be grateful to him for the loyalty and support he has always shown to me and for shouldering the whole burden while I was away.

This needs no reply as I know how busy you will be with Ralph and the children.
All good wishes,
Tegla

---

[179] Paul Cadbury, Tegla Davies, John Fleming, Harold Watts: all were leading Quaker members of the FAU

For my Mother it was undoubtedly a period of enormous strain, giving up her own home, moving from house to house, first to Honor and Christopher Cadbury's when I was born and then to Wolverhampton and bringing up two children in someone else's house albeit her sister's and brother-in-law's. In addition, all through the period of nearly four years, letters to and from this country took uncertain and variable lengths of time to reach their destination, with the constant worry of not knowing the danger my Father might be in, or, when he was very ill, whether he would recover. That their relationship survived and that they were able to regroup after the war, says a great deal for both of them and their loyalty and devotion to each other, as attested in their many love letters written during this extremely testing and difficult time, some of which I have cited above. They clearly show their trust and love in each other and I feel sure, as I said before, that they will undoubtedly form the basis of another book.

Finally, it should not be forgotten, there was the necessary readjustment to civilian life. For my Father, starting back at the Trust after five years away, during which time he had seen continuous action during an adrenalin filled time, travelling continuously from place to place, leading his mission and being responsible to HQ, cannot have been easy. It was a long period of great camaraderie, with people of shared values and a common desire to serve in trying and often impossible conditions, with whom he had seen scenes of unimaginable carnage and terribly wounded soldiers, many of whom died from horrific wounds. It is little wonder that he didn't talk much to us children about his wartime life and even his memoirs, written specifically for us, are mere outlines of these years; the deeper experience is scarcely touched on. How humdrum, the running of an inner city Housing Estate must initially have seemed after the end of those five years.

For my Mother, there was first, yet another move, not just back from Wolverhampton to Birmingham, but from Linden Road to Swarthmore Road and sorting out the house from the years Granny Barlow had lived there. There was also Lydia[180] to contend with, a Nurse come Housekeeper inherited from her Mother-in-law, who had treated her very much as a servant who should know her place. My Mother had a totally different attitude, treating her as part of the family, but having been used to doing everything herself, it was inevitably an adjustment for her to get used to having someone else to help with the chores. But we children came to be very fond of Lydia and I remember she used to ask David or I to go down to the local Post office to purchase her regular packet of Craven A with its trademark black cat, the first of the cork-tipped cigarettes. Both of us would have been well under 10, yet in those far off days before Health and Safety wreaked its havoc, no-one showed the slightest concern! Then there were the post war problems common to all, living with ration books and late 1940's austerity and my Father's none too generous salary from the BVT. And then in 1945 with the birth of Stephen and 1947 with Rosemary, two more children to bring up on a salary from the Bournville Village Trust, which to say the least, was not inflation linked!

At the end of his memoirs my Father sums up his time with the Unit as follows:

"I was very doubtful about the rightness of leaving the unit. I was not well and perhaps I did not fully realise how far from well I was. But I suppose that as long as they wanted me at Gordon Square, I could have carried on. I did not want my health to be an excuse for getting me back to Bournville. I did not want my friends to feel that I was deserting them. But although I had many regrets about leaving, I did not share other people's forebodings that I should find my life at home dull. But though I felt I could have carried on, I was advised by Christopher Taylor and Paul Cadbury, on the recommendation of a specialist to leave and live at home. So with many expressions of regret and much kindness, I left the Unit and went to live at home

---

[180] Lydia Brookes, who had worked for Granny Barlow, and helped look after us as well as about the house.

again, this time without fear of further partings hanging over my head which was marvellous. One can enjoy the pleasures of life at home so much more when one can really become a part of it; this is so different from short leaves and weekends. I did not ultimately find difficulty in settling down, which was, of course due to Joan, who is the most marvellous wife. I have two charming children and I am very proud of them and very grateful to Joan for having brought them up so well. We are indeed lucky. A reunion and a return after so long wandering and waiting seemed almost too good to be true. We were very fortunate and very thankful."

I might end this chapter by quoting from Tegla Davies' book on the FAU, which I think sums up the feelings of most of those who were in the Unit during the war.

"It was our Unit, and we were proud of it, not with uncritical pride, but with the pride of those who for better or worse, had made it what it was. The Unit started with the war and we who became its members were the Unit....We all had ideas of what we wanted it to be, of what we wanted it to do. We argued and we laughed and we sweated over it: for the war years it became our life: it bounded our horizons: our friends were in it: we talked little of other things: and only when we left it did we realize fully what it had meant to us."

The growing family immediately after the war: l to r - David, Antony, Rosemary and Stephen

Chapter 20
Ralph and Joan - life after the war

Inevitably this chapter of our family story is going to be much more subjective and reliant on my recollections. But although in places, it may seem to be too much my personal account of the lives of my brothers and sister, I hope that it always reflects the broader picture of the home life that our parents made for us. So here I will tell the story in some detail, of our family unit, first six, then seven when Nicholas was born in 1958, up until the time we grow up and leave home, either to get married or settle down with partners. This is not the story of all our subsequent lives, except to show in a very general way the interaction of my parents with the widening family circle. That story is for someone else to tell at a later time. This chapter will detail the story of my parents' lives from the end of the war until my Father's death in 1980.

Once the war had ended in 1945, my Father returned to the Bournville Village Trust and remained there until he retired in 1972. The Trust was his life's work as it had been his Father's and he believed it was a vital part of the larger Quaker community, to which he dedicated himself. My Mother had left Wolverhampton with David and myself, probably with some relief, to join my Father back in Birmingham and live in her own house once more. Gradually life began to return to normal, though our Father was never to be as physically strong again after his debilitating wartime illness. But as children of course, we were scarcely aware of this, because he used to love taking us on extensive walking or cycling holidays in the Cotswolds, or climbing in the Lake District or Snowdonia. I remember David aged 8 and myself only 5, proudly climbing all the way up the famous pig track to the top of Snowdon with him, disdaining the easy option of the train!

With a growing family to bring up and educate, my parents never had much money. But despite this, they always made sure we had wonderful holidays, not only in this country but also on trips abroad, to Holland just after the war, or staying with friends in Norway and Switzerland. So to begin with I want to tell of those holidays, as they say a great deal about the family we were and the happy home life in which we grew up.

It might however, be instructive if I say a little about this immediate post-war period, as of course from today's viewpoint it is an utterly different world. It is not just the technological advances that have changed, significant though those are, it is much more the way everyday life has altered so completely. It was a much safer world then, when my parents did not worry as they let us go on the bus to school unaccompanied, nor fret about letting us go on foreign trips with unmarried Scoutmasters or even that many of the masters at our boarding schools were single. It was a world of the BBC Home Service and Alvar Lidell, of 'Much Binding in the Marsh'[181] and Flanders and Swann,[182] the latter who had been in the FAU with my Father. Televisions were expensive luxuries and we didn't have one until the sixties.

We made our own entertainment, dressing up in my Father's FAU uniform for instance, which was the nearest we ever came to playing soldiers! Or acting in the little plays my Father devised for us, which we would perform at Woodbrooke or Fircroft[183] Colleges, or even sometimes at the annual Christmas gathering at the old Midland Institute in Edmund Street, then a centre for the Arts. We would help in the garden, digging, weeding, planting seeds or pruning.

---

[181] A very popular comedy programme on the Radio, starring Richard Murdoch, Sam Costa and Kenneth Horne
[182] Michael Flanders and Donald Swann, an acclaimed duo whose show 'At the Drop of a Hat' ran for some years in the 50s.
[183] Fircroft is a residential college, occupying a former Cadbury family home, in six acres of beautiful grounds in Selly Oak

Now we are four – or six!

The augmented Barlow family
(Above) **Now four children: Stephen, Antony, Rosemary, David in a field near Llanthony in 1949**

(Below) **or six: with Parents, amongst the ruins of Llanthony Abbey in 1951**

We were encouraged to learn how things worked so that we could mend them, such as the old sash windows in most houses at that time. These windows had counterweights on either side, attached to the sashes, using pulleys of braided cord and Dad used to show us how to take the window out, extract the broken cord and feed the new one down, weighted by a lead 'mouse'! We would learn how to mix cement and mortar and to build a simple brick coal house; how to use carpentry tools and make shelves or a book case; and we could mend a fuse when the lights went out and change a tyre when it punctured.

Our parents read us books, which in our early childhood were of course, Beatrix Potter, *Winnie the Pooh* or *Alice in Wonderland* but as we grew older, progressed to the *Just So Stories* or *The Jungle Book*, delighting us in the adventures of Mowgli with Shere Khan the Tiger and the wolves Bagheera and Baloo.

It was a more rigid world, in which people did a weekly shop, and made a joint of meat last most of the week, eating it hot on Sundays, cold on Mondays, minced on Tuesdays and as rissoles on Wednesdays. The washing was done on Mondays, in an old fashioned hand-operated machine with a mangle, and the ironing completed on Tuesdays; the house cleaning was done on Wednesdays and shopping on Fridays. We knew the names of the people on the Green who ran the shops; Mr Ward in the electrical shop, Mr Honeybourne the butcher and Miss Batchelor with rather goofy teeth, in the Greengrocers. The Barrows Stores' Rep came on Tuesdays to take our main grocery order and their vans delivered on Thursdays. The milkman from nearby Lucas' farm, delivered milk in bottles with wide tops that had a cardboard stopper with a perforated hole in the middle, which one pressed to lift it out.

We mended and made do; socks were darned, trousers and jackets were patched and shoes soled and heeled. Mr Waddle, a local shoemaker, used to call to collect any shoes that might need repairing and returned them a few days later. My Mother knitted us sweaters and pullovers and thick woollen socks to tuck inside our boots. We had tricycles and then bicycles and we would go out with our Mother to visit friends and neighbours unannounced or they would call on us and be given cups of tea and home-made cakes and biscuits. As we grew up, our Father would take us over to his office on a Saturday, then opposite Cadburys' main factory, and let us sit where his secretary, Miss Darling usually sat. We were taken round Cadburys to see how the chocolate was made, in the days when they still showed a film of the 'natives' collecting the cocoa beans in the Gold coast and of them loading the big bags on to the boats that brought them to England and thence to Bournville, often on the old canal or the train that pre-Beeching, came right into the works.

We visited our cousins, locally the Barlows in Northfield and the Hazels in Sutton, or further afield, the Rutters in Wolverhampton or the Barbers in Canterbury, and the Braithwaites in London. We drove in a succession of second hand cars, never owning a new one. There was the old Morris Oxford, which still had orange indicators that came out of the side and a crank handle to restart when the ignition failed. There was a black Austin ten and a beige Hillman Minx and they all had a fixture on the back to which we could attach a trailer to carry all the luggage we needed for a large family holiday. A khaki uniformed AA man on a yellow motorbike with a yellow side car with all his tools in, would salute as he passed by and we would salute back, or sometimes make a rude gesture when our parents weren't looking! It was a different world but a happy one. As to our holidays, we had two favourite destinations. One was at Llanthony in the Black Mountains and the other was at Whiteslea Lodge on Hickling Broad in Norfolk. Before the war, my parents used to regularly frequent the Black Mountains with their friends Jeff and Margaret Gillett, as guests of another Quaker family, the Elliotts

Favourite holiday places - Llanthony valley in the Black mountains

The 'camp' at Llanthony – caravan and two tents

The Author writes:

"Partly what attracted us children to staying 'at the caravan', was the ability to enjoy a pretty primitive life style."

David and Dad, with young Mr Trevor Griffiths, on the farm

who owned a home-made caravan, which I think had only ever made the one journey, just as far as this Welsh valley. They must have shown their great fondness for the place, for when the Elliotts became too old they generously gave it to my parents. Mr Elliott had constructed this simple, but effective home away from home and taken it down to a corner of a field between the little village of Llanthony with its ruined Augustinian Priory and the neighbouring hamlet of Capel-y-ffin.

The field belonged to a local farmer, Mr Griffiths who had very kindly allowed first the Elliotts and then us, to leave the caravan there in perpetuity for only a nominal rent. We would drive down there with our car and a trailer packed with warm clothes and blankets plus food enough to feed an army. On arrival we'd pitch camp, gather fire wood and light a fire ready to cook our first meal. After that we would rush to inspect all the familiar haunts – the stream at the bottom of the field, the heather covered hillside beyond the stream and then later, we'd make the treck up the rough path to the farm house to collect fresh eggs or milk direct from the cow, only briefly passed through a fairly simple cooling machine before we quaffed it down. The Griffiths were a wonderfully indulgent couple who happily taught us basic farming skills such as how to milk a cow or drive a tractor, all of which would undoubtedly come under the strictures of 'Health and Safety' inspectors in today's risk free world.

Partly what attracted us children to staying 'at the caravan' was the ability to enjoy a pretty primitive life style. We washed in the cold running water of the stream at the bottom of the field, disappeared into its secluded corners, carrying a spade, to dig a hole for our toilet, lit a simple fire to cook our meals, which often consisted of wild rabbits freshly shot by Mr Griffiths or a few fish from the stream. We climbed over the neighbouring foothills of the Black Mountains and down into the next village of Longtown, picking bagfulls of juicy, black bilberries from the slopes, on the way.

In Longtown we came across the most beautiful garden, full of every flower imaginable and whenever we were there, we would peer through the wrought iron gates, marvelling at the profusion of colours. One day, a lady wearing a wide-brimmed straw hat, who had a rather grand appearance, came and asked us if we would like to look around, which of course we did. This was a Mrs Molyneux, a lady who had lived in the area for many years and who regaled us with all kinds of local gossip, including the fact, whispered under her breath, that a writer by the name of Peter Wildeblood had a cottage on the slopes above our caravan. Not knowing who Peter Wildeblood was at the time, it meant very little to us children. But questions as to who this mysterious man might be, were met with non-committal answers, with my Father pretending as though he hadn't heard the question![184] Only years later did I discover about Wildeblood and his involvement with Lord Montagu and both their subsequent imprisonment for gay carryings on, and that this quiet and quite lonely valley was Wildeblood's bolt hole to escape the attention of the media, following his release. Mrs Molyneux, was thus associated in our minds with intriguing mysteries as well as the wonderful teas with delicious home-made cakes with which she regularly refreshed us after our long walks.

We drove up over the as yet unmade-up road to the still unspoilt village of Hay, where there were splendid wild Welsh ponies on the hillside. And we clambered over the ruins of the Priory with its 'temple-haunting martlets', as Shakespeare calls Martins, which flitted in and out of

---

[184] Wildeblood was a journalist and playwright who was caught up in a notorious case involving Lord Montagu and Michael Pitt-Rivers where 'homosexual acts' had supposedly taken place on the Beaulieu estate in 1953, for which they were both imprisoned. The case and Wildeblood's book, *Against the Law* were very influential in helping to set up the Wolfenden Report in 1957 and eventually changing the law ten years later in 1967.

Ruined Llanthony priory and little Capel-y-ffin

"The ruins of 12th century Llanthony Priory, with its 'temple-haunting martlets'

"The neighbouring Chapel at Capel-y-ffin that lies in the Honddu valley"

The joys of basic holidays in Llanthony

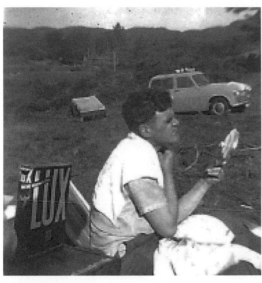

The Author writes:
"Dad shaving in an old saucepan lid and David washing in the stream or just cycling around the lanes on old cycles with not even a Sturmey Archer gear."

the old stones. It was in many ways an idyllic place for children to grow up and we all became inordinately fond of it, except perhaps our dear Mother who gradually found its very primitiveness a little much as she got older and would often indulge in the greater comforts of a small station hotel in nearby Pandy, where she was gently cossetted by the delightful owners Mr and Mrs Best!

Mr Griffiths used to keep an eye on the rickety old caravan for us and not possessing a telephone, would often scrawl the briefest of notes in the most succinct words possible and send it post haste to my Father. One which went down in family folk lore read simply "Last night your roof blew off!" This occasioned precipitate action, so we gathered reinforcements from the maintenance department at the Trust, together with its corpulent head, Mr Stewart who resembled no-one so much as the Reverend Audrey's big fat Controller from Thomas the Tank Engine and off we went. With Mr Stewart driving us in his new Vauxhall, we drove at top speed down to Llanthony, the quicker to make emergency repairs. The roof had indeed blown off and could be seen lying strewn across the field. But we all set to with a will and in next to no time, my Father astride a ladder, with advice from below from Mr Stewart and ably assisted by my brother and I handing up hammers and screwdrivers, nails or screws as required, had effected some running repairs, enough to survive a few more months of Welsh weather that could often blow up the valley with destructive ferocity.

We got to know the valley well over many years and we would introduce our friends and relatives to it too, to come down and share with us the joys of this amazing place. I remember particularly, from amongst a host of visitors, my cousin Graham, two friends from Norway, Tor and Lars, my great childhood friend Antony Platten, Quaker family friends, the Ransomes, and later our school and University friends, all joining us on various occasions.

The other place we loved almost as much as Llanthony, was Hickling Broad, where we stayed at Whiteslea Lodge which belonged to the Norfolk Wildlife Trust, of which Christopher and Honor Cadbury were Trustees, having donated much money to it over the years. A white clapboard building, right on the very edge of the broad, it offered the most perfect view out over the wide expanses of water surrounded by golden reeds and narrow inlets, stretching as far as the eye could see.

Once the residence of Lord Desborough, it had long been a nature reserve providing a veritable haven for birdwatchers. At almost any time you might see varieties of waders such as Red Shank or Green Shank as well as birds of prey like Ospreys or Harriers and always in the distance was the far off, deep resonant boom of the Bitterns. Further out in one of the inlets you could regularly spot moustachioed Bearded Tits or tiny, male Reed Buntings with their striking black heads and white collar, darting in and out of the reed beds. And if you were very lucky, you might even spot a rare visitor such as a Spoonbill. Come late April or early May there would inevitably be swallowtail butterflies or rare dragonflies flitting gracefully along the water's edge.

Inside, the Lodge was a friendly family house with several bedrooms, a homely kitchen with a big old fashioned stove and a large living room with a big log fire always kept burning in the chill, early Spring weather. The walls of each room were covered with the complete hand-coloured prints of John Gould's Birds of Britain. These are justly famous with impressive pictures of Eagles, Harriers, Gulls or Swans, but for me the finely delineated small birds were the most beautiful. Numerous different Finches or the many varieties of tits were, to my mind amongst the finest of all his illustrations, often with exquisite details such as a worm in the

Favourite holiday places - Whiteslea Lodge on Hickling Broad

Whiteslea Lodge on the edge of Hickling Broad

Mum and Dad with ever present binoculars back from a bird outing

beak being brought to feed a brood of hungry babies just visible at the edge of the nest, or perhaps a butterfly landing on a sprig of blossom hanging from a nearby tree, all helped to make them great paintings as well illustrative pictures from a book. There were also four long friezes in the sitting room, painted by another fine bird artist, Roland Green, who had made his home in Hickling, where he set many of his paintings and whose distinctive style perfectly captured the wild beauty of this region.

Spring was a perfect time to be there with all the rare migrant waders coming in to feast on the rich pickings to be found either in the water or the mud flats at the edge. And whilst we were there, the two game keepers, Mr Piggin and Mr Bishop, used to take us out in one of the punts and show us perhaps a Bearded Tit's nest in amongst the reeds or maybe, skulking on the Broad's edge, a buff-coloured snipe, with its short legs and long straight bill poking around in the mud for food. Another day we might find maybe a well-camouflaged batch of Plover's eggs, nestling on the ground amidst the corn stalks and a little further afield, over towards Thetford, one could find Golden Plovers gracing the air with their distinctive gold and black plumage.

Each day we'd drive into one of the local villages, either Hickling or Potter Heigham for provisions, where the proprietors of the local shops would greet one with their broad Norfolk accents, which delighted us children as we tried to imitate it. Back at the Lodge we loved to take one of the punts out on the Broads, as we learnt to handle the long pole, pushing the boat slowly forward, manoeuvring between the narrows of the reed beds. We also learnt to sail, out on the more open expanses of Hickling Broad itself, and once in a moment of rash exuberance, I managed to capsize the boat, trapping my Father under the sail and leaving poor Mr Bishop floundering in the muddy waters, apparently unable to swim, whilst helmsman Antony swam unheroically for the shore! Luckily we hadn't got further than one of the narrow inlets and somehow, no thanks to me, everyone made the shore, soaked and shaken, but happily safe.

Not far from Whiteslea, was a small island known as Miss Turner's island, named after Emma Turner, an ornithologist and bird photographer, who lived and worked for part of each year on the Broads and who used to stay in a small hut on the island, which we delighted to visit, as it afforded us good views from the hides that she had left there, from which we could observe, unobserved.

Both the Black mountains and Norfolk were special holiday places for us children. Our parents taught us to love the outdoors and nature; to acquire skills such as sailing or cooking and to be self-sufficient. We looked after ourselves and we brought our friends to share the sort of holidays we enjoyed.

Then there were the foreign holidays. My parents were always wonderfully hospitable to generations of foreign students from Woodbrooke, many of whom stayed with us, or regularly came to our house for meals. They all became close friends of the family and very often reciprocated my parents' friendship by inviting our family or sometimes just my parents, to stay with them when they returned home. One of these families was Sis and Einar Myrebøe and their children Tor and Lars, from Oslo, with whom we had a wonderful holiday in the summer of 1952 at their island house near Oslo on Larvik's Fjord. Tor and Lars had also been over to stay with us down in Llanthony in the Spring of that year. One time my parents were invited to join them on their own, for a skiing holiday up in the mountains, near Lillehammer. They had a wonderful time getting thoroughly into the spirit of it as can be seen in the happy photograph of them on the slopes. My Mother, who was an excellent knitter, had made jumpers for both herself and my Father, which they are wearing.

Holidays in Norway

**Mum and Dad skiing in Lillehammer, Norway in 1950 with Sis Myrebøe,
who with her husband Einar (who took the photo) they had known from Woodbrooke.**

Lars and Antony on Larvik's Fjord, Summer 1952

There were other friends from Woodbrooke, including Mamdouha As-Sayyid, a Lebanese lady of whom we were very fond, who went on to work at the United Nations and eventually married the American businessman Elmer Bobst, but often visited us on her visits to this country. Then there was Erica Laübli and her photographer husband Walter from Switzerland, with whom we spent a very happy holiday first at their home in Zürich and then in Engelberg in 1953, where we went climbing in the Urne Alps. I think one's first ever view of the Alps stays with one for ever and as the plane came into land at Zurich airport, it was quite simply breathtaking.

Like my Father, whose quoted love of mountains I mentioned previously, I too became completely awe struck by the extraordinary glamour of this Alpine scenery. One day we were very excited I remember, as our Father told my brother and I we were to get up very early the next day, as he had arranged with a local mountain guide to take us both up the nearest peak, Mount Titlis which was some 10,000 feet high.

We were all agog as we donned climbing boots and warm, protective clothing, with my Father's old rucksacks swung over our backs, replete with sandwiches and a thermos. Off we set, roped together like seasoned mountaineers, very early indeed so that we should avoid the heat and glare of the midday sun and reach the top in good time to make the descent before dusk. It was an exhilarating, if strenuous climb and at the top we were able to enjoy a spectacular view in the crystal clear sky over towards Berne and Lucerne. We soon got talking to a group of local Austrian climbers who were swigging a bottle of an enticing looking drink, which they were happy to offer to us thirsty mountaineers. Thinking it to be merely orange juice, I quaffed it down in one healthy gulp, only to splutter as I choked on what turned out to be something much stronger; a local schnapps, much to everyone else's great amusement.

This was our first close encounter with the beauty of the Alps and we fell in love with all things Swiss. I bought a model chalet which was also a music box, and played a well-known Swiss yodelling song 'Mir Senne hei's Lustig' ('We shepherds have fun!') when you lifted the chalet roof, which I still possess. I also remember making a terrible fuss when I was told I couldn't have a Swiss army penknife, as they were too expensive and my Father eventually taking me to a shop to find a cheap one, to keep me quiet!

Every Christmas after that holiday, I remember Erica did her best to satisfy our love of things Swiss by sending us some Lindt chocolate, which was quickly devoured by all the family, even though we secretly thought Cadbury's was superior!

One other foreign holiday about the same time, that stands out because it gave us our first experience of flying, was when David and I were given permission to leave The Downs before the end of term to join my parents on a trip to Holland, where my Father had to attend a housing conference. It was shortly after the end of the war and I recall my Father being very impressed, that although the dam over the Zuiderzee was yet to be fully repaired after the Germans had severely damaged it in the closing days of the war, the Dutch had, nevertheless, rebuilt the major cities with impressive speed.

We travelled throughout Holland, not only to Amsterdam and Rotterdam but also making a special trip to Delft to visit the pottery factory, where my Mother bought some of the famous blue Delftware. My parents were always keen that we should learn to appreciate fine art and of course we visited the Vermeer centre and though we were still very young, something must have remained with us, as reading Tracy Chevalier's delightful book *The Girl with the Pearl Earring* years later, it all seemed remarkably familiar.

Holidays in Switzerland

Family Barlow in Switzerland 1953 with Erica Laübli and Mount Titlis just visible in the background. Photo taken by Erica's husband, Walter Laübli, a very well-known photographer.

The Author writes:
"David and Antony with a group of Austrian climbers, exhausted on top of Mt Titlis, having had a healthy quaff of some orange juice, which turned out to be schnapps!"

As children we were intrigued by the country, with its canals and old bridges and windmills and everywhere hundreds of cyclists. I always liked to bring home little mementoes from a country that would remind me of its specialities and in Holland not only did I buy a miniature pair of clogs but also a real full size pair which I fondly imagined myself wearing round the house. It's unlikely, of course, that I ever wore them again!

Since then I've returned several times to Holland, always with pleasure and I took my Mother there some few years after my Father died when we had a nostalgic trip down memory lane, revisiting the places where we had been on that visit. It was one of the coldest Springs on record and we shivered in the unseasonable weather I remember with both of us struggling to smile for the camera!

Not all our friends were Quakers by any means. There was Ralph Pugh, an old high Anglican friend of my Father's and Duncan Wood's. Exactly how and where they met I am unclear, though his first entry in the visitors book is 1945. Typically, however, for Ralph, having omitted to sign on his first visit, he signed on the next, against the place where my Mother had written his name, with the legal Latin tag 'Nunc pro Tunc' – now for then! He was the same age as my Father, but the two Ralphs couldn't have been more different. Ralph Pugh was a true eccentric, an enthusiast for precision, whose manners were very formal and who gave sight-seeing as his recreation in Who's Who. There was more than a deal of truth in this, for he was a distinguished academic and Editor of the Victorian County Histories and on his frequent visits to stay with us, my Father would always contrive to take him to view some country house or place of historic interest. He had a curvature of the spine and became increasingly incapacitated as he got older, but he was wonderfully kind to David and I as we were growing up, often taking us to lunch at his club, The Reform, and on to a play afterwards on our Long Leave days from Leighton Park. I recall with amusement how we would wander through the then dark and smoky, Victorian rooms of The Reform with Ralph giving a discreet running commentary as we progressed past the leather armchairs, indicating the silhouette of an elderly member asleep under a copy of The Times, saying that "that was Lord Ponsoby" or some such, a no-doubt distinguished member of the great and the good. David also remembers going to see Becket's *Waiting for Godot* and the two of them walking out in disgust!

But perhaps our family's closest friends were the Plattens, Michael and Elizabeth and their children Antony, Angela and Michael junior, always known as Charlie. They initially lived very close to us in Selly Oak, before they moved to a large house in Meriden called 'Strawberry Bank'. Michael was a Doctor and had been in the Navy during the war on the Atlantic convoys and with our Father away as well, my Mother and Elizabeth became close friends. Their eldest son and I were born within a few months of each other, grew up together and went to school together. We were both called Antony, spelt without an 'h', after Antony Knebworth who had died in a flying accident, aged only 30 a few years before and had been immortalised in a famous book called simply 'Antony', by his Father the Earl of Lytton, that depicted the golden youth as supremely talented and who in the preface by J M Barrie, no less, was characterised as one "who had he lived, might have given to England, gifts of leadership and imagination which she sorely needs, and a selfless service which none who knew him could doubt for a moment." Not much to live up to then!

As children, Antony and I were always in and out of each other's houses and when they moved to Meriden, we would have what today's children call 'sleep overs' and we became the closest of friends. The two families shared many holidays together, most often in their beloved Scotland, far up near Oban or by the Kyle of Lochalsh, to the West of Inverness, to where in those halcyon pre-Beeching days, you could still ease the journey from the South, by putting your car on the train.

Close family friends

(Above) Michael Platten and Antony P just off fishing

**Elizabeth Platten with the two Antonys, rods lying to the left,
enjoying a warming cup of tea after the fishing**

We all loved the outdoors and though my Father never cared much for fishing, he and Mum would relish the spectacular mountain walks, with their steep-sided glens and the many picturesque fishing villages and of course, the bird life. High up amongst the Scots pines you would find the little crested tits and once on a visit to the isle of Mull, we saw a Sea eagle. But Michael and Elizabeth, with Antony and I would regularly go off fishing to a loch somewhere high up in the hills perhaps on Ben Cruachan. Michael, was an expert fisherman, who had been taught in turn by his Father and he would show us how to tie a fly and how to land a line on the evening water of the loch as light as gossamer. Like theatre folk, climbers and fisherman can be very superstitious and we were instructed always to appease the mountain spirits by leaving a sweet buried under a cairn on the way up, so that we might all descend home safely, untrammelled by the impenetrable, late evening mists.

Because of having the same name, we two Antonys were known respectively as AP for Platten and AB for Barlow and remained so. We stayed in a rented cottage in Minard, a small village on the western shores of Loch Fyne not very far from Oban, from where one year, we took the ferry over to Mull. We hired a small bus, I remember, to take all ten of our two families plus some other friends the Waynes, who came for a few days and we drove across the island. Walking, climbing, fishing and bird watching were our indulgencies and how we all relished them. Like the Black mountains and Norfolk, Scotland became another of our favourite holiday destinations.

In later years, my Father had less energy and often enjoyed just relaxing with my Mother back at the cottage, reading and smoking his pipe and just being in each other's company. They were both voracious readers and I have a number of little pocket books that they kept, with lists of books that they had read, or reviews of books to read in the future. My Father often read and reread the King James translation of the Bible, enjoying its beauty of language as much as its teachings.

Sadly, as Antony P grew older, we grew somewhat apart. He became a Doctor like his father, got married and had children and I went into the Arts and became a Theatre Administrator and settled down with my partner. And then one day out of the blue, I received the terrible news that AP had killed himself. Some years ago, his children asked me to tell them about the Antony I had known and remembered and as best I could, I told them of our shared childhood and early years; of the fun we had had, of the discussions, the arguments and of our shared hopes for our lives ahead. It was a terrible tragedy, as brutal as it was unpredictable and his family and ours, and all who had known him, mourned the loss of a brilliant friend and human being.

The year after Antony died, my parents accompanied Michael and Elizabeth to Italy to help them get over the shock of that tragedy. The two families remained good friends all their lives and friendships continue down the generations, as I am still close friends with Angela and her husband, Sam Dastor, with whom I was at The Downs School and I am Godfather to Angela's daughter Emma by her first husband Chris.

I have dwelt on the holidays of our childhood as they reveal a great deal about our parents and the values they taught us. We seldom, if ever stayed in hotels and not just because we couldn't afford it, but rather because it was a lifestyle choice. In true Quaker custom, we eschewed frippery and espoused simple pleasures instead. We walked and cycled, we climbed and went camping; we learnt to cook and looked after ourselves. We were a happy family and there was much love. There was firm discipline but without corporal punishment and our parents didn't fall out. There was a close circle of friends, most of whom, though not all, were from a Quaker background and had a shared core of values. We grew up with the children from such families; the Darbys and the Ransomes, the Gilletts, and the Plattens plus our cousins on both sides.

A family holiday in Llanthony with family and friends

A picnic with close family friends, the Ransomes near Llanthony 1950's
l to r: Rosemary, Stephen, David, Hilda Ransome, Mary Ransome, Cousin Graham Barber, Antony, Edwin Ransome, Robert Ransome, Dad, Dinah Ransome, Jill Ransome. Photo taken by Mum

We read the Bible on Sundays, taking it in turn as we grew older to read a passage, which when it was my turn, I remember to my embarrassment, misreading 'hunger and thirst after righteousness' as 'hunger and thirst after rhinoceroses', which seemed like the nearest equivalent I could make out! We went to meeting on Sundays, had roast dinners afterwards and would often go for a walk in the grounds at Woodbrooke, where we knew all the Quaker staff and came into contact with the surviving group of that remarkable older generation of Quakers from my Grandparent's generation, Horace Alexander, H G Wood and Wilfrid and Winifred Littleboy. These all came from old Quaker families and had born witness to their pacifist faith through two World Wars. Their example influenced our young lives as we grew up in the knowledge of the extraordinary heritage to which we too were heir.

My parents, like many Quakers before them, were members of many Friends' institutions such as the old Midland Institute, the Quaker Book Club and the Essay Society, all established in an earlier age, when families made their own entertainment. The Essay Society was made up of members who each contributed an essay on some topical subject and read it out to the others in the group. It was a very formal occasion and involved wearing tail coat and full evening dress, much to my Father's annoyance who hated any sort of pompous dressing up, although I remember he rather prided himself that he could still - just - get into the dress clothes he was married in!

I still have some of the Essays they wrote, several on serious topics such as 'Some Thoughts on the 17th Century' in which my Father wonders whether Quakers put too great an emphasis on the writings of George Fox and neglected others such as Shakespeare, Milton and the metaphysical poets and suggests that we should try to *"understand what these poets have to say about man in relation to his fellows and to God and about the great questions of life, death and eternity."* And there is an equally intellectual one by my Mother on 'Victorian Poetry' in which she discusses how, though many of the poems depict situations where *"disaster may lurk around every corner, nevertheless the ideals and framework of society seem reassuringly safe."* Serious matters. But equally there are more light-hearted ones, for instance on 'The Fascination of Press Cuttings'. My parents were excellent writers of great style and enjoyed the research and preparation for such events. In later years they would often get annoyed with other members, who as many began going on holidays to far flung corners of the planet, would show their holiday slides instead of delivering an Essay. Not good!

Never happy in a suit or formal attire, my Father was much more relaxed in casual clothes, mucking about in the garden, which both he and my Mother loved doing. They were both very knowledgeable on matters horticultural and my Father was also a good garden designer and when later, I had a garden of my own in Clapham, he came and laid it out for me. Together they regularly won prizes for the best garden on the Bournville Estate and in later life when he could do less and had stopped entering, he would often be one of the judges.

My Father was often very good at coming up with surprise treats for the family, usually centred on special national occasions. In 1951 I remember he took my Mother and David and I down to London for the Festival of Britain on the South Bank. We all stayed at his sister's house in Golders Green and though I recall being very sick on the big dipper in Battersea Gardens and my brother catching a wallet that had fallen out of someone's pocket as they whizzed round upside down, of anything I might have seen in the Dome of Discovery, my memory remains a blank! But even at age ten, I began to fall in love with London and the excitements to be had in a big city.

Two years later my brother and I came down with my Father and his brother to the Coronation. My Mother stayed in Birmingham with Stephen and Rosemary and as we still didn't possess a television, they all joined up with Mum's sister and family in Wolverhampton and watched theirs. Unlike the Festival of Britain, I recall the Coronation very vividly, as we slept out overnight in the Haymarket in the pouring rain, to be sure of a good view. The streets were all bedecked with bunting and everyone carried a bedraggled little Union jack under their umbrellas, which they waved enthusiastically on every possible occasion. As dawn broke, I remember it being announced over the Tannoy system to much shouting and cheering, that Everest had been climbed by Edmund Hilary and Sherpa Tensing. The rain seemed to go on for ever, but there was such an atmosphere that I do not recall it spoiling the day. I can also still remember as the coach bearing Sir Winston Churchill came past, his horses started to rear up, affrighted by the cheering crowds, upon which Churchill lent out of the window and cheerfully gave us the Victory sign. Then there was the redoubtable six foot tall, Queen Salote of Tonga with all four foot eight of the Emperor Haile Selassie, completely dwarfed, sitting beside her. She endeared herself to everybody watching, by riding through the streets in an open carriage, smiling and waving in the pouring rain. Of course the whole procession was extraordinary; a riot of colour from uniformed soldiers and golden coaches to flags and decorations but perhaps unsurprisingly, to a twelve year old, it is the unusual incidents that seem to stand out more in my memory than actually seeing the Queen's coach.

I was quite small as a young boy, unlike David who was, even at sixteen, already nearly six foot, and I struggled to be able to see very much at all. Happily, someone took pity on me and let me squeeze through to the front of the pavement from where I had the best view of all. After the procession had returned from the Abbey following the ceremony, we somehow picked our way through the crowds down the Mall to Buckingham Palace, the better to see the fly past by the RAF. Then, tired and exhausted we made our way to Golders Green, to collect the car and drive home and I remember, before we had gone less than thirty miles, my Uncle John began to nod off much to our consternation, at which my Father took over to take us the rest of the way home. I seem to remember too that we arrived home too late to take my Mother and younger brother and sister to see the big firework display, much to her annoyance. But my Father had wanted us to witness this uniquely British pageantry, as he said it was unlikely that we would live to see another like it and if the present Queen lives as long as her Mother, that may yet turn out to be true.

One further occasion also stands out in my mind, which comes into the long list of my Father's 'Unexpected Surprises'. For my seventeenth birthday, not long before our youngest brother Nicholas was born, perhaps as much a treat for my Mother, prior to having a young child again, as for me, my Father had arranged for us all to visit London. This was not in itself too unusual, as we had often been to places like Whipsnade Zoo, not far from Luton and then later stayed at Millior and Alfred's in London. But on this occasion, he wondered out loud, in a roundabout hypothetical, Christopher Robinish sort of way, what plays my Mother and I might like to see, just supposing we were to visit London. And then, lo and behold, a few days later he announced that he really had bought tickets for us to go to the theatre; to see Margot Fonteyn in *The Firebird* at Covent Garden, which was my Mother's choice and then the next day to go to the Old Vic to see *King Lear,* with their leading Shakespearean actor Paul Rogers, which was my choice. Little did I know it at the time, though fate sometimes works in an uncanny way, that I would find myself in that milieu only twenty years later. Perhaps my Father intuited something about me that I wasn't even yet aware of myself, but as it turned out, it was uncannily prescient, as I was later to work as General Administrator for Dame Margot at The Royal Academy of Dancing, of which she was President and later with The Old Vic/Young Vic under the aegis of that theatre pioneer Frank Dunlop, where one of our actors just happened to be Paul Rogers' daughter Emma! So perhaps things do turn out as they are supposed to and maybe it sparked a flame inside me, as I remember being completely bowled over by *The Firebird*, with Stravinsky's music, quite unlike anything with which I was familiar, the ravishing designs by Natalia Goncharova, which created a rich riot of colour and of course, the extraordinary performance of Fonteyn, a dancer whose vivid stage presence is something once seen, remains forever.

As for Shakespeare, it has been probably the one constant that runs throughout my love of the theatre and though I've seen many Lears since then, including greater actors such as Olivier, Gielgud, Laughton and Jacobi, the first, inevitably makes a strong impression and that of Paul Rogers' remains fixed in my mind's eye even now fifty years on. So I remain eternally grateful to my parents for passing on their love of the theatre to me and indeed to all of us, for it has enriched all of our lives.

The postscript to this London visit made a slightly unfortunate ending to an otherwise very happy few days, as arriving back from the Old Vic on a high, our bright disposition was soon shattered as we realised that my Aunt's house had been comprehensively burgled in our absence. Every draw in my Uncle's desk, had been opened and the contents scattered willy-nilly like so much confetti over the furniture and floor. I remember my Father, torch in hand, grabbing a poker from the fire place, stalking through the house, opening every door and cupboard, in case there was still someone lurking in the house, ready to attack us! Happily, the Police soon arrived and were able to reassure my Father and the rest of us that the intruders had long since fled. They also told us that every other house nearby, had seemingly been broken into as well, which made us feel slightly better, though I was aware that ringing my Aunt and Uncle, who were in America, wasn't going to be something my Father would relish!

Visiting the theatre however, was not an unusual occurrence. It was something both my parents loved and they regularly took us to the Alex[185] to see visiting productions and Barry Jackson's famous Birmingham Rep[186], initially to see the famous Christmas productions written by Nicholas Stuart Grey and then as we got older to both new and classical plays with actors, many of whom were to become household names such as Derek Jacobi and Albert Finney. But my own love of the theatre and Shakespeare in particular, came from my parents and living in Birmingham, we were only forty minutes away from Stratford-upon-Avon and its Memorial Theatre. It was a beautiful drive through the lanes of Warwickshire, a countryside that a young William would still have found familiar. The journeys however, were often spoilt for me, as I was an inveterate car-sick child. On one embarrassing occasion I even contrived to throw up in the aisle of The Memorial Theatre, just as the curtain was rising. Nevertheless, I was not to be deterred from travelling with my siblings to the theatre, where growing up during a golden period of English acting, we were able to see many legendary Shakespearian performances by such actors as Laurence Olivier and Vivien Leigh, Diana Wynyard and John Gielgud or Paul Scofield and Margaret Leighton.

Every Christmas as well, Stratford would play host to a visit from the D'Oyly Carte Opera company and even my Father, a most unmusical person, enjoyed their operettas. D'Oyly Carte at this time, before the copyright ended, was still performing the operettas in the original versions with Martyn Green and Peter Pratt in the patter roles, with every choreographed repeat included, some of which, if pressed I could probably still perform myself! My Mother was someone who kept everything from newspaper cuttings to theatre programmes and amongst

---

[185] The Alexandra Theatre, run by the Salberg family, housed visiting touring productions.
[186] Barry Jackson was the founder of the old Repertory Theatre in Station Street as well as the Malvern Festival.

boxes of items I discovered after she died, were innumerable programmes from concerts and plays from the thirties onwards, with musicians like Yehudi Menuhin and Fritz Kreisler or actors as varied as Cicely Courtneidge and Jack Hulbert, Noël Coward and Gertrude Lawrence or indeed Godfrey Tearle, whom my Father thought the greatest Othello he had ever seen. These all bore testament to an extraordinarily diverse cultural life, which they both regaled us with as we grew up, so that these people felt as much a part of our lives as those we actually knew.

So far, I have only lightly touched on our education and perhaps I should bring this in here. Our parents were anxious that we should have the same sort of education that they had enjoyed. Both had been to Quaker boarding schools where they had been happy and wished the same for us, even though it was to stretch their budget to breaking point. So my brothers David and Stephen and I went to The Downs and then on to Leighton Park and despite inevitable homesickness and in those days only seeing parents once a term, we were for the most part, happy. The Downs in those days was a wonderfully outgoing school, where practically everyone learnt a musical instrument, sung in the choir or played in the orchestra. David learnt the piano with a large, voluble Italian lady, Miss Lloyd and I the violin with tubby Miss Mitchell, known as 'Barrell' and our indulgent parents bravely listened to our no doubt excruciating musical performances at the end of each summer term. I rather feel that brother Stephen wisely opted not to take up an instrument.

In some respects following an elder brother could always be difficult. After David went to The Downs and later LP, each succeeding boy had to cope with being the elder one's brother. Inevitably I was Barlow junior to David and Stephen was Barlow II when he joined me and we both had to cope with comparisons and make our mark in our own way. David excelled at intellectual pursuits, I perhaps at more artistic activities, whilst neither of us was very sporty. Stephen on the other hand loved games and participated with a will.

But the school was good at helping each boy to find his own niche. We all had the opportunity to learn a hobby from woodwork and metalwork to painting or pottery and our brave efforts of metal ashtrays (David), wooden toast racks (Antony), or clay vases (Stephen), where proudly exhibited at the end of the summer term for parents to admire.

There were garden plots where we could learn about horticulture and grow vegetables and best of all, there was a small gauge railway which encouraged generations of enthusiasts, who learnt about engineering and how to lay tracks and build tunnels. It had been Geoffrey Hoyland's[187] philosophy that every boy should learn something that interested him and at which he could excel in addition to classroom subjects, which is why it suited us all in our different ways.

Geoffrey Hoyland was succeeded by his brother Frazer Hoyland,[188] who established an amazing tradition of drama productions. It was under his inspirational guidance that plays as seemingly beyond the scope of Prep school boys as Maeterlinck's 'The Blue Bird' and Eliot's 'Murder in the Cathedral', were staged and brought brilliantly to life with wonderful sets designed by Maurice Field, the school's gifted and much loved Art master. Being an all boy's school, of course we played the woman's parts too and my own triumph was as the Maid in Rattigan's *The Winslow Boy* with a cast including Jan Piggott, subsequently Head of English at Dulwich College as the Mother, Grace Winslow, the distinguished artist Christopher Stevens as Catherine Winslow and Sam Dastor as the barrister Sir Robert Morton, which decided him on his future career as an actor and who was to become a founder member of Olivier's National Theatre, as well as, incidentally the husband of my friend AP's sister Angela.

---

[187] The second Headmaster of The Downs, whose guiding genius set the ethos for the school.
[188] The third Headmaster of The Downs.

Downs Headmaster, Frazer Hoyland and his wife Phyllis encouraged drama at the school

Frazer and Phyllis Hoyland outside the gym at one 'Commemoration Day' c 1953

The Winslow Boy' 1952 with l-r Jan Piggott, Chris Stevens, Julian Ormond, Antony Barlow, Michael Ware, Julian Hipsley, Robin Lewis.

I am quite certain too in my own mind, that following the play acting that we had done at home with my Father, I leapt at the chance to be involved with more at school, which I was later to continue at Leighton Park in a memorable production of Shakespeare's Henry IV with a fine cast that included, future BBC Administrator, brother David as Westmoreland, Ambassador Plenipotentiary in waiting Richard Thomas, playing Mortimer, distinguished Reuters correspondent to be, Colin Fox a memorable Hotspur, Richard Kay as Hal, who prior to his untimely early death, was another member of the fledgling National Theatre and 15 year old me as a glamorous Lady Percy, my career path inexorably set!

The staff at The Downs were, on the whole, a dedicated group, many of whom stayed there for life. In particular, the Art master, Maurice Field, known to everyone as 'Parsy'[189] was an extremely gifted artist, who had a talent for inspiring the untalented and we learnt not only how to draw and paint, but how to use charcoal, mix oil paints and prepare a canvas. He sketched and painted many of the boys at the school over a period of nearly thirty years and one summer holiday, came to stay at our home, making some delightful sketches of all of us children[190].

The distinguished painter and Art teacher, Sir William Coldstream, described him as *"one of the most outstanding teachers of art of his generation."* He later returned to The Slade, where he had himself studied, inspiring graduate artists including Francis Hoyland, Anthony Fry and Sir Lawrence Gowing, who had attended The Downs as a young boy and described Field as *"among the unsung influences on British painting."*

W H Auden had been a master at the school in the thirties and wrote of Field: *"The Downs is one of the very few preparatory schools were the boys are taught to paint in oils.....and though most boys will not become professional painters, the results of having once painted themselves is bound to inspire an interest and appreciation of the pictorial arts."*[191] I think I can positively say that I owe my own love and understanding of art to Maurice Field's inspiration.

Amongst the many others, were Donald Boyd who taught me not only the disciplines of Latin grammar, but gave me a life-long love of the short stories of 'Saki', which he often used to read to us; Ken Ricketts, known as 'Snappy', instructed me in the basic skills of carpentry as well as inspiring me to acquire the ability to perform a handstand and a backflip; and then there was Gus Miller, a pedantic Scotsman, who instilled in me the rudiments of sentence construction and to whom I owe any skill I have in writing.

We were entrusted out on the Malvern Hills in small groups with just a pack leader only a few years older than we were, and enough money to buy some food which we cooked on a fire we built from sticks. On Sundays we walked or cycled to Malvern Quaker meeting and raced down the Wyche Cutting back to school in time for lunch and a piece of home-made fudge. We wrote letters home once a week and we looked forward eagerly to tour our parents' replies. In the summer term we wore Aertex shirts and khaki shorts and bathed naked in the open air swimming pool.

We built tree huts that Health and Safety would have deemed dangerous and helped produce a school magazine called The Badger which published our early attempts at essays and poetry. There was a system of democratic self-governance by Leaders who went on a 'Leaders' Week' in Snowdonia in the September prior to assuming the role, and during term time we had regular meetings with the Headmaster to discuss problems that might arise.

---

[189] Usually thought to have been derived from 'Parsley', which grew in a field!
[190] Reproduced courtesy of Rosemary Howells
[191] Preface to the catalogue for 1937 exhibition at The Redfern Gallery.

The School Orchestra and drawings by Maurice Field

**The Downs was a very musical school.
Here the orchestra is rehearsing, with Antony second violin far left**

**The Art Master, Maurice Field was an extremely gifted artist and sketched (left) Stephen and myself
and (right) Rosemary one summer, staying with the family**

It was possibly this early training and experience in Leadership that was one of the most valuable aspects of the wide education the school offered and as Jim Brown says in his book 'The First Five'[192], *"the principles of leadership gained in the last year at The Downs remained with pupils for the rest of their lives."* In many ways, no school could have been closer to the ideals that our parents' instilled in us, as previously described, in the holidays we enjoyed together as a family. As Jim Hoyland[193] has written in the Forward to Jim Brown's history of the school:

"Quaker foundations were absolutely fundamental to the ethos of The Downs, with its caring and compassionate 'family', in which each boy was encouraged to develop his individual talents, as well as his imaginative and creative faculties in the service of his fellow man."

That, I would say was as much our parents' philosophy as that of The Downs and I suspect that it was bred in my Father in part during his own years at the school, years before. Herbert Jones, who founded The Downs, and had laid down the Quaker principles which governed its future, had also previously been Headmaster of Leighton Park. It is hardly surprising, therefore, that the two schools had much in common. So when we graduated to Leighton Park, we found ourselves very much in familiar territory, where all the attributes I have described at The Downs, were developed, only in a way that prepared us for University and adult life.

We continued to progress our 'hobbies', which in my case included carpentry to a high standard, as well as continuing my violin studies to a point where I could at least have a go at a Mozart Violin concerto, though like Algernon in *The Importance of Being Earnest*, it could have been said "I played not very accurately, but with great feeling." As recounted, we continued to act in plays and my brother David, a good public speaker, entered and won the prestigious JB Hodgkin speech competition. We became members of the Head, John Ounsted's prestigious Poetry Society for which we wrote meaningful poetry, which was dissected by both Ounsted and the other members and gave us confidence in our own abilities. We formed strong and influential friendships, in my case with people who helped to develop my burgeoning beliefs in holding the government to account for their actions, especially on the burning issue of the day, nuclear weapons. And it is to LP's great credit that they allowed me and these fellow school mates of mine, John Hoyland and Dan Elwyn Jones to join the Alermaston march. I shall not readily forget Dan's parents, writer Pearl Binder and Harold Wilson's Lord Chancellor, Lord Elwyn Jones cheering us on and feeding us with nourishing cups of warm soup along the way. Similar to The Downs, there was a School Council, comprised of us boys and although Masters could be invited to attend, we were the officers and the ones who took many important decisions about School affairs. It was another way in which we learnt about leadership.

As the booklet 'Seven Years'[194]says:

"We wish to teach young people how to think, instead of what to think.......at Leighton Park liberty is increased according to a person's ability to use it......it is a school, where right thinking is the final arbiter, where corporal punishment is non-existent because unnecessary, and where freedom is tempered with sane restriction."

Again this echoed very much our parents' beliefs about both learning and discipline. They gave us free rein to discover ourselves, let us make our own mistakes, offered help and guidance without prejudice and still loved us when we went contrary to their advice.

---

[192] 'The First Five: The Story of a School' by E J Brown 1987.
[193] Geoffrey Hoyland's son.
[194] Leighton Park, Seven Years 1948-1955. LP Publications

A School council at LP and a school play

David 4th left back, facing table. Classics master, Firth Barlow (no relation) back with glasses.

Shakespeare's Henry IV

The Author writes:

"A fine cast including future BBC Administrator, brother, David Barlow as Westmoreland, Ambassador Plenipotentiary in waiting Richard Thomas, playing Mortimer, distinguished Reuters correspondent to be, Colin Fox as Hotspur, future member of Laurence Olivier's National Theatre company, Richard Kay and future Arts administrator Antony Barlow as a glamorous Lady Percy."

I have a typically wonderful letter from my Father, following a substantial disagreement we had, which says – *"We understand and must respect your decision, not that we think it is the right one, but you are still our dear son and one of the family."* It echoes so much a letter that his Mother wrote to him in 1942 - *"Do not think you have disappointed me dear. Tho' we have differed at times, it has never severed our love."* I still find both these letters deeply moving and I firmly believe they espouse a deep Quaker understanding of the meaning of family and love, which was embedded in the very fabric of their make-up. And I am sure it has been passed on to us, as one generation succeeds another and finds its own far off echo of the lives of those who have gone before, such as Betty Sutton, John Barlow, Eliza Nicholson, my Grandparents and my parents.

As a past Chairman of the Governors wrote in the forward to the history of the school[195]: *"Leighton Park was an extraordinarily human place. It was a school to which almost any child could be sent with confidence of prospering, of gaining in breadth and social responsibility and not becoming arrogant. It has done particularly well by youngsters who do not necessarily thrive on intense competition, including many with a strongly original talent and it is a good sign that ex-pupils are to be found in a wide range of occupations, all over the world and that they are very much themselves, not conforming to any standard pattern. Education at LP has proved a congenial place in which pupils can grow at their own pace and in what proves to be their own distinctive direction."*

That too concurs with my parents' outlook on life. While being ambitious for us to do well, they were more concerned that we were content and forged our own futures in a way that suited us best. My sister Rosemary went first to Whitford Hall School, which was then in Bromsgrove, as a weekly boarder, which she greatly enjoyed, before transferring to the Church of England School in Birmingham. This proved slightly less conducive to her free and open nature, but even so with her customary determination, she achieved the necessary A levels to gain entrance to Homerton Teacher Training college in Cambridge, a place where she was supremely happy. Here she gained the sort of confidence and independence of spirit that we boys had perhaps had at our boarding schools and eventually enabled her very soon after qualifying to embark on a highly successful teaching career.

Through all the decisions our parents took regarding our early lives, their greatest wish was always to do their best and to enable us to have as good a training as possible for our future careers, whatever and wherever that might be. In that they succeeded, though inevitably at considerable financial cost to themselves. Up to now, I have talked quite a lot about the early years of us four children, which though now over fifty years ago, are still very vivid. But this is only incidentally a book about us. It is, and will remain essentially about our parents. Where we feature, it is hopefully, to illustrate some facet of my parents' lives. The home life we had, the schools we went to and the holidays we enjoyed, were symptomatic both of our parents' philosophy and consequently of our happy home and the love and security with which we felt surrounded.

Of course not everything was idyllic. As Katherine Hepburn, playing Eleanor of Aquitane, in the film 'The Lion in Winter' remarks, in her famously husky voice, of her turbulent relations with Peter O'Toole's Henry II, *"well, every family has its ups and downs"* and there were certainly 'ups and downs'. But our parents believed firmly in the words of Saint Francis that *"where there is discord, may we sow love...and where there is sadness may we bring joy"* and in the end, most differences were resolved and the family survived the stronger for it. And in the long run these problems are not the story here; they are for another time, if at all.

---

[195] 'Leighton Park, The First 100 Years' by Robert Maxwell.

Mum and Dad in the Cotswolds and their Silver Wedding

The Author writes:

"My parents just prior to Nick's birth. There's a slight air of posing with Mum, looking perfect in a summer's dress and necklace and a bouquet of wild flowers, and the head turned judiciously for the camera! It's a perfect picture of them both."

My parents' Silver Wedding 1961
back l to r: Stephen, Antony, Rosemary and David.
front l to r :Mum, Dad, young Nick aged 3 and (right) Jill, David's wife

The family enjoying themselves

Prior to Nicholas' birth in 1958, these show the type of outdoor holidays the family enjoyed.

Rosemary canoeing in Scotland

Stephen on a cycling holiday

David rowing on Hickling Broad

**Dad, Antony, Stephen and Rosemary at
Burnham-on-Sea 1950's**

Antony riding on Exmoor

By the end of the fifties my parents were in their mid-forties, not far from their Silver Wedding anniversary, David was about to get married and go to Oxford, I was shortly to leave Leighton Park and Stephen and Rosemary would soon be going on to Leighton Park and the Church of England School respectively. So perhaps the arrival of another sibling was understandably not amongst our immediate expectations, for like most children we rarely contemplated the possibility that our middle aged parents might have sexual relations. That surely was something that young things like us were about to discover! But in August of 1958 we had the happy addition of another brother, named Nicholas Phillip.

This meant a complete change of life for my parents and for us too, if Nick was not to grow up an only child. For my Mother, it meant getting to know a new set of parents who had young children and for my Father, whatever thoughts he may have had of early retirement, had to be put on hold. For us, we all had to rally round and do our best to be a presence for our young brother, so that we would not be strangers.

So it could have been a difficult time, with extra strain on my Father's slender financial means, determined as he was that a late arrival should not miss out on the advantages that the rest of us had had either educationally or otherwise, and my Mother coping in middle age with a young child and the strains that can involve, including it should be said, having a rinse in her hair, so that, as she admitted to me in later years, 'when collecting a young Nick from school, he might not be embarrassed with a grey-haired Mum!' That my parents succeeded triumphantly in incorporating us all into the new family unit, speaks volumes for the people they were.

The next period is more difficult to relate as I was not at home so much. I was away studying Drama and English at Manchester University for three years, though still living at home in the vacations. But I was having the greatest of fun, busy discovering about myself, and then in 1965 setting out on a career in the theatre. David had married Jill Roberts and after he finished at Oxford set up home and he too began his working life, first with the British Council and then with the BBC.

Inevitably, when one is fast becoming an adult oneself and busy with one's own concerns and living at home less and less, young children seem to grow up very suddenly. When it was just the four of us, we seemed to advance together. But with Nick, one day he was a child off to his first school, and the next almost imperceptibly, he was a young adult graduating from University. Of course, Nick wasn't really on his own. David and I visited as much as we could and after Stephen left LP[196] to study Hotel Management at the College of Food, he lived at home with Rosemary, who was then studying at the Church of England school, which meant Nick always had some family around him. Then there were family gatherings, of which the most important was always Christmas.

Being the sort of family we were, Christmas was a special time, when we were all together and when we followed our own particular rituals, firmly established since childhood. Our parents filled our Father's old FAU long-stockings with little gifts, tangerines, chocolates and nuts and somehow managed to hang them over the ends of our beds without us ever suspecting.

Back in early autumn, we had helped stir the pudding and put old silver threepenny bits or lucky horseshoes inside the rich mixture, for some lucky recipient to find on Christmas day. Each year we would search in the box room for the bags that we had carefully marked 'Christmas decorations' the year before and prayed that the baubles and lights hadn't been broken in the intervening months.

---

[196] Sadly, Stephen's time at LP was one of the casualties of my parents' increasingly tight financial budget. He left after 3 years in 1962, finishing his schooling at Bournville College before going to the College of Food 1963-66.

Nick grows up fast and a family wedding

**Nick in 1966 aged 7
on his first day at Hallfield School**

Nick at his graduation in 1981

**Rosemary and Richard's wedding 1971
Richard Howells, Rosemary, Nick, Dad and Mum**

Everyone helped to decorate the Christmas tree with coloured balls, pretend parcels and silver glitter as well as, in the old days, live candles, which we balanced precariously on the frail branches, heedless of the possibility of fire. Finally, we would place an increasingly dilapidated fairy, made from an old toilet roll and coloured paper, uncertainly on the top.

On Christmas Eve we all had a token present from under the tree, before retiring reluctantly to bed. In the morning, inevitably, we awoke at crack of dawn, too excited to sleep and tried to guess what presents might be in our stockings, which we would take as soon as decently possible into our parents' room to open. After breakfast, we would rally round to help my Father stuff the Turkey; chestnut one end, sage and onion the other. Then at last, amid cries of 'presents, presents', we rushed to the drawing room, where the youngest member of the family would hand them out from an old laundry basket, in which they had been piled high, while Mum did her best to keep track of who had given what to whom. Even so, some 'thank you' letters inevitably said vaguely 'Dear Aunt and Uncle, thank you so much for your 'present', it was just what I wanted.'

Then too full to move, someone, my Father usually, would suggest that we all went for a stroll to walk off our lunch. Slowly, amidst groans and grumbling, we would rouse ourselves and, wrapped in our winter scarves, many newly acquired as gifts that very morning, we would head inexorably towards a wintry Woodbrooke for a brisk walk round the pond, with a quick game of 'Pooh sticks', before returning home for Christmas cake and mince pies.

Afterwards, like families everywhere, we would listen to the Queen's broadcast and, as my Father tried to smoke his annual cigar and Mother had an unaccustomed Cointreau, we promptly fell asleep, another Christmas over.

But there were many other occasions when we, 'the family', came together, most often inevitably, for weddings or funerals. I particularly recall during this period the happy occasion of our parents' Silver Wedding in 1961; and sadly, the death of our much loved maternal Grandmother, Granny Barber in 1966.

Then too, there were the family weddings of my brother Stephen and sister Rosemary. I'm not sure if choice of venue says anything about the characters of either of them, though possibly it might be said that Rosemary was more of a traditionalist, choosing to marry Richard Howells at the splendid old Tudor building, Minworth Greaves[197] in Bournville. While Stephen, on the other hand, an avid sports enthusiast, opted to celebrate his marriage to Linda Cairns at Birmingham Cricket ground!

And there were still the holidays of course, albeit in smaller groups. Stephen and Rosemary recall in particular, two memorable holidays with Mum and Dad and a four year old Nick, on the West coast of Ireland in the early 60s. They stayed in Roundstone, a beautiful village in Connemara set on one of the most spectacular coastal drives in Ireland overlooking the Atlantic. It was here, with my Mother's innate gift for making friends that they met a special couple, Kay and Percy Hughes, who later became close friends of all the family and with whom I stayed at their home in Manchester during my first year at University.

---

[197] Thought to date to 1250, Minworth Greaves was originally in Sutton Coldfield. It was saved from destruction by George Cadbury and rebuilt by Laurence Cadbury in 1932.

Family weddings and holidays

Stephen's marriage to Linda Cairns 1970

Mum and Dad in 1965 at a family wedding, with Dad just squeezing into his dress clothes!

The Author writes:
"Wherever Dad went, he always had his binoculars round his neck, and Nick came to be as keen as he." On holiday, Dad and Nick, with Mum and Antony.

They seemed to be always jolly with a great sense of humour and we all became very fond of them. They were the most wonderful couple to be with during that first University year, as they took an interest in everything I did and came to see all the drama productions of the Department and were always there with moral support when needed.

I too remember a holiday, which I was able to join in with the family, in the early 70's when Nick was about twelve. This was in Arles in the Camargue, the little town that so appealed to van Gogh. The family drove the car all the way down to the South of France following a route map supplied by the AA, in the days when every vehicle had to display a GB sign and carry yellow filters so as not to dazzle native drivers with the superior brightness of the British headlights. For some reason now lost in the mists of memory, I travelled down by train some days later. I missed the one my Father had said he would meet and only just caught the next, which must have been the slowest and oldest train ever, with hard wooden-benched carriages, occupied inevitably by garlic-chewing locals who eyed me suspiciously. I arrived several hours late at Avignon and in those pre-mobile phone days, there was much consternation about my safety. We stayed in a little pension somewhere near where the Rhône divides into the Grand Rhône and the Petit Rhône, and the patron and his wife rustled up some food and a welcome glass of the local wine for a tired and hungry traveller. It is glorious countryside and the weather shone on us and I remember playing around in the river and having to listen over and over to some popular song of the moment, which was constantly being played by teenagers nearby. It was a time of much fun and laughter when my youngest brother and I were able to spend what in today's jargon would be called 'quality time' together and so were able get to know each other properly for the first time.

Wherever we were, Dad always had his binoculars round his neck and Nick came to be as keen as he, and is the one who proudly follows in his bird-watching footsteps, being now as knowledgeable as Dad once was. In some ways, as Nick was at home with Dad until he was 13, much longer than David and I were, and because he shared the same love of sport and birds, they were able to bond more. As a result Dad became very close to him, in a way perhaps he hadn't with us. Also in that strange way people sometimes do as they get older, and in the knowledge of his less than robust health, I think he may have had a premonition of his early death. Because of that he was increasingly anxious to enjoy as much of his youngest son's life as he possibly could. They did a great deal together, watching Birmingham City play football or organising countless birding trips, in a way that he used to when he was a young boy himself with Duncan Wood.

Our Father retired from the Trust in 1972 and like his Father before him, had praise heaped upon him for his lifelong dedication to the BVT from as far back as 1932. This came both from countless people on the Estate as much as from those with whom he had worked. This included the official minute which records:

"In all his activities with the BVT, Ralph Barlow identified himself with the Bournville community and has interpreted the aims and purposes of the Trust, both to residents and visitors....He will be remembered for the help and advice he has given freely and with the sympathetic way he always dealt with people's troubles and complaints. The Trustees record their sincere thanks for the enormous contribution he has made for over 40 years."

He thoroughly enjoyed his retirement, being able to devote his time to doing all the things he loved, which meant primarily of course, spending as much time as possible with our Mother whom he adored, as Ben Jonson once said 'this side idolatory'. They lovingly tended their garden, they read to each other and they attended a course of religious study at Woodbrooke in the Autumn of 1977.

Dad's 70th birthday gathering

My Father's 70th birthday gathering, with the birthday boy, typically hiding away at the back!

Back row:
David, Dad, Stephen and Antony

2nd row:
Richard Howells (Rosemary's husband), Millior, Mum, Rosemary, Linda (Stephen's wife), Jill (David's wife) Carol Braithwaite (cousin)

Front row:
John, Andrew, Simon (David's children), Colin and Christopher (Stephen's children), Jenny and Sally (Rosemary's children)

70th birthday party at 17 The Park 1980

Mum and Dad at Millior's on his 70th birthday

His retirement echoed in many ways that of his Father's fifty years before. Now he too was besieged from all sides with invitations to take on a host of commitments. But wisely, he limited himself, agreeing only to write the history of Woodbrooke, of which like his Father, he was a Trustee; and to remain on various committees with which he had been long been associated, particularly that of Copec, a voluntary housing movement, whose board he had been on for most of his life, and which in 1982, opened a garden in his memory.

As he approached his 70th birthday, he set himself three targets. Firstly, despite increasing frailty, he was determined to see Nick finish his education, for which in a way he felt especially responsible; secondly, to complete the book on Woodbrooke, a place dear to his heart as it had been to his parents, to whom he dedicated the book; and lastly to celebrate his 70th birthday. As it turned out, he completed practically all of his aims before he died in 1980, after suffering a fatal heart attack after 'Log Night' at Woodbrooke.

The family celebrated his 70th birthday only months before, with a glorious party at his sister Millior's house in London, surrounded by children and grandchildren. I had seen in a Bird magazine what I thought would be an ideal present; a beautiful replica edition of John Gould's Birds of Britain, which he had so much loved from our many holidays at Whiteslea. We all decided to club together to buy this and indeed, it turned out to be just the right gift.

Some of the last photographs of my parents, were at his adored Woodbrooke. One taken by the lake, where we later planted one of his favourite trees, a Golden Acacia in his memory. The other was of myself with my parents, out looking for siskins and redpolls, which had been sighted there, on what turned to be the last of our famous Christmas after dinner walks in 1979. Possibly the very last photograph of him was taken in the garden of his sister's house in Golders Green on his 70th birthday, which turned out to be the last time I ever saw him as I went off on a business trip to America. Tragically by the time I had returned he had died. I can still recall the numbness I felt, when on my return, I rang home to say I was back, only to have the phone answered by my Aunt Win, who was comforting my Mother and told me of his death. Though he had seemed frail before I left, I had not the slightest apprehension that he would not be there when I returned. My brother Nick too was in the States, staying with our cousins Michael and Marjorie and both of us, I think, felt a certain guilt that we had not been here to support Mum at the time. So I like to remember my Father, sitting with my Mother in the quiet of a summers's evening at 17 The Park, as I left to catch the plane.

The history of Woodbrooke was all but finished, needing only some final editing, which my parents' great friend and senior Woodbrooke lecturer, David Gray brilliantly did, completing it in 1982,[198] with help from our Mother and my brother Nick. In her moving 'Forward' to the book, Gillian Hopkins[199] writes:

"As an ardent bird watcher and gardener, Ralph was a man with an eye for detail and beauty, with patience and a sense of the changing seasons and with the rugged honesty which comes of never fooling oneself. He has used all these talents in writing this book...Those of us who had the good fortune to be at Woodbrooke in the Autumn term of 1977, when Ralph and Joan were students, will recall his quizzical, sometimes caustic comments about the College....but in writing this loving account, it is obvious that he is won over to whole-hearted support of the aims and visions of the institution. Above all this is an account of people like Ralph, who have given service joyfully, arduously and faithfully. He has indeed made a truly significant contribution to Woodbrooke over many years, as a member of the Trust, as well as in the care and love he gave to its garden, and now with this account of its recent history."

---

[198] Woodbrooke 1953-1978
[199] Gillian Hopkins, daughter of Thomas Hopkins, 'Hoppy', the much loved Gym master at LP, and herself a Clerk of YM

David Gray in his Preface also manages to sum up my Father's qualities perfectly, when he writes:

"Ralph's kindly wisdom, his warmth and his sense of humour has managed to string many varied impressions together on a thread that is distinctively and lovingly his own. Ralph collapsed and died in the Common Room at Woodbrooke, surrounded by Woodbrooke staff, students and friends and with his wife Joan, at the end of the happy Log Night which closed the 1980 term. As we gathered later that evening in the Quiet Room, to give thanks, we knew that no ending for him could have been more fitting."

A short while later, we had a beautiful memorial service for my Father, held at Woodbrooke, which was attended by over 200 people, a tribute to the regard in which he was held. Amongst the many there, apart from family, were many of his closest friends with whom he had grown up, including Duncan Wood, Michael and Heather Cadbury, Ralph Pugh and Jeff and Margaret Gillett. Only Horace Alexander, who was by then a rather frail 91 and living in America, was sadly unable to make the journey. For us children, it was a very special occasion and we will always treasure the indelible memory his life made on our family as well as the wide circle in which he moved.

Dad's favourite spot at Woodbrooke, with the lake in winter frost

My Father

The Author writes:
"My Father as I like to remember him, in a typical pose, binoculars to hand, by the lake in his beloved Woodbrooke shortly before he died."

Chapter 21
Joan Barlow - solo

It was, of course, a terrible shock to my Mother when Dad died. It had been such a close relationship, the one dependent on the other, and finding herself on her own after over forty years of marriage, was inevitably going to be very difficult. To my recollection, all matters of business and finance had been left to my Father, so she had to acquire a new set of skills; budgeting and paying bills on very little money. I have already hinted that the BVT were not over generous in the salary they paid my Father and consequently, his pension was not large either. Naturally, she was worried as to how she would cope and be able to manage on such slender means. The family, of course, rallied round but in a very short time she learnt to live on a limited budget. Throughout the next twenty five years, she managed consummately, never once becoming overdrawn.

Throughout their married life, my Mother had been as active as Dad on many committees such as the Middlemore Homes for orphans, as well as being Chief Commissioner for the Girl Guides, which she took over from her great friend Honor Cadbury. After my Father's death, she was asked to become Secretary of the Old Woodbrookers, a job which she came to love very much. The Edward Cadbury Trust supplied her with a Morris Mini-Minor, which enabled her to drive over to the little office she had at Woodbrooke and which also gave her independence. She was extremely popular there and as always, she made many friends, including people such as Elizabeth Holmgaarde, the much loved Head of the Catering staff and indefatigable weaver of tapestries, and being Mum, sooner or later they would be invited back to her home for coffee or a meal.

When her brother-in-law Llewellyn retired from his post as Regional Medical Officer in Nottingham, he and my Aunt Win decided that they would move back to Birmingham to be near her and were always wonderfully supportive. They joined the QQ Book Club, of which my Mother and brother Nicholas were members, they took her to the theatre and they would both visit each other on alternate Sundays for sherry and a roast lunch. The QQ Book club was ideal for my Mother as she adored reading, just as her own Mother had done, always with several on the go, devouring with relish an unbelievable number over a year. She kept a list of everything she read in a little booklet, recording not only the titles, but also adding a succinct summary of each one. For instance during the year 1991 she starts with Peter Mayle's 'A Year in Provence' - 'a fascinating and amusing diary-like account of the author's first year in their new home' - and goes on through Iris Murdoch's 'The Bell'- 'an author I can't say I really enjoy' - to titles as diverse as 'Three letters from the Andes' by Patrick Leigh Fermor, 'Period Piece' by Gwen Raverrat and 'The Story of San Michele' by Axel Munthe, which amounts to a fair cross section of the literary output of the year in question.

With her elder sister Bobby, her brother Reg and her Mother now all dead, the other members of the wider family took on a greater emphasis. Win and Llew became her constant companions, but she also liked to visit her sister-in-law, Vera Barber, especially since she too had been widowed early and additionally lost her eldest son Graham in a plane crash. Vera moved into Graham's bungalow in Hampton, which she proceeded to keep as a shrine to his memory, with all his belongings left as they had always been, liking only to revisit the places that had been dear to him and seeing people whom Graham had known. Mum had always forged her own life since Dad died, dearly remembering, but never wallowing and so she found visits to Hampton increasingly difficult, as on each occasion, they repeatedly did the same

Mum at 80

A lovely 80th birthday portrait of Mum

Mum opening the Ralph Barlow Gardens
Cousin Anna and family in Blackheath

Sir George Young, MP unveils the plaque at Ralph Barlow Gardens, with him is Mrs. Joan Barlow, the widow of the man the scheme was named after.

B'ham Evening Mail 8/4/82

Tribute paid to housing champion

A Birmingham Housing Trust has named its first sheltered housing scheme in memory of one of its long-serving management committee members Ralph Barlow

From The Birmingham Evening Mail 1982

Cousins Anna and Carol (left) in Anna's Blackheath home c. Christmas 1997 with Alex (hidden), Anna's husband, Callaghan, Mum and Antony

things and constantly drove over the identical routes where Graham had so often taken her. Occasionally she would visit Mum in Birmingham or accompany us to family gatherings such as when we joined Bobby and Les' daughter Sue and her husband Clive for their 40th wedding anniversary at their farm in Shillingford, near Exeter, but as the years passed, sadly she retreated further and further into her shell.

Following Dad's death, Mum lived alone, but soon made a new life for herself, taking up many of my Father's duties, keeping up with BVT functions and ensuring that the memory of her beloved husband's work should not be forgotten when she opened the Ralph Barlow Rooms at the Dame Elizabeth Hall and the Ralph Barlow gardens in North Birmingham as part of the COPEC housing community. Each summer she joined the Shakespeare studies course under David Gray at Charney Manor; she was an active member of the 50 Club and most typically she adored spending time with old friends and relatives. These included her niece Anna, of whom she was very fond and close friends whom she had known over fifty years, some of whom she'd grown old with like Margaret Gillett and her children, whose husband Jeff had died comparatively young like my Father, or Michael and Elizabeth Platten and their family, with whom she had shared a lifetime.

Elizabeth and Michael Platten had been stalwart friends of Mum's for fifty years, from their early married life, to our joint holidays, with my Mother always a sympathetic listener to the ups and downs of their difficult marriage and a comfort in times of sorrow, that had endeared her as a wise and understanding friend no matter how stormy the weather. So in 1999 their Diamond wedding was an emotional celebration of a deep and lasting friendship. The family closeness continues into the next generation, with myself and AP's sister, Angela who long ago had invited me to be Godfather to her daughter Emma, by her first husband Chris Berry, and now she and her second husband, the actor Sam Dastor and I are good friends. Ironically - or not, - Chris, Sam and I were all at the Downs School together, though our interlocking relationships were scarcely on the horizon back then!

There were also friends of Dad's with whom he had been in the FAU, like Henry Headley and Ronald Joynes and their respective wives Mary and Peggy, with whom she kept in touch all her life. Mum never forgot a friend and even if they lived abroad like Blanche Ammoun whom she had known since her teens in the Lebanon and who latterly lived in Paris, or Henry and Lydia Cadbury who were in America, there was a constant correspondence.

When Mum and I visited Paris in 1996 she eagerly looked forward to seeing her old friend Blanche once again, still living in the same cluttered apartment in Avenue Mozart in the 'seizième arrondissement' as I remember staying in as a teenager on my first trip to Paris. Blanche had married André Lohéac, an Army Chief who worked for SHAPE[200] and they had three children, Gwen, Lynne and Frank. I went to stay with them in 1956 when I was fifteen and enjoyed an unexpectedly wonderful two weeks. They allowed me the run of the city, unchaperoned and I discovered my own Paris, walking alone along the Seine, taking the Bateaux Mouches on the river, exploring the galleries and finding out how the Métro worked. I learned to love French cuisine and acquired a taste for the French wine served with each meal.

They also taught me how to speak French 'comme un Français', without being easily detected! Later the same year Gwen came to stay with us at our home in Birmingham, so for a while our two families were very close. André had died some years before and in the thirty years that had

---

[200] Supreme Headquarters Allied Powers in Europe, formerly in Paris now in Mons in Belgium.

Mum with her sister and sister-in-law

Mum and Win in the late 1990's

Mum with Vera (right) and Vera's sister Irene Harrison at Hampton

Mum with old friends

Mum with Margaret Gillett (left), daughter Alison and Anthony, her then partner

Elizabeth Platten, Angela, Mum, Sam Dastor and Michael Platten in 1999

elapsed since they had last met, much had happened to both Blanche and her family as to my Mother and hers. There had been much happiness as well as sadness, but it was just as though their conversation had been rudely interrupted and so they resumed where they had left off, with their friendship as vital as ever and the reunited families passed a wonderful day together.

My Mother also loved to see her nephews and nieces, like Anna Braithwaite, Millior's daughter, for whom my Mother had always been a favourite Aunt. Our families had spent much time together when we were young, on holiday in Burnham or at their home in London and had become close friends as well as cousins. Carol and my sister Rosemary were of an age and had remained in touch over the years as I had with Anna and after my Uncle Alfred had died relatively young and later my Aunt Millior too, perhaps even more so. Anna moved to live first in Peckham in South London, which was one of the reasons I moved there myself in 1982. Little did I know then until I began researching this book, that our Quaker ancestors had close links with the area which had been a large centre of Quaker life in the mid nineteenth century.

Later when she married Callaghan[201], she moved to a large and beautiful, family house right on the edge of Blackheath with a breath-taking view out over the common with its myriad kite flyers and children playing all sorts of games. Anna often invited my Mother to stay there and as both my cousin and Callaghan enjoyed family gatherings, there was very likely to be any number of relatives from Anna's children from her first husband and their partners, as well as step children from Callaghan's first marriage.

Her friends remained always a central part of her life as indeed did the wider family of first and second cousins, aunts and uncles. It was important to my Mother for her children to feel a part of the old Quaker diaspora, which was part of a strong Quaker tradition and she remained, as her mother before had been, the centre of a large and expanding family, presiding over her children as a benign and loving matriarch. But for Mum, the immediate family was always paramount and she would take it in turns to visit each of her children and she delighted in watching their families grow up, for whom she was an equally wonderful Grandmother and subsequently great Grandmother, never once forgetting any of their birthdays. She relished the company of her Grandchildren and great Grandchildren and I am sure in later years when they recall their childhoods, they will remember a gracious, gentle, kind and lovely Grandmother.

Though I know she never stopped missing our Father, her widowhood was nonetheless very happy, as she was able to enjoy doing things that perhaps she hadn't been able to do whilst Dad was alive and her children, Grandchildren and great Grandchildren gave her continuous happiness. She was remarkably active almost up to the end, dying peacefully after only a short illness on March 3rd 2007, aged nearly 93.

She believed in the family first and last and was always anxious that her children and grandchildren should do well as her Mother had wished and striven for her. She had a special gift for friendship and everyone who knew her, loved her dearly. She was not only a very special mother to her five children, Grandmother to her thirteen Grandchildren and great Grandmother to her six great grandchildren, but someone who served the community in a wide variety of ways, gave wholeheartedly of herself to a vast circle of friends and lived a truly Christian life through her Quaker beliefs.

---

[201] Anna divorced her first husband Jimmy Kerr and married second, Callaghan OHerlihy.

"Mum never forgot a friend, wherever they may be"

**Henry Headley and Ronald Joynes had both been in the FAU with my
Father and they and their wives, Mary and Peggy respectively
remained lifelong friends**

**Likewise, Blanche Ammoun, (left in Aleppo in 1935) whom my Mother had met originally in the
Lebanon as a teenager, remained a friend all her life and Mum and I revisited them in Paris in 1996.
(Right) In Blanche's Paris apartment with Lynne, Antony, Mum and Blanche.**

All together for Mum's 90th birthday in 2004

Nick, Antony, Rosemary, David, Mum and Stephen

David and children with Mum

(left) Mum with David in Shoreham and (right) at Mum's 90th birthday 2004

David's 60th 1997 with Mum and Lucy and David's eldest, John

David with Rosemary and Mum 1999

Chapter 22
Endpiece - Mum with her children

Mum's widowhood wouldn't be complete without showing her developing relationship with her children and Grandchildren. So the following pages depict her at the centre of the family, with love and concern for her children. Having no children myself, I show instead, my Mother together with myself and my friends. She came to love and be loved by all of them, some of whom were from the world of the Arts like myself, but some were just close friends of many years standing, but her fondness for them all demonstrate her tremendous gift for friendship. The section, devoted to myself and my friends is a little longer than that for my siblings, but that is not to downplay their part in the overall picture. From just a few photographs of our Mother with my brothers and sister and their children, the close relationship they enjoyed, is immediately apparent; it takes a different range of photos to perhaps make another point about friendship. So as the author, I make no apology for the space self-allocated!

Mum was the very opposite of the typical Mother-in-law. She welcomed all her children's friends, partners and spouses into the family and was adept at making them all feel at home. She could be critical but was never censorious; she was occasionally disapproving, but never judgemental; and if sometimes she might cast aspersions, she never condemned. She always sought to be inclusive rather than exclusive and to bring people into the family fold. But as I have mentioned before, this is not the place to tell the full story of my parents' children. That is for hereafter and for others to tell.

David

A parent's relationship with their firstborn is always unique and though they never showed partiality, they did I know, rightly reserve a proud and special corner for the head of the family. David initially studied PPE at Oxford before he joined the British Council, prior to being recruited by the BBC, where he remained for the rest of his career. He has amply filled his role as the family's head, and in his turn he has had an outstanding career at the BBC, including a spell in a senior role in Regional Broadcasting as well as the Senior Administrative post, of the Secretary of the BBC. As a brother, though he has not always enjoyed the private happiness[202] that he would have wished for, he remains one of whom we are all justly proud. And despite of difficult times, I think both Mum and David were always conscious that above the fray, there was an allegiance to family, and she always did her best to be a part of his life wherever it led, and he to acknowledge, what we all owed to her, in remaining the still yet vibrant centre of it at all times.

---

[202] David married Jill Roberts in 1958, adopting three children; in 1981 he married Sancha Oppenheimer, from which there were 3 more children. Both marriages sadly ended in divorce, but he is now happily married to Stella Hewer.

David with Mum at the Downs and at the Ralph Barlow room

David and Stephen (far right) with Mum at an Old Downian reunion in 1990 at the school, with two Headley brothers, Lewis and Henry (centre).

Mum with David and Stephen at the opening of the Ralph Barlow rooms in memory of Dad in the Dame Elizabeth Hall, Birmingham 1993

Antony – Mum's gift of friendship

Discovering that one of their sons was gay, was I know not easy for my parents, and I am sure it was not what they had envisaged, especially back in the sixties. But it was a fact with which they did both come to terms and eventually to accept. In a true Quakerly manner, they sought the advice of Kenneth Barnes, who had written extensively on the subject for Quakers, especially in the formative and far seeing *'Towards a Quaker view of Sex'* published in 1964, and gradually, they came to acknowledge my sexuality. Though perhaps it was more difficult for my Father, he did become reconciled to my then long term partner Ven Hart, whom I had met at Manchester University in the Drama Department and with whom I shared my life for over ten years. As I mentioned earlier, my Father wrote a wonderful letter telling me that whatever our differences, I was still his 'beloved son' and that meant so much. A few years after Dad died, my dear Ven succumbed to the deadly HIV virus and Mum supported me wonderfully through a difficult time, as she had inevitably become very fond of him and his family and was truly upset at his passing.

After he died, I had other partners, though no-one compared and sadly they didn't always work out. However, after Dad's death, I think Mum found it much easier to accept my sexuality. This had a lot to do with discovering that my late Cousin Graham, was also gay, which meant she and his Mother, my Aunt Vera, had a mutual bond. In the early days after Ven and I settled in London, Graham had been our guide and mentor in the faltering steps we took together in this new world, having been there before us. I missed him tremendously when he died, as he had been like a brother to us both and his wisdom had been invaluable. To lose my partner and then my close Cousin within a short space of time, was a tremendous blow and it took a long time to recover. But I also owe a great deal to Ven's family, his adorable parents, Barbara and Ken and brother Andy, who were like a second family to me and during my time running the Kenton Theatre in Henley-on-Thames, I always stayed at their home near-by. Later they came to live next to us in Chelsea and we were always in and out of each other's houses.

After Ven's death, being largely on my own, and with no children or grandchildren for Mum to cherish, I introduced her to my friends. Some were gay, like my oldest friend, the late writer and Publisher, Eric Inglefield with whom Mum shared a great love of gardening; the wonderful and effervescent John Morley, pantomime King who was ever a joy to know, and whom Mum just adored and missed almost more than any when he suddenly died; Richard Bayliss, Head of VIP travel for BA, an old and loyal friend, whose lovely house in Windsor, Mum and I often visited; the American artist Bruce Church, who painted a beautiful picture of her bungalow for her 90th birthday; or my Swedish friend Tord von Dyrssen, Head of Ralph Lauren Europe, a staunch friend to Mum and I at all times, often taking us both, along with his Mother, to the opera and out to a meal.

Then there are those friends I met through my long career in the Arts[203], such as Vi Marriott, whom I met at The Young Vic; musician friends, such as the great Viennese pianist, Katherina Wolpe and the ineffable German Cabaret singer, Eva Meier with her ebullient husband, the German Cultural Attaché, Frank Burbach. Mum met and became fond of them all and they in turn adored her for her natural enthusiasms and unaffected humanity, to which they responded instinctively. She gave them her love with just the same attention as if they had been family and they in return loved her. My Mother never tired of coming to London and often said that she felt the same excitement coming to the big city as she had as a young girl, and on her many visits to stay with me I tried to give her something of a different experience.

---

[203] General Manager, Royal Academy of Dancing with Fonteyn; Head of Press London Festival Ballet and The Young Vic; Freelance Arts PR for The Kirov and Bolshoi companies, Nureyev, Baryshnikov, Makarova, Howard Keel amongst others.

My first boyfriend and beloved partner Ven

My beloved Ven Hart, whom I met at Manchester University and lived with for 10 years.
Here on holiday at the caravan in Llanthony valley in the Black Mountains in 1960's

My mother with my friends -
Vi Marriott

I have known Vi Marriott for nearly 35 years since I first worked at the Young Vic with Frank Dunlop in 1980. Vi first started in the theatre when she joined the Old Vic in 1946 as Assistant to the General Manager, during the legendary seasons at the New Theatre, where they had moved when the theatre was bombed during the war, with Laurence Olivier, Ralph Richardson and John Burrell. When the company moved back to its home in the Waterloo Road in 1950, she went as PA to the new Director, Hugh Hunt, who coincidentally was to be my Professor of Drama at Manchester University in the 60's. In 1955 Vi joined Hugh in Australia, when he was invited to run the Elizabethan Theatre Trust in Sydney, a prototype Australian National Theatre. After five years, when the Trust was fully operational, she returned to the UK and whilst running her own Public Relations firm with Roger Clifford, she met Frank Dunlop who had been invited to become part of Olivier's young National Theatre, temporarily at The Old Vic while the new National Theatre was built. Vi went with Frank to help plan The Young Vic, a theatre designed to encourage young audiences, which opened in 1970, and where she remained for the next twenty one years. She has also worked tirelessly, helping other companies and received an MBE in the Birthday honours of 2009, for 'services to the theatre'.

Vi became my most loyal and trusted friend, always there when one needed and never one to let you down. She and Mum became very good friends and whenever Mum came to stay, Vi who lived only a few doors down in our picturesque corner of Peckham, would always join us for drinks or a meal. We also went on several overseas trips together, as they both loved travelling, visiting Paris and Amsterdam. Mum and Vi were mad about ballet and in Paris we visited that most exquisite of opera houses, the Garnier, to watch the oldest and possibly the finest ballet company anywhere in the world, the Paris Opéra Ballet where my old friend Patrice Bart, formerly Principal dancer with London Festival Ballet, was then Maître de Ballet. He arranged the best seats in the house for the three of us and treated my Mum and Vi like visiting Royalty with drinks in the VIP room in the intervals. They were memorable evenings. It was some years since Mum had been to Paris and so we went to all the familiar sites such as Montmartre as well as a few of my own favourites, such as having a drink in the bar at that grandest of Hotels, the Crillon on the Place de la Concorde!

It was even longer since Mum had been to Holland, and we stayed in a really old family run Hotel in Amsterdam, where I had stayed in the past, and where one was looked after with traditional Dutch courtesy. Nostalgically, we visited all the places we had been to shortly after the war, including Delft and its famous pottery shops, and of course, in Amsterdam we took a boat on the canals, visited the Rijk's Museum and saw the Nederland's Dans Theatre, then run by my friend Wayne Eagling. The international dance world is really one great big family and dancers move around the world from one company to another with consummate ease and you often find dancer friends from London turning up as Directors in another city. So it was in Amsterdam, where Wayne, a former Royal Ballet Principal, was now the Artistic Director of NDT and once again Mum, Vi and I were entertained with gracious hospitality.

Vi also stayed several times in Birmingham, as with her love of dance, the Birmingham Royal Ballet became one of her favourite companies and though she seldom cared to stay in strange houses, she always made an exception for Mum's house, where she knew that there would not only be a warm welcome but, she claimed, one of the softest and most comfortable mattresses she had ever slept on!

Mum in Paris and Amsterdam with Vi Marriott

Mum and Vi in Montmartre 1996

Vi and Mum in our favourite Crillon Hotel 1996

Mum and I in Delft on a very cold day 1997 – taken by Vi

Eric Inglefield

Another friend was the writer and Publisher Eric Inglefield, who I had known for nearly forty years. He was an only child from quite a poor background but made his way to Nottingham University where he read Spanish and French and was subsequently a Senior lecturer in Spanish at Sheffield University. He left academia and entered the world of publishing, becoming Senior Editor at Hamlyns and later at Macdonalds. He was also a writer of distinction himself, authoring a number of books, such as the popular Kingfisher Guides for children, on such varied topics as Birds, Horses, Wild Flowers or Flags.

He was always a keen traveller, and would drive all over the world in one or other of a series of ever more trendy two-seater sports cars that so appealed to him, exploring his chosen area and writing several wonderful travel guides on places as different as Egypt or France as well as a comprehensive guide for AA Publishing, *Travelling Across America*, still a staple today.

His working class background inclined him to the left politically and he was a much respected Father of the Chapel for the print Union. He was a wise old cove and I learnt a great deal from him politically, sharing many an animated discussion. But he was superb company and had a wonderful sense of humour, making me laugh inordinately at ridiculous absurdities.

Eric often joined Mum and I for Christmas day with his Icelandic partner, Oskar Orlygsson and she loved visiting his Chiswick house and delightful garden too, as like her, he was an expert gardener and they used to swap tips as to the best way to nurture this or that plant. In return, Eric came up several times with me to stay in Birmingham and on every occasion, they would exchange cuttings from each other's garden.

Sadly in the last years of his life Eric suffered from Alzheimer's, and as he gradually receded into another world he ceased to recognise his friends, which was a great sadness to all who loved him, especially Oskar, who looked after him with much loving care until his death in 2012.

Christmas crackers 1998 with (left) Eric and Vi and (right) Mum, and Eric's partner Oskar Orlygsson

My oldest friend Eric Inglefield

Eric Inglefield and I in his lovely garden in Chiswick, photo taken by my Mother in 1990's

Katharina Wolpe

Working in the Arts, I was lucky enough to become close friends with many distinguished artists and musicians and without exception, they all adored my Mother and I was often in serious trouble if I didn't arrange for them to see her when she was in town. One of these was my dear friend, the much loved pianist Katharina Wolpe. Katharina belonged to the last generation of brilliant musicians to escape from Nazi Austria, whose interpretations of the great Viennese classics had become collectors' items. She was a close friend and colleague of mine for nearly thirty years and the Wigmore concerts which I arranged for her, were occasions of supreme musicianship and treasured memories of both Mum and I.

Kathi, as she was known, had endured a traumatic childhood, as her Father, the composer Stefan Wolpe, had left both her and her Mother in Vienna, moving first to Palestine and from thence to the States, when she was only a small child. Although she and her Mother eventually managed to escape Nazi persecution in 1938, they were forced to remain in hiding for nearly eight months, before finally escaping and walking all the way to Serbia. Hearing her in her maturity, it was hard to believe that she only began to play as a young girl when she first came across a piano in the refugee camp where she had ended up with her Mother, and discovered that she had a natural talent for the instrument.

Despite a difficult marriage, her natural generosity of spirit and humanitarian politics, as well as her love of all the arts led her to form a performing partnership with Vanessa Redgrave and one of the great privileges of my life was working with these two great artists when they invited me to join with them, raising money for refugees and the work of UNHCR as well as Vanessa's numerous other causes on behalf of the many abandoned peoples, less fortunate than herself. Katharina was wonderful company, a warm and generous woman, who took enormous pleasure in welcoming one into her beautiful Hampstead home and feeding us with her truly special vegetarian dishes. Kathi thought the world of my Mother and visiting her in Well Walk and sitting in her beautiful garden was always a highlight of Mum's visit to London. Her death from cancer in 2013 deprived us too early of this gracious and wonderful artist.

Katharina Wolpe before a concert

Mum with 'Kathi' in her Hampstead garden

Frank and Eva Burbach

Through my friendship with Kathi, I got to know the German Cultural Attaché, the brilliant and engaging Frank Burbach and his wife, the captivating cabaret singer Eva Meier and their two talented daughters Julia and Jana. Eva seemed to move effortlessly from being the elegant and sophisticated wife of an Attaché to that of the most expressive chanson singer of a latter day Dietrich with consummate ease. She managed to bring her own unique style to the great songs of the Weimar-era with their mix of passion and cynicism and no-one who heard her sing *Mack the Knife* or *Surabaya-Johnny* could ever forget it.

She was a hugely popular performer wherever Frank's career took her, but perhaps nowhere was her impact greater than in London, singing at Wigmore Hall, The Purcell Room and The Linbury Studio or as she frequently did on the BBC. Eva was always a wonderfully engaging singer, drawing an audience in, with an almost confidential tone yet managing to reveal a world of love and pain behind the lyrics. Chanson is not an easy genre to pull off, but Eva was the mistress of the art, with a haunting stage persona.

On another occasion, however, you would find her being the Diplomatic hostess. She and Frank were the still point of a fantastic cultural mêlée and at the frequent gatherings at their elegant Knightsbridge home you might bump into anyone from sculptor Antony Gormley to the violinist Anne Sophie Mutter. Consummate hosts, they welcomed everyone from somebodies to nobodies, painters to writers, television presenters to journalists and artists of all sorts.

Generous to a fault, they always made a big fuss of my Mother and many a Christmas time we were invited there to join in their family celebrations with Eva's parents and though Mum spoke even less German than Eva's elderly parents spoke English, they always said they could understand her every word because of the clarity of her diction, which pleased Mum greatly. Frank Burbach was the epitome of the perfect Diplomat: always courteous, charming, witty and generous-hearted. If he knew Mum was in London, he would often provide tickets for a concert that he had helped to sponsor or arrange, and ensure that we were invited to the reception after. We had some very special times not just with Frank and Eva, but together with their whole family.

Left: Frank and Eva arriving at Peckham

Right: Eva Meier in cabaret

Mum and Eva at my house in Peckham

Christmas in Peckham – Mum and Eva Meier

John Morley - The Pantomime King

Another friend of mine, of whom Mum was very fond, was the puckish John Morley, known to everyone as the 'Pantomime King', with whom I worked for some twenty years. John had started out as a revue artist in his youth, but described himself as a 'panto-scriptwriter' having written well over 250 pantomime scripts. In the days when The Palladium Pantomime was the major Christmas event in town, John was their creator, writing for everyone from Evelyn Laye to Arthur Askey and Les Dawson to Danny La Rue.

Like our family, John was a Birmingham man and had seen his fist pantomime at the old Prince of Wales Theatre in Broad Street, sadly destroyed by a bomb in 1941, which my Mum remembered well from her own childhood. They struck up an immediate, if surprising rapport. Mum relished his somewhat camp sense of humour and always genial temperament, whilst he in turn, adored Mum's old fashioned hospitality and courtesy. He stayed with us several times in Birmingham, loving the chance to revisit the areas of Edgbaston where he had been brought up and she loved the two occasions we stayed with him and his boyfriend Terence Hopkins, in their beautifully furnished home on the sea front in Hove.

John was not just a script writer, but also an eminent Pantomime historian and archivist and his comprehensive 'Encyclopedia' of the genre was a wonderful mixture of scurrilous personal reminiscences, historical facts and anecdotal gems, which I had the fun of promoting for him. Mum came down especially for the launch at the Theatre Museum and was presented with a specially signed edition, which she greatly treasured, the more so, as only a few weeks later, John suffered an unexpected heart attack, dying very suddenly in Brighton hospital. He had been due to pay another visit to Birmingham, and my Mother was really heartbroken to lose this dear and lovely man of whom she had become so fond.

I arranged the funeral at the actors' church, St Paul's in Covent Garden at the invitation of John's brother Dick, and Mum cancelled other appointments so that she could be there. I was quite overwhelmed by the number of offers from every major artist in the business who wanted to come and pay their tribute to him. In fact it was difficult to limit the service to a reasonable length without offending someone; as it was, the Impresario Charlie Vance remarked to me afterwards that 'it was longer than an Evening with Ken Dodd'! But in its way, it was entirely appropriate for John, being really more like a pantomime in itself, with hilarious stories from Roy Hudd, June Whitield, Lionel Blair and Fenella Fielding and everyone emerging afterwards in fits of laughter rather than tears.

"John Morley the Pantomime King"

John Morley in his Brighton home surrounded by scripts. Photo taken by Mum

Dick Morley and Mary Sales

I suppose it was inevitable that our friendship with John should also engender another great relationship with John's brother Dick and his wife Mary. Mum immediately took to them as she had to John and before long they were under her spell too, and in next to no time we were up in Durham staying at their historic house with its exquisite walled garden exchanging horticultural tips and sharing funny stories as we had with his brother. In contrast to John, Dick and Mary were both academics at Durham University, but delighted in the same off-beat humour. They often came to stay with Mum and would always bring gardening clothes to help with pruning, weeding, hedge-cutting or some necessary task demanding attention. They loved to visit country houses and National Trust properties and I recall going to Coughton Court on one of their trips to stay in Bournville and then later, on our return visit north to their lovely home, being given an authoritative guide round Durham city and its great cathedral.

Dick Morley and his wife Mary Sales with Antony after a spell of gardening in Bournville

Bruce Church

Talking of artists, I must make mention of the tremendously gifted landscape artist Bruce Church, whose paintings adorn several galleries around the world. In true bohemian style, Bruce lived in an exotic, converted old church off Ladbroke Grove with a very high roof and everywhere, just as in any artist's studio, his paintings decorated the walls. Mum had admired his work for a long time, especially after seeing a charming painting he had made of John Morley's house. So when my Mother was 90, I thought an ideal present would be a similar painting of her bungalow in Westholme Croft in Bournville. The family clubbed together and as a surprise, when she was staying with me for her birthday, Bruce came over for supper, bringing the painting with him, which she unveiled to her joy and amazement. Bruce was inordinately fond of Mum and as she got older was so gentle and kind towards her, that she always loved to visit his somewhat eccentric home. Bruce is an American, and an old fashioned gentleman and though he has lived here most of his life, he still possesses the typical outgoing bonhommie of his fellow countrymen. In a long life he has travelled the world painting, often to Italy, where many of his best paintings have been executed. He was also an expert in trompe l'oeil and much of his home was decorated in that style, so that it was not always easy to say which was real and which not.

Bruce and Mum with the painting Bruce did of Mum's Bungalow in Bournville

Sir Reresby and Penelope Sitwell

Often when I think of Mum, it is her ringing laugh that comes first to mind and it was when I took her up to Renishaw Hall, the Sitwell's famous home in Derbyshire, that I can still recall hearing her, hardly over the threshold of the ancient house, already enchanting the then head of the family, Sir Reresby and his wife Penelope with glorious heart-warming laughter. Although then in her eighties she was still a beautiful lady, crowned with the most brilliant white hair and her face lit up with a smile that brightened any occasion.

At the time in 1997, I was organising a memorial exhibition on Maria Callas, with my friend, Impresario Alan Sievewright, to mark twenty years since the singer's death in 1977, which we assembled initially at Renishaw, before transferring it to the Royal Festival Hall. It was in a converted barn on the estate which is now the family museum, housing the long history of their distinguished forebears including Edith and Osbert and Sacheverell. Mum and I stayed in this extraordinary house, now nearly 400 years old, with its rambling corridors, creaking floorboards and ghostly presences, that could easily be the ideal setting for either Jane Austen's *Northanger Abbey* or Oscar Wilde's *Canterville Ghost*! The stunning Italianate gardens are justly famous, laid out in the late 19th Century by Reresby's eccentric Father, Sir George Sitwell. The lakes are a haven for wildlife, with rare butterflies, dragonflies, and birds and Reresby took great pride in showing us the vines which he had planted in 1972 which must be the most northerly vineyard in all Europe. Just the sort of place with its history and gardens that Mum loved and I was especially happy that I was able to take her there and let her enjoy such surroundings while she still could. The Sitwell's delightful daughter, Alexandra and her husband Jack Hayward (former Chairman of the Wolves' football club) were also staying there, and together it made for a very happy family weekend. Since Sir Reresby's death in 2008, Alex is now head of Renishaw and lives there with her husband and their five children.

Sir Reresby snapped by Mum, in a typical pose outside Renishaw

Mum and I at Renishaw with the Sitwells

Mum in the Italianate Gardens at Renishaw 1997

Lady Penelope, and Sir Reresby with Antony at Renishaw in 1997 taken by Mum

Richard Bayliss

I first met Richard Bayliss in the 1970's when he was working for British Airways, looking after VIP travel arrangements, in particular for many of the people I worked with, such as Margot Fonteyn and Rudolf Nureyev. His lovely house at Windsor was always a favoured place for weekends away and other guests would regularly include many well-known dancers from Lynn Seymour to Anthony Dowell and Leanne Benjamin. A wonderfully generous host, he was a good and true friend and Mum always treasured our weekends with him. His death in 2010 deprived us all of a much loved person.

Mum and Richard Bayliss, in Windsor Christmas 1999

Maria Garzón

I must have known the distinguished Spanish pianist, Maria Garzón for about thirty years; indeed I cannot now recall where we first met. But I have been putting on concerts for her as long as I can remember and in addition we did a series of concerts together with me introducing and talking about the music. But Maria and her writer husband, Carlos Lopez, have long ceased to be just clients, being amongst my closest friends, being best man at their wedding. Mum and I have holidayed in their isolated house in Anna Riglia

Maria Garzón in Bournville

in the Peloponnese and Maria often stayed in Birmingham when, for several seasons, she was a regular performer at the Barber Institute concerts. Her popular record of Spanish music regularly topped the Classic FM's list of most requested CDs and remained one of Mum's favourites too. One memorable Christmas we stayed with Maria and Carlos at their home in North London, enjoying warm Spanish hospitality. Mum seemed to love the company of musicians and Maria was no exception.

Mum at Glyndebourne

My regular birthday treat to my Mother after Dad died, was to take her to her beloved Glyndebourne. Over the years, the day established its own routine, driving down through the winding Sussex lanes to Lewes, where we would always stop for lunch in the beautiful garden at Shelleys Hotel, before driving on to Glyndebourne. I think my Mother's favourite production over all the years we visited, was Peter Hall's miraculous staging of Britten's *A Midsummer Night's Dream* in 1981 with Ileana Cotrubas and James Bowman, which always remained our touchstone.

Sometimes it was just she and I, but we often went with others such as my boyfriend Ven Hart, or other close friends including Eric Inglefield and Vi Marriott or as here, my very good Swedish friend Tord von Dyrssen, when we saw Rossini's *La Cenerentola* in 2001. In the old days we would wander round the picturesque gardens and find a picnic spot, but latterly sitting on a rug on the lawn was more difficult for her and so we would treat ourselves to dinner in one of the restaurants, either Middle or Over Wallop.

Mum and I at Glyndebourne, enjoying the Sussex countryside in the long interval.

Tord von Dyrssen and I at Glyndebourne, taken by Mum

Left – the supper interval.

Some guests would arrive very early to set out their tables with candelabra and all the accoutrements of a very grand dinner party and as the walk from the car park is some way, several journeys are required! This particular year, in a fit of extravagance, I ordered a picnic from M&S which came with chairs, tables, ice buckets and everything included and all laid out for one in advance. Wonderful!

Stephen and family with Mum

Mum and Stephen in 1998

Mum with Stephen and wife Linda, with their two boys, Christopher and Colin in 1982 at the opening of the Ralph Barlow Gardens in memory of Dad.

Stephen

Stephen has inherited, perhaps more than any of us, our Father's placid nature. Fate has not always been kind to him, yet he has born every set back with equanimity and an uncomplaining acceptance, exactly as our Father did and that is undoubtedly an outstanding quality. His initial work in Hotel Management, and his success in running the family owned Norfolk Hotel in the centre of Birmingham, led subsequently to his meeting with Linda Cairns and later to their marriage. This has been a very happy relationship and their children Christopher and Colin have been a credit to them. Mum I know, was very proud of the children, especially in the way they have continually helped their Mother cope with her increasing disability after she contracted MS soon after Colin was born. When the Hotel was sold to new owners, my brother, unhappy at developments, bravely set up a Milk franchise on his own, which he developed with indomitable stamina and determination. He was backed by a very loving and supportive family, who have learnt how to cope with adversity and move forward. They have been a fine example to everyone. To Stephen, family and tradition mean a lot and he has always instilled this in his children, bringing the best from the past to the future. Both he and Linda are people of whom no-one could ever find a bad word to say and that is an inspiration in itself.

Rosemary

After three boys, my parents always longed for a girl, so when Rosemary was born, it was a great thrill. Though only six, I recall the occasion vividly, being allowed to go up and look at the new baby, before going off to school and announcing to everyone that I had a sister. It was also memorable for being one of the stormiest March nights on record, with trees blown down and chimney pots dislodged, that always reminds me of Glendower's remark in *Henry IV* "*At my nativity, the frame and huge foundation of the earth did shake!*" Whatever omen the weather portended, she has been all that parents could hope for a daughter, always there with sensible advice and a generous nature, and though she was my parents' only girl, she and husband Richard Howells fully supplemented the deficit with three more girls, Sally, Jenny and Lucy, of great individuality, character and charm. Always a great support to Mum, especially as she became frailer, she and the children were constant visitors, which gave her enormous comfort and reassurance. My sister was a gifted Primary school teacher, a profession she returned to when the children grew older, and which daughter Jenny also pursued. Sally worked in the field of social wellfare until she met her partner Olly Dowson and the birth of Wilfred in January 2015, as did Lucy prior to her marriage to Owen Claridge in 2011 and the birth in 2012, of their first child Summer.

Rosemary and family with Mum

Rosemary and Mum at Ro's home in Shoreham

Mum with Rosemary's girls, Jenny, Sally and Lucy

Nicholas

Nick and Caroline at the time of their marriage

Being born in my parents' mid-life, Nick was always playing 'catch-up' with his siblings, but Mum and Dad always tried to give him the same childhood and education that we had enjoyed. As he grew up and graduated, then started work and married, he was a great support to Mum after Dad died and I know there was a special closeness, as very often he was the only one of us around. Nick made a special point of joining in with the activities that Mum particularly enjoyed such as reading and music. He became a member of the QQ Book club that Mum had joined soon after she got married, so she always had someone with whom she could discuss the books.

Similarly with music, which I think she had missed out on in her life with Dad, who had not a musical bone in him, and was something she was able to take up again with relish after his death. Nick generously took out an annual season ticket for the City of Birmingham Symphony Orchestra concerts and throughout the Simon Rattle years, he devotedly accompanied Mum, first to the old Town Hall, and later to the new Symphony Hall, which gave her very real pleasure. Though the youngest, Nick was in many ways the oldest, often taking responsibility when others weren't there and he was a constant source of joy and comfort to her. I know it was a sadness to Nick that Dad didn't quite live to see his youngest son's graduation from Reading University in 1981 with a BSC, which I know would have made him very proud. Instead it was his proud Mother and I who were there for him and I recall a very happy day, bringing back memories of my own graduation all of 16 years earlier!

Being so much younger, also meant that he married and started a family that much later. He met Caroline Cooper about 1989/90, while they were both working at the old family firm of Chartered Surveyors, James and Lister Lea in Birmingham. However, the Company disapproved of them continuing a relationship whilst still working for the firm, so eventually they decided to leave and set up on their own. They also got married, and that has proved an enduring and very happy relationship. Fortuitously, during their time with Lister Lea, they had already established a strong working association with Lord Aylesford at the Packington Estate near Meriden and he was able to continue doing that, which he still does successfully today as well as looking after other clients. Living and working near Meriden proved a happy conjunction of coincidences. Firstly it is very close to where our Grandfather Barber's family came from in Coleshill and secondly, our family's very close friends the Plattens had long lived in Meriden and we spent so much time at their home 'Strawberry Bank', that Meriden was almost a second home!

With a very ornithological Father, who took every possible opportunity to look at Birds whatever the weather and with our frequent 'birding' holidays at Whiteslea on the Norfolk Broads, it was inevitable that we would all grow up with quite a reasonable knowledge of Birds. But Nick is the one who has inherited our Father's knowledge and skill the most, and he would think nothing of driving for hundreds of miles to catch a siting of a rare migrant. Like our Father he has also been an active member of the West Midlands Bird Club and photographs of Nick relaxing usually depict him with Binoculars round his neck!

With Nick's marriage being later, Mum relished the joy of having more Grandchildren after the others had already grown up and the photograph of Mum with Nick's three children in 1998, then aged about 4, 2 and 1, is typical of her love of being with them. Now they too are nearly ready to fly the nest and start out on their own. How quickly 'the whirligig of time' comes round, with yet another generation about to move out, settle down and have families of their own. Perhaps they will one day look at this history of their ancestors and marvel at their achievements and even write the story of their own families for their children and grandchildren.

Mum with Nick and Caroline's children, Sophie, Matthew and Laura in 1998

I hope this chapter shows the very special person our Mother was and how she loved and cherished all her children and their children and their children's children as well as their friends. And in a way, there couldn't be anyone better with whom to round of this history, as in her way she epitomises all the best qualities of those who preceded her and sets the template for those who follow.

Mum and Nicholas out birding

THE END

Chapter 23
Postscript

"All this was a long time ago, I remember. And I would do it again, but set down this. Set down this: were we led all this way for Birth or Death?"   *('The Journey of the Magi' by T S Eliot)*

What of Quakers today? Where are they now? Looking at the photograph of all the Cousins in 1948 (Ch.14), seems today like those photos of the pre 1914 generation, still all youthful hopefulness, unminded of what the future may hold. All those families gathered together post Second World War, all related, still believing that their future will replicate that of their Fathers and Mothers and Grandparents.

We, the children of those born in the early years of the last century and the grandchildren of those from as far back as the 1850's, brought up in the Quaker traditions of our forebears and expected to follow them and be torchbearers of the next generation. We, the scions of old Quaker families, many of whose ancestors have led distinguished and exemplary lives, most recently braving the opprobrium of public opinion as Conscientious Objectors in two world wars, we of whom great things were expected. And, we who were educated at Quaker boarding schools, still further underlining our historic dissenting continuity, find now as we too grow old, that within but a few short years, all this is disappearing, as though it had never been.

Up and down the country, Quaker meetings are being sold off, with groups downsizing to smaller halls and those that remain, peopled by the newly 'convinced', no longer sustained by the gravitas of the revered old families, who for generations have been such stalwarts of the faith, established nearly 400 years ago. At such a time, it seems to me all the more important to remind ourselves of our history and traditions, before we too vanish like our family archives, consigned to dusty libraries.

Yet, we refuse to go away. All over the world, Quakers fight well above their strength in numbers. Behind many of the global trouble spots, members of the Society bear witness to the Peace Testimony and influence the ongoing debates in the corridors of power. They engage in arguments over the serious issues of the day; fighting courageously for greater rights for those of different sexuality; working tirelessly for those who find themselves imprisoned, inspired as ever by the sufferings of the early founders of the society; and they represent those whose minority views bring them into conflict with the establishment.

Thus in many and varied ways, the Society is still as vital as it ever was; defending the corner of the unrepresented, upholding lost causes and the values for which Fox and his followers fought and suffered. So I believe very strongly, that it is ever more important to chronicle the history of those who went before and bore witness to the ideals of the Founder. The history of my forebears and those like them, should be acknowledged and proclaimed before it is lost irrevocably. It was heartening for me, therefore, to hear Ben Pink Dandelion's 2014 Swarthmore lecture in the presence of vast numbers of fellow Quakers of all ages, for its affirmation of our heritage and its reminder of the eternal truths established by our many distinguished forebears and what it is possible to achieve when we listen to the positive voices from our past. In this book I have endeavoured to honour my family who have endowed me with so much and which I have tried to recount in order to inspire future generations.

THE LANCASTER & NICHOLSON FAMILY TREE

JAMES LANCASTER (1618/21- 1699) = m.1652 MARGARET (1631-1682?)
(Owner of the Family Bible)

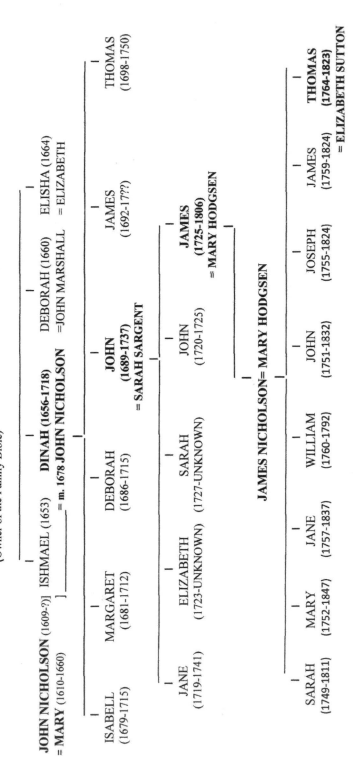

JOHN NICHOLSON (1609-?)] ISHMAEL (1653)   **DINAH (1656-1718)**   DEBORAH (1660)   ELISHA (1664)
= MARY (1610-1660)   **= m. 1678 JOHN NICHOLSON**   =JOHN MARSHALL   = ELIZABETH

ISABELL   MARGARET   DEBORAH   **JOHN**   JAMES   THOMAS
(1679-1715) (1681-1712)   (1686-1715)   **(1689-1737)**   (1692-17??) (1698-1750)
                                          = SARAH SARGENT

JANE   ELIZABETH   SARAH   JOHN   **JAMES**
(1719-1741)   (1723-UNKNOWN)   (1727-UNKNOWN)   (1720-1725)   **(1725-1806)**
                                                                  = MARY HODGSEN

JAMES NICHOLSON= MARY HODGSEN

SARAH   MARY   JANE   WILLIAM   JOHN   JOSEPH   JAMES   **THOMAS**
(1749-1811) (1752-1847)   (1757-1837)   (1760-1792)   (1751-1832)   (1755-1824)   (1759-1824) **(1764-1823)**
                                                                                                  = ELIZABETH SUTTON

For the issue of Thomas Nicholson and Elizabeth (Betty) Sutton see next page

265

NICHOLSON FAMILY TREE CONTINUED

THOMAS NICHOLSON (1764-1823) = m.1793 ELIZABETH (BETTY) SUTTON (1769-1834)

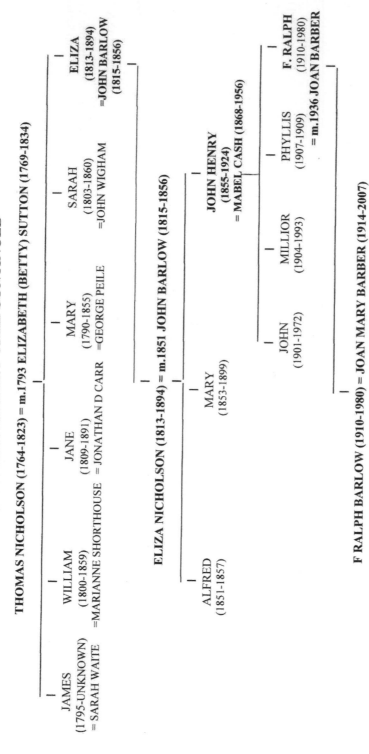

JAMES
(1795-UNKNOWN)
= SARAH WAITE

WILLIAM
(1800-1859)
=MARIANNE SHORTHOUSE

JANE
(1809-1891)
= JONATHAN D CARR

MARY
(1790-1855)
=GEORGE PEILE

SARAH
(1803-1860)
=JOHN WIGHAM

**ELIZA
(1813-1894)
=JOHN BARLOW
(1815-1856)**

ELIZA NICHOLSON (1813-1894) = m.1851 JOHN BARLOW (1815-1856)

ALFRED
(1851-1857)

MARY
(1853-1899)

**JOHN HENRY
(1855-1924)
= MABEL CASH (1868-1956)**

JOHN
(1901-1972)

MILLIOR
(1904-1993)

PHYLLIS
(1907-1909)

**F. RALPH
(1910-1980)
= m.1936 JOAN BARBER**

F RALPH BARLOW (1910-1980) = JOAN MARY BARBER (1914-2007)

DAVID JOHN
(b.1937)

ANTONY RALPH
(b.1941)

STEPHEN HUGH
(b.1945)

ROSEMARY JOAN
(b.1947)

NICHOLAS PHILIP
(b.1958)

For the issue of Ralph and Joan Barlow's children see Barber family tree
For Barlow family tree see next page

266

THE BARLOW FAMILY TREE

HENRY BARLOW (1664-1720) of Over Alderley, Cheshire, Yeoman = Hannah (1663-1712)

MARTHA **JOHN (1694-1758) = MARGARET KEAVE (1693-1766)**

JOHN (1717-1732)

ISAIAH (b.1718-?)

HENRY = m.1744 MARY BOLTON (1720-1799) (1723-1795)

PETER (b.1723-?)

JOSEPH (b.1726-?)

HANNA (b.1728-?)

ISAAC & JACOB (b/d 1730)

ELIZABETH (1746-?)

JOHN = m.1786 ELIZABETH BEELY (1748-1818) (176?-1821)

MARY (b.1749-?)

HANNAH (1752-1779)

HENRY (1754-1803)

ANN (b.1756)

SARAH (1759-1786)

THOMAS (1761-1770)

HENRY (b/d 1787)

JOHN = m. 1812 DEBORAH NEILD (Daughter of RALPH NEILD of Cheshire, cousin of John Camden Neild)
(1789-1846) (1783-1850)

JOHN (Professor) = m. ELIZA NICHOLSON (1815-1856) (1813-1894)

ELIZABETH (d.1860)

HANNAH (1818-1896)

MARY (1819-1881)

HENRY (d.age 8½)

DEBORAH* (1822-1879)

THOMAS (1825-1897)
= JOHN THISTLETHWAITE **MARY ANN EMMOTT**

**Issue: Sir John Emmott Barlow (1857-1932) 1st Baronet 1907= 1895 Hon Anna Denman
Grandparents of the current title holder, the 3rd Baronet Sir John Kemp Barlow (b.1934)**

ALFRED (1851-1857)

MARY (1853-1899)

JOHN HENRY= m. 1895 MABEL CASH (1855 -1924) (1868 -1956)

For John and Mabel's children : John Cash (1901-1972), Mary Millior (1904 -1993), Phyllis (1907-1909), **Ralph** (1910 -1980) see Nicholson tree
*Deborah Barlow and John Thistlethwaite's daughter married a Darby, and were the great Grandparents of Michael Darby, who was at school with the author

267

THE CASH FAMILY TREE

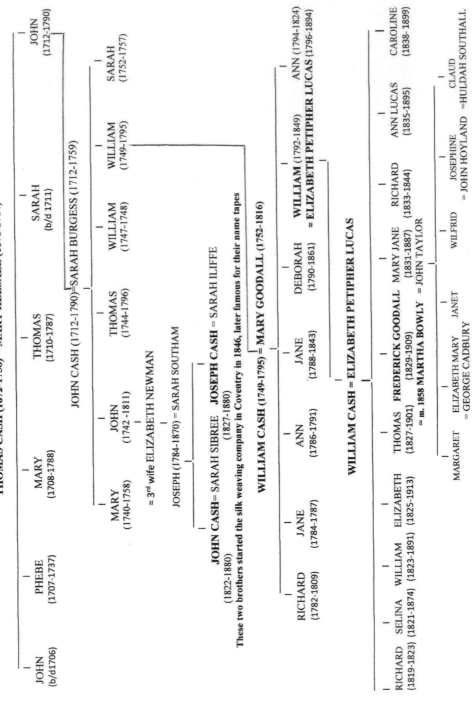

THOMAS CASH (1672-1758) = MARY KELSALL (1671-1714)

JOHN (b/d1706)

PHEBE (1707-1737)

MARY (1708-1788)

THOMAS (1710-1787)

SARAH (b/d 1711)

JOHN (1712-1790)

JOHN CASH (1712-1790)=SARAH BURGESS (1712-1759)

MARY (1740-1758)

JOHN (1742-1811)

THOMAS (1744-1796)

WILLIAM (1747-1748)

WILLIAM (1749-1795)

SARAH (1752-1757)

= 3rd wife ELIZABETH NEWMAN

JOSEPH (1784-1870) = SARAH SOUTHAM

JOHN CASH= SARAH SIBREE   **JOSEPH CASH** = SARAH ILIFFE
(1822-1880)   (1827-1880)
These two brothers started the silk weaving company in Coventry in 1846, later famous for their name tapes

WILLIAM CASH (1749-1795) = MARY GOODALL (1752-1816)

RICHARD (1782-1809)

JANE (1784-1787)

ANN (1786-1791)

JANE (1788-1843)

DEBORAH (1790-1861)

WILLIAM (1792-1849)
= ELIZABETH PETIPHER LUCAS (1796-1894)

ANN (1794-1824)

WILLIAM CASH = ELIZABETH PETIPHER LUCAS

RICHARD (1819-1823)

SELINA (1821-1874)

WILLIAM (1823-1891)

ELIZABETH (1825-1913)

THOMAS (1827-1901)

FREDERICK GOODALL (1829-1909)
= m. 1858 MARTHA BOWLY = JOHN TAYLOR

MARY JANE (1831-1887)

RICHARD (1833-1844)

ANN LUCAS (1835-1895)

CAROLINE (1838-1899)

MARGARET

ELIZABETH MARY = GEORGE CADBURY

JANET

WILFRID

JOSEPHINE = JOHN HOYLAND

CLAUD = HULDAH SOUTHALL

For Frederick Goodall Cash and Martha Bowly see next page

268

CASH FAMILY TREE CONTINUED

FREDERICK GOODALL CASH (1829-1909) = m. 1858 MARTHA BOWLY (1836-1901)

GERTRUDE (b.1859) =Joseph Taylor = Ernest Hutchinson

LOUISA MARY (b.1861)

WILLIAM (1863-1865) died young

FREDERICK SEYMER (1865-1873) died young

MABEL CASH (1868-1956) = **JOHN HENRY BARLOW** = Sarah Bond from Iowa

HERBERT THOMAS (1871-1920)

OLIVER HAYHURST (1875-1931) = Eva Hunt from Ohio

JOHN HENRY BARLOW (1855-1924) = **m 1895 MABEL CASH** (1868-1956)

JOHN CASH BARLOW(1901-1972) MARY MILLIOR(1904-1993) DEBORAH PHYLLIS(1907-1909) **F RALPH BARLOW (1910-1980)**

= m. 1926 Enid Priestman (1900-1991)   = m 1939 Alfred William Braithwaite (1901-1975)   = **1936 JOAN MARY BARBER (1914-2007)**

DAVID ANTONY STEPHEN ROSEMARY NICHOLAS
(see Barber Tree for more)

Roger Barlow (b.1930) = Mary Biddle
| (1933-1997)

Annabel Barlow (b.1963)

Anna Millior (1942-2011)   Caroline May (b.1948)   = Moussa Saker (b.1943)

= m.1. Jimmy Kerr   Adam (b.1984)
                                                     Sami   (b.1987)

1.Abigail Kerr (1972-2008) ptrnr Chris Rowell
   Issue: Rosalie Anna (b.2002)

2. Jane Kerr (b.1975) = Duncan Bewley (b.1970) (div)
   Issue: Scarlett Abigail (b.2009)

= m. 2. 1992 Callaghan OHerlihy
   No issue

THE LUCAS FAMILY TREE

WILLIAM LUCAS (b.1676) = ELIZABETH WHITEHEAD

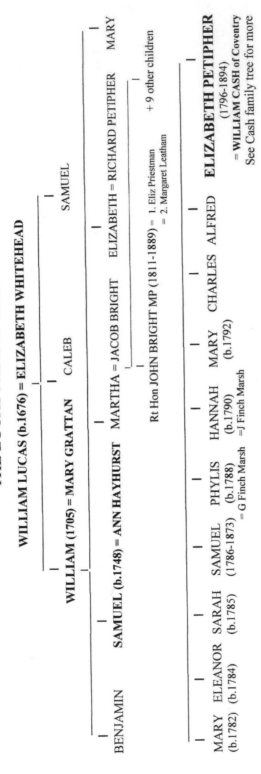

WILLIAM (1705) = MARY GRATTAN

CALEB SAMUEL

BENJAMIN **SAMUEL (b.1748) = ANN HAYHURST** MARTHA = JACOB BRIGHT ELIZABETH = RICHARD PETIPHER MARY

Rt Hon JOHN BRIGHT MP (1811-1889) = 1. Eliz Priestman
= 2. Margaret Leatham

+ 9 other children

MARY ELEANOR SARAH SAMUEL PHYLIS HANNAH MARY CHARLES ALFRED **ELIZABETH PETIPHER**
(b.1782) (b.1784) (b.1785) (1786-1873) (b.1788) (b.1790) (b.1792) (1796-1894)
= G Finch Marsh = J Finch Marsh = **WILLIAM CASH** of Coventry
See Cash family tree for more

THE HAYHURST FAMILY TREE

WILLIAM HAYHURST = m 1680 LADY ELEANOR MONCK (Sister of General George Monck)

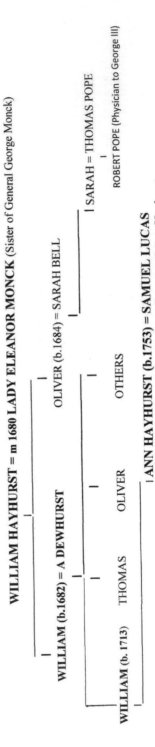

WILLIAM (b.1682) = A DEWHURST OLIVER (b.1684) = SARAH BELL

WILLIAM (b. 1713) THOMAS OLIVER OTHERS SARAH = THOMAS POPE

ROBERT POPE (Physician to George III)

ANN HAYHURST (b.1753) = SAMUEL LUCAS
See above for continuation of Samuel Lucas and Ann Hayhurst

270

THE SUTTON FAMILY TREE

JOHN SUTTON (d.1686) = ANN TINKLER (d.1714)

EDMOND (d.1688)   BARBARA (1659-1706)   REBECCA (d. 1662)   THOMAS (1665- 1712)   **DAVID (1670-1740)** | +RUTH, MARY
& m. 1. DORCAS JACKSON1698 = m. 2. **ESTHER BOND**   & JENNET

DAVID SUTTON = ESTHER BOND (1680-1766)

JOHN (b.1700)   **WILLIAM (1705-1792)**   DAVID (1707-1789)   BARBARA (1709-1711)   ESTHER (b.1711)   + ANN, MARY, BENJAMIN
= **m. 1730 MARY SAVAGE (1706-1802)**

WILLIAM SUTTON= m.1730 MARY SAVAGE

WILLIAM (1731-1815)   DAVID (1736-1829)   THOMAS (1741-1783)   +SARAH, JOHN, THOMAS, JOSDEPH
= **BETTY ROBINSON**

WILLIAM SUTTON = m. 1762 BETTY ROBINSON (1732-1813)

ELIHU (1765-1768)   MARY (b.1765)   **BETTY (1769-1834)**   WILLIAM (1771-1842)   NANCY (b.1773)   ELIHU (1778-1852)
= **m. 1793 THOMAS NICHOLSON (1764-1823)**

JAMES 1795-1855   MARY 1798-1855   WILLIAM (1800-1859)   SARAH 1803-1860   JANE (1796-1856)   **ELIZA (1813-1894)**
= SARAH WAITE   = GEORGE PEILE   = MARY SHORTHOUSE   = JOHN WIGHAM   = J D CARR   = **m.1851 JOHN BARLOW**

For continuation of Eliza Nicholson and John Barlow family see Nicholson family tree p 263

271

BARBER FAMILY TREE

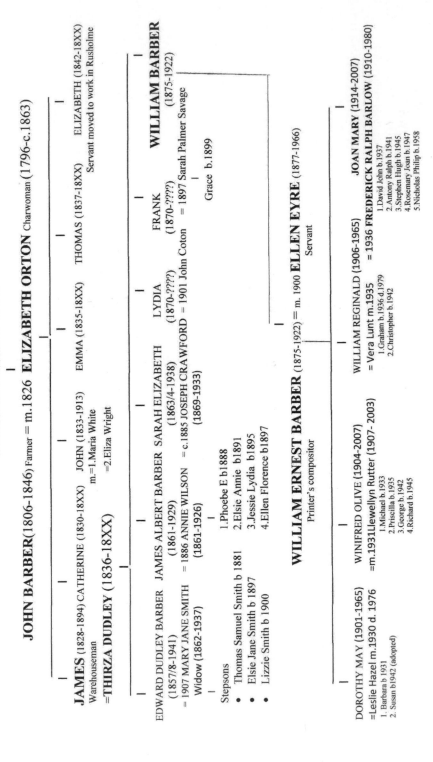

JOHN BARBER(1806-1846) Farmer = m.1826 **ELIZABETH ORTON** Charwoman (1796-c.1863)

JAMES (1828-1894) CATHERINE (1830-18XX) JOHN (1833-1913) EMMA (1835-18XX) THOMAS (1837-18XX) ELIZABETH (1842-18XX)
Warehouseman
=THIRZA DUDLEY (1836-18XX)
m.=1.Maria White
=2.Eliza Wright
Servant moved to work in Rusholme

EDWARD DUDLEY BARBER JAMES ALBERT BARBER SARAH ELIZABETH LYDIA FRANK **WILLIAM BARBER**
(1857/8-1941) (1861-1929) (1863/4-1938) (1870-????) (1870-????) (1875-1922)
= 1907 MARY JANE SMITH = 1886 ANNIE WILSON = c.1885 JOSEPH CRAWFORD = 1901 John Coton = 1897 Sarah Palmer Savage
Widow (1862-1937) (1861-1926) (1869-1933)

Grace b.1899

Stepsons
1.Phoebe E b1888
2.Elsie Annie b1891
3.Jessie Lydia b1895
4.Ellen Florence b1897

- Thomas Samuel Smith b 1881
- Elsie Jane Smith b 1897
- Lizzie Smith b 1900

WILLIAM ERNEST BARBER (1875-1922) = m. 1900 **ELLEN EYRE** (1877-1966)
Printer's compositor
Servant

WILLIAM REGINALD (1906-1965) **JOAN MARY** (1914-2007)
= Vera Lunt m.1935 = 1936 **FREDERICK RALPH BARLOW** (1910-1980)
1.Graham b.1936 d.1979
2.Christopher b.1942
1.David John b.1937
2.Antony Ralph b.1941
3.Stephen Hugh b.1945
4.Rosemary Joan b.1947
5.Nicholas Philip b.1958

WINIFRED OLIVE (1904-2007)
=m.1931Llewellyn Rutter (1907- 2003)
1.Michael b.1933
2.Priscilla b.1935
3.George b.1942
4.Richard b.1945

DOROTHY MAY (1901-1965)
=Leslie Hazel m.1930 d. 1976
1. Barbara b 1931
2. Susan b1942 (adopted)

See next page for next generations of Barber, Hazels, Rutters and Barlows

272

NEXT GENERATION OF HAZELS, RUTTERS, BARBERS AND BARLOWS

HAZELS

Dorothy Barber/ Leslie Hazel

1. BARBARA HAZEL=SCOTT STUART
1.ROBERT b. 1955
=1.1980 Gisela Gschaider (div) = 2. Jill Deeley
2.MATTHEW b. 1956
=Rosemaery Vickerstaff
1.Joanne
2.Christopher

2. SUSAN HAZEL= 1962 CLIVE BOYCE
1. ANDREW CLIVE b.1965
= 1.1995 Nancy Canda (div 08)
Bazzil b.1997
=2. 2013 Melody
Charley b.2013
2. TIMOTHY b.1967 = 2012 Rachael
3. SIMON b.1971 single

RUTTERS

Winifred Barber/Llewellyn Rutter

1.MICHAEL RUTTER= m 1958 MARJORIE HEYS
1. SHEILA b.1960 = 1982 Stephen Mellish
Twins: James, Laura
2. STEPHEN b. 1963 = Eleanor Millward
1.Bill 2. Albert 3. Mabel
3. CHRISTINE b. 1964
Ptnr = Edward Parry
1. Rachel 2. Lauren

2.PRISCILLA RUTTER=GEORGE SIDRAK
Margaret Sidrak=Robert Lalor (div)

3.GEORGE RUTTER=CAROLYN – No issue
4.RICHARD RUTTER = JANE
1.WILLIAM 2.VICTORIA

BARBERS

Reginald Barber/Vera Lunt

1.GRAHAM – SINGLE
2.CHRISTOPHER BARBER=1.BRIDGET
1. Katherine Margaret b. 1967.
2. Andrew Christopher b.1969 = 1997 Fiona
1. Elliot b.1998 2. Harriet b.2002
3. Edward William b.1969 = 2001 Rachel
1. Hannah b. 2002 2. Nicholas b.2006 3.Richard
=2.CHERYL no issue

BARLOWS

Joan Barber/ Ralph Barlow

1.DAVID JOHN BARLOW= 1958 1. JILL ROBERTS b.1936 (div)
1. JOHN (Adopted b.1965) = Hilary (div)
1. Girl 2. Girl
2. ANDREW (Adopted b.1966) = Tracey Graily (d. 2012)
1. Son 2. Daughter
3. SIMON (Adopted 1968 d.1989/90)
DAVID J = 1982 2.SANCHIA OPPENHEIMER(b.'51)
1. IMOGEN b.1984
2. LUKE b. 1986
3. NATHAN b.1989
DAVID J =3.STELLA HEWER – No issue

2. ANTONY RALPH- Single
3. STEPHEN HUGH = 1970 LINDA CAIRNS
1.CHRISTOPHER b. 1971 = 2004 VICTORIA GRAVENOR
1. Hannah Joy b. 2005 2. Stephen John b.2007
2. COLIN LAUDER b.1974 =1999 1.MERÂL OGAN (div 08)
Connor Pele b. 2000
=2009 2. LYDIA MASON
1. Georgia Rose b. 2010 2. Eleanor Grace b. 2013
4. ROSEMARY JOAN = 1971 RICHARD HOWELLS (b.1943)
1. SALLY b.1974
2. JENNY b.1978
3. LUCY b.1980 = 2011 OWEN CLARIDGE
Summer Rose b. 2012
5. NICHOLAS PHILIP = 1991 CAROLINE COOPER
1. LAURA JANE b.1994
2. MATTHEW CALLUM b. 1997
3. SOPHIE MIREILLE b. 1998

EYRE* FAMILY TREE

(*Spelling is often erratic in this period and the version Hair, later turns up as Ayre and only eventually as Eyre)

JOHN HAIR (1825-1895) = MARTHA UPTON (1833-1889)

b. Overseal Leics., Labourer in Iron works, Darlaston   b. Horton Street, Darlaston

| THOMAS (b.1846) Iron works lab | HANNAH (b.1851) Servant | ALICE (b.1862) Servant | ANN (b.1864) Servant | JOSEPH (b.1866) Iron works lab | BARNABAS (b.1870) Iron works lab | WILLIAM (1856-1885) engine driver at iron works |

WILLIAM HAIR/AYRE/EYRE (1856-1885) = **SUSANNAH AMOS** (1857-1883) see below

b. Regent Street, Darlaston.   (m. at St Peter's Church, Walsall 1874)   b. Darlaston

William, an engine Driver at Jones' Iron works, killed in industrial accident July 11 1885   Susannah died in childbirth at Station St, Darlaston from Pelvic Cellutisis

EMILY (1875-19??) Servant   **ELLEN** (1877-1966)   WILLIAM JOSEPH (1880-19??) Electrical engineer's toolmaker   JAMES ALFRED (1882-1956) Iron works   SUSANNAH BUTLER (1883-1885) died young

EMILY =m.1902 JOHN PATRICK WYLDE
1. LESLIE
2. ROLAND
3. THELMA

ELLEN =m.1900 **WILLIAM ERNEST BARBER**
1.DOROTHY b.1901
2.WINIFRED b.1904
3.WILLIAM REGINALD b.1906
4. JOAN MARY b.1914

See Barber family Tree for continuation

WILLIAM JOSEPH m.1906 HARRIET WILDAY d.1916
1.WILLIAM b.1907
2.DAISY LOIS b.1909

JAMES ALFRED m.1.1917 1. FLORENCE KIMBERLEY
1.JOHN b/d 1918
2.MARGUERITE 1919-1929
3.HARRY LESLIE b/d 1920
4. OLGA 1926-1970

m 2. 1921 2. ALICE KING A widow (née Baker)
1.ELLEN b.1923= m 1. WALTER PENNY LINES
1.PAULINE
=2. HERBERT GIBSON
half brothers: Leonard,Thomas and Albert King
half sister: Alice King

* When Susannah Eyre died in childbirth in 1883, the Father looked after the children, but then after William died too in 1885, the children were eventually taken into care in 1888 – Emily and Ellen went to Crawley's Orphanage for Girls in Erdington and William and James to Josiah Mason's Orphanage. Quite where they lived between 1885 and 1888 is not yet clear.

AMOS FAMILY TREE

JOHN AMOS (b.1835) = m. c.1853 **MARY** (1839-1901)
Miner   Servant

ELLEN b.1854   MARY ANN b.1856   **SUSANNAH** (1857- 1883) See above   JOSEPH b.1860

DAME ELIZABETH CADBURY'S 90th BIRTHDAY
Family Gathering at The Davids, Northfield, June 24th, 1948

Identification of people in photo on page 80. See next page for key to numbers

Key to photo of Dame Elizabeth Cadbury's 90th birthday, June 24th 1948

1. Elizabeth M Cadbury
2. Virginia Bridget Cadbury
3. Roger Victor John Cadbury
4. Peter Hugh George Cadbury
5. Antony Ralph Barlow
6. Constance Mary Taylor
7. Janet Elizabeth McGregor
8. Shea Sinclair
9. Susan Sinclair
10. Susan Elizabeth Taylor
11. Richard Charles H Taylor
12. Katherine Mary Crosfield
13. Eleanor Jane Crosfield
14. Edmund Cadbury Hambly
15. Elizabeth Cadbury Hambly
16. Clare Henderson Taylor
17. David Bright Gillett
18. Henry Francis Hambly
19. Martin Bevis Gillett
20. Marion F E Wharton
21. Peter William Allen
22. Elizabeth Anne Wharton
23. John Christopher Gaman
24. Patricia Mary Gaman
25. Anthea Karen Cadbury
26. Jeanette E Bryony Cadbury
27. John Breeze
28. Christopher James Cadbury
29. Mary Breeze
30. George Breeze
31. Rowland Cash
32. Mabel Cash Barlow
33. Marion Janet Greeves
34. William Edward Greeves
35. Denis Malet Lambert
36. Elizabeth Ursula Lambert
37. Celia Jeanette Cadbury
38. George Norman Cadbury
39. Geoffrey Hoyland
40. Elsie Dorothy Hoyland
41. Bertram Fothergill Crosfield
42. Eleanor Crosfield
43. Dorothy Cadbury
44. Edward Cadbury
45. George Cadbury
46. Henry Tylor Cadbury
47. Mary Isabel Wilson
48. Kenneth Henry Wilson
49. Lucy B Cadbury
50. George Adrian Hayhurst Cadbury
51. Jocelyn B Laurence Cadbury
52. Barrow Cadbury
53. Annette L K Cadbury
54. Ian George H Cadbury
55. Helen C A Dixon
56. Frances Marjorie Watts
57. M Isabel Lefebure
58. Huldah Mary Gaman
59. Julie Huldah Gaman
60. Isabel Taylor
61. George Timothy E Cadbury
62. Roger Wilfred Tomkinson
63. Eleanor M Tomkinson
64. Elizabeth M Hambly
65. Veronica Cadbury
66. Caroline M Gillett
67. H G Wood
68. Janet K Wallis
69. Elsa Fox
70. Joyce Ilbert
71. Yvonne Fox
72. Margery P Cadbury
73. Huldah R Taylor
74. Egbert Cadbury
75. Joyce Cadbury
76. Laurence J Cadbury
77. Rachel E Cadbury
78. Anita Glaisyer
79. Hannah H Taylor
80. Dorothy Taylor
81. Mary F Cadbury
82. Betty Potts
83. C L Potts
84. Emmeline H Cadbury
85. Margaret Bradley
86. Neville Bradley
87. Arthur Nicholas Gillett
88. Jean Elizabeth Gillett
89. William George Gaman
90. John Knox Taylor
91. George Breeze
92. Honor M Cadbury
93. Eveline A Cadbury
94. Marion B P Cadbury
95. Elizabeth C Clark
96. Catherine Cadbury Lambe
97. E Margaret Sinclair
98. Robin N Cadbury
99. Brenda Wallis
100. Enid P Barlow
101. Michael H Cadbury
102. M Heather Cadbury
103. Mrs Leonard Appleton
104. George Bertram Crosfield
105. Richard Watts
106. Dorothy A Cadbury
107. Christopher B Taylor
108. Robert C Taylor
109. Marjorie L Taylor
110. Eleanor M Wharton
111. Elizabeth A Lambert
112. Cicely C Lambert
113. Celia Judith Cadbury
114. John Clark
115. Miss Newell
116. Miss Cook
117. Thomas William Greeves
118. J Christopher Cadbury
119. Charles W Gillett
120. Doreen Gillett
121. Albert Clark
122. David C Cadbury
123. George M Greeves
124. Julian St John Cadbury
125. John C Barlow
126. G Ross Wood
127. Elizabeth M Wood
128. Margaret W Gillett
129. Joseph A Gillett
130. Leonard Appleton
131. Joshua Watts
132. Elizabeth R Glaisyer
133. Edward P Cadbury
134. Mary C Cadbury
135. Christopher L Wharton
136. Alfred Brian Taylor
137. John S Hoyland
138. Martin G H Cadbury
139. Kenneth J Wilson
140. Harold Watts

276

Index
nb refers to text reference at foot of page

The future generation

The great grandchild of Ralph and Joan Barlow, Summer, born January 2012, with her parents Lucy and Owen Claridge. Lucy is the daughter of Richard and Rosemary Howells (née Barlow), now establishing a new dynasty.

Bon voyage!

Photo courtesy of Lucy and Owen Claridge

Hitchen Market Place in 1842 by Samuel Lucas

Painting of Hitchen Market Place in 1842 by Samuel Lucas, Elizabeth Lucas' brother. Frederick G Cash went to Isaac Browne's school in Hitchen at the time. The painting features many well-known Friends and prominent townsmen. (see next page for key)

Key to people in painting of Hitchen Market Place 1842 on p 283

Key to the picture of Hitchin Market;
by Samuel Lucas.

1 — Edward Blush
2 — Sigismund Van Church
3 — Doctor Mansell
4 —
5 —
6 —
7 —
8 — Mr quest reed
9 — Croft (the Herbalist)
10 —
11 —
12 —
13 — Mr quest reed
14 — William Lewin
15 —
16 —
17 —
18 —
19 — Nat Baldock
20 —
21 — Jim Draper

22 — Isaac Newton
23 — Oswald Tindin
24 — John Ransim
25 — William Lewin
26 —
27 — Mrs Draper
28 — J P Odnus Ratcliffe
29 — Col Odnus Ratcliffe
30 — Draper
31 —
32 — Doctor Niblock

33 — William Lucas
34 — Samuel Allen
35 — Superintendent
36 — John Faulkner
37 — John Wilshire
38 —
39 —
40 — Ann Lucas
41 —
42 — Clergy of Priston

43 — Edward Burr
44 — Charles Hersy jr (P.Om)
45 — Thomas Hailey (Postman)
46 — John Whiting
47 —
48 — Ned Baker
49 — Joseph Lucas
50 — Roland Oakley
51 —
52 — Jack French
53 — Betsy Beadle
54 — Jack the Huntsman
55 — R Huntsman (Butler)

284